University of Liverpool

University of Liverpool

1

OCCUPATIONAL CHOICE

OCCUPATIONAL CHOICE

A selection of papers from
The Sociological Review

WITH AN INTRODUCTION BY DR. CYRIL SOFER

EDITED BY
PROFESSOR W. M. WILLIAMS

London
GEORGE ALLEN & UNWIN LTD
RUSKIN HOUSE   MUSEUM STREET

First published in 1974

This volume © The University of Keele 1974

All the material in this Volume is copyright under the terms of the Brussels Convention and the Copyright Act 1956

ISBN 0 04 371025 5 hardback
0 04 371026 3 paperback

Printed in Great Britain
by W & J Mackay Limited, Chatham

Contents

Notes on the Contributors

S. ALLEN	Professor in Sociology, University of Bradford.
S. BOX	Lecturer in Sociology, University of Kent at Canterbury.
M. A. COULSON	Senior Lecturer in Sociology, Preston Polytechnic Designate.
J. FORD	Senior Lecturer in Sociology, Enfield College of Technology.
B. S. R. GREEN	Until recently Assistant Professor of Sociology, York University, Ontario, Canada.
ALISON M. GREGORY	Administrative Assistant, Open University, Newcastle-Upon-Tyne.
J. HAYSTEAD	Lecturer in Sociology, Dundee College of Technology.
E. TERESA KEIL	Lecturer in Sociology, University of Technology, Loughborough.
W. LIVERSIDGE	Was group leader on a project undertaken by students reading for the Diploma in the Social Psychology of Education at Leicester. He has now left academic life.
P. W. MUSGRAVE	Professor of Sociology of Education, Monash University, Australia.
C. RIDDELL	Lecturer in Sociology, University of Lancaster.
K. ROBERTS	Lecturer in Sociology, University of Liverpool.
CYRIL SOFER	Fellow of Queens' College, Cambridge and University Reader in Industrial Management.
D. S. STRUTHERS	Lecturer in Sociology, University of Strathclyde.
S. R. TIMPERLEY	Lecturer in Organizational Behaviour and Management Studies, London Graduate School of Business Studies.

Preface

Individual articles in the *Sociological Review* have, from time to time, stimulated original papers on similar or cognate themes and occasionally, critiques and rejoinders. It is, however, very unusual for a series of papers on a major issue to persist and develop over a period of years. The discussion of occupational choice is perhaps not yet complete after more than ten years—and this may in part account for the great interest shown in these papers. It is this sustained interest which has encouraged us to embark on this collection; and in order to produce a volume as quickly as possible the papers remain as they were originally printed in the *Review*, apart from such minor changes as page numbers and types of reference. These papers are introduced by a specially written review by Cyril Sofer.

I wish to record my gratitude to the authors of the papers for their willingness to allow reprinting here, and to Anthony Evans and Jean Thomas for their patient assistance at every stage of the enterprise.

W. M. WILLIAMS
School of Social Studies,
University College, Swansea

Chapter One
INTRODUCTION
Cyril Sofer

The central issues to which the reprinted papers in this book address themselves are: how do people form occupational preferences and implement them or try to implement them; what role does personal preference play in determining first or early occupations; what factors other than personal preference determine occupational fates and shape the distribution of persons between occupations at any given time?

The term 'occupational choice' appears in the title of the book and in several of the papers because it is commonly used as the label for the particular field of inquiry dealing with the entry of young people into work. Its use has certain disadvantages. It can be taken to imply that people enter the occupations they do after careful and systematic consideration of the alternatives open to them, that the attempt to implement preference is a distinct and discrete act and that the overall distribution of persons between occupations in our society is what it is as a result of the cumulation of several million personal decisions made in this way. Our contributors realize that personal preference is only one of several variables affecting the way a person opts when faced with concrete alternatives; that such choices are not necessarily systematic and are the crystallization of long-term processes, and that 'external' social influences and institutions play a crucial role in canalizing people toward one occupational stream or another and therefore in affecting the overall distribution of persons between occupations. Indeed, most of the contributors emphasize the importance of social and economic forces as determinants of actual occupational entry. Some of the most searching and illuminating papers argue that such forces shape even the motives, values and therefore the preferences with which young people approach the occupational structure.

Nevertheless, the term 'occupational choice' recurs from time to time even among our contributors and other writers they or I quote in a way that implies that preference is crucial, that choice is systematic or that our occupational distribution is the result of such preferences deliberately exercised. This is partly no doubt a result of the fact that, as in many branches of social science, the individual is the most convenient unit for research (even if not necessarily the critical unit for explaining his behaviour) and most studies of entry into occupations consist of research on the individual entrants. The far greater difficulty of getting a grasp of the social processes and institutional forces and how precisely they have their impact on the person should not deter us from maintaining a dual analytic framework which includes sociological and social psychological variables alongside those that may be said to reside within the person.

I begin with some preliminary comments on the importance to society and to individuals that persons be effectively and satisfactorily allocated to work roles; on the broad social institutions for handling this; and on the difficulties entailed in the process, particularly for the prospective or new entrant into the occupational world. In the next section I describe certain key studies in the theory of occupational choice.

Several of the papers start from the one or more of the three important prior formulations (all American) in this field of E. Ginzberg and his associates, of D. E. Super, and of P. Blau and his colleagues. In some cases their conclusions are summarized or reviewed, but usually very briefly and from a perspective that bears on the particular point the writer of the paper wishes to make. I therefore set out my own summaries of their contributions. I have handled these rather differently from the authors of the papers. As summaries they are fuller (and hence potentially more helpful to readers without a detailed background in this area). I think they do more justice to Ginzberg, Super and Blau because I use their work for exposition rather than for the debates appropriate to the pages of a technical journal, and therefore put as much emphasis on their contributions as on their short-comings. I have also tried to bring out points in them which make them relevant to more of the papers in the book than actually refer directly to them. Occasionally, I interpose a comment that I think readers will find helpful to bear in mind in reading the *Sociological Review* papers.

I then turn to the reprinted papers. Although these were written by different authors and over several years, there is a certain continuity between them, and certain themes or problems recur. I discuss these below in sections headed: accuracy of appraisal of occupational choices; purposiveness and rationality in occupational decision making; the role of school experience in adjustment to work; frustration or potential frustration in the job; 'occupational choice' as a process; commitments in the decision process; and structural aspects of 'occupational choice'.

SOCIAL AND PERSONAL IMPORTANCE OF THE ALLOCATION PROCESS

While all societies divide in some orderly way the work to be done, Western industrial societies have a particularly complex division of labour and inevitably intricate arrangements for manning the tasks that are divided and co-ordinated.

Our highly developed division of labour (and the allocation to specialized roles of persons who are or become experts in these) appears to be one of the main pre-conditions for massive production, effective distribution and a high standard of living. From the overall social point of view, specialization is most effective when tasks are allocated to those especially fitted for them. It is true that some jobs have been so broken down that practically anyone can do them and can gain in speed and proficiency as they concentrate on them. But adolescents and adults differ markedly in their ability to do various kinds of work involving different physical, mental, perceptual and cognitive abilities and the maintenance of different types of social relationships (however such differences have developed and whatever discriminatory mechanisms may have ensured that some get better chances than others to develop such abilities). It is therefore important to the members of a society collectively that it is on the whole the people who are better able to master the tasks available who find their way to them.

Apart from the social importance of the allocation of persons between occupations, occupation in Western society plays a central role in one's personal life. It is often critical in determining such matters as one's income; standard of living; health; self-esteem; social relationships; the quality of one's life; and the environment one can provide for one's family, including the chances of one's children to enter particular occupations.

Substantial differences exist between the life experiences of different occupational sub-cultures in our society. This is most immediately evident in the differences between the work experiences of persons who find themselves in the white-collar and blue-collar occupational sectors. A variety of studies has indicated that membership of either of these categories is closely correlated with:

(1) how satisfied one is with one's work
(2) how much autonomy one has in the way the work is to be done
(3) how interested or bored one is by one's work
(4) how meaningful one finds one's work (for instance, whether one regards it as an end in itself or primarily as a means to other ends)

(5) how close a connection one feels to exist between personal merit and social success

(6) how alienated from or integrated with, the rest of society one feels

(7) how much one expects one's opinions and wishes to be taken into account in connection with the way things are run

(8) The image of society one possesses, e.g. whether one sees society as divided into two basic power and status groups or as a series of layers between which movement is possible.

INSTITUTIONS MATCHING PERSONS TO WORK ROLES

Society develops mechanisms for placing square pegs into square holes. The classic distinction is between ascription and achievement. Under an ascriptive system of bringing people and jobs together it is assumed that some categories of persons have, from birth, qualities that automatically fit them better than others for entry into certain occupations. Under an 'achievement' system, occupations are not reserved in this way but are left open to be reached through competition and individual effort.

In the real world, the distinction is less clear cut. Although in Western societies occupational positions are normally allocated on the basis of merit, certain competitors even of equal, or initially equal, merit start off with advantages that give them superior chances of acquiring those posts that they particularly want or that are materially or psychologically most rewarding. These advantages include a superior economic or social class position of family of origin, economic capacity to stay at school and university longer than others, access to higher quality education, more accurate information about occupations, and the motivational support, advice and influence of relatives and friends. Also we limit the process of achievement by allowing only certain people to start, e.g. women cannot be starters for military leadership, nor peers for Prime Ministership. Foreign nationals, even though resident in the U.K., are eligible here for free primary and secondary schooling but not for grants to finance undergraduate study or postgraduate university research.

Modern societies emphasize the importance of filling occupational roles through achievement. This is partly because it is impossible to fill posts in a highly specialized and differentiated economy by reference only to an individual's prior social category. If we did so we would not be able to draw on the services of female computor operators, administrators and members of Parliament or of dons, editors and Prime Ministers drawn from the working class.

A second reason for emphasizing the importance of filling occupational roles through achievement lies in the existence today of a liberal philosophy based on the free development of the individual personality. That is, we regard it as not only economically desirable but also, in current moral terms, as a right of the individual to compete for the kind of work for which he is qualified or fitted to become qualified.

A third reason for emphasizing the importance of filling occupational roles through achievement lies in the importance we assign to work as an indication of a person's social worth. One can hardly judge a man on the basis of his occupation unless he had some scope for decision in entering it.

Difficulties in matching persons to work roles

Taken overall, a substantial amount of social investment is put into efforts to increase the probability that persons will enter roles in which they will contribute to the economy and which they will feel congenial to them or, at worst, tolerate. The institutions contributing to this process include educational streaming, academic examinations, diffusion of written and oral information, school tours, vocational counselling, recruitment campaigns, and personnel selection. The instruments of guidance and selection range through intelligence tests, aptitude tests, trade tests, diagnostic personality procedures, vocational interest inventories, occupational histories, application forms, interviews and interviewers' rating scales.

In spite of the social and personal importance of matching persons to roles, and in spite of a multiplicity of institutions and procedures designed to improve such matching, the process is a rough and ready one, involving misfits, readjustments, errors and miscalculations by employers, employees and advisers. Costs are probably heavy in terms both of economic output and personal regret. This is perhaps inevitable in a society in which economic efficiency is only one of the many values we pursue; in which education is more than preparation for an occupation; in which we prefer the existence of multiple sources of decision taking to centralized direction; in which employers compete for labour; and in which we regard it as proper for individuals to try to secure for themselves the occupational experiences they value. Most of us would regard as intolerable such alternatives to our present system as occupational allocation according to social categorization or direction of labour.

The problems of getting people into the right jobs—either right for the economy or right for them—stem from many sources other than and additional to our plural system of values and the interplay between those values. The problems stem partly from the complexity and variability of modern occupational systems. There is an immense range of working roles, many of them unknown in detail to all except those who perform them and to their immediate colleagues. This is partly a consequence of the privacy in which most work is performed. Demand changes for various types of worker, because of market factors, technological innovations, shifts in the roles of central and local government, shifts in relations between nations. Long-established occupations become obliterated by new techniques of production and distribution. New occupations supersede them.

The problems stem partly from the complexities of the human personality, our limited understanding of personality and our limited capacity to predict how a person is likely to develop and change or will respond to particular forms of education, training or work environment. Every person has a unique constellation of attributes between which a dynamic relationship exists. The concept of personality type is no more than a labelling device, a form of categorization through which we seek to impose order on complexity; it is consequently of limited usefulness to try to decide from 'personality type' what occupation a person should seek for himself. Our impressions of personality may be illusory: what we see in others (or experience in ourselves) may be relative only to particular social situations. Most people are fit for or could cope with a variety of work roles. Personality and identity (or at the least overt behaviour) can change appreciably during adulthood, especially during the early phases when a transition is made from education to work. Criteria for success in one context (for instance, school) may be an insufficient indicator for success in another (e.g. a factory, an army unit or a civil service department).

The problems stem partly from our limited knowledge of the relation of personality to competence or success in a job. Almost no work role can be played in only one way. There is usually a looseness of fit between role and person, and the 'same' job can be done by different people minimally, optimally, or equally well but differently. There are many work roles which we do not understand well enough to predict exactly who will succeed in them—or even to communicate to others what it would be like to fill them. It is easy enough to list the duties and rights attached to a role but difficult to grasp the essence in terms of how the occupant might choose to relate or order the various duties, or to describe what enters sociologically and psychologically into them. There can be a sharp difference between the 'nature of the work' and the social setting in which that work is done. A prediction based on the former can easily go wrong because of the latter. The success, or even competence, of a person in a work role often depends closely on the characteristics of the particular colleagues he is put to work with, and on the relations that develop between them. Apart from situations in which people resign or are dismissed, it is difficult to specify what constitutes competence, success, satisfaction to a worker or satisfactoriness to an employer. On the worker's side, whether he is reasonably satisfied and feels competent obviously depends largely on his expectations, his standards, his reference groups and the place of work in his life. On the employer's side, his acceptability will depend on the availability of alternative workers, the nature and enforceability of the contract entered into, current wage rates, current and potential union support, and so on. Workers' standards of expectation and of success will fall during a depression and rise under conditions of full employment. The employer's standards will move in contrary directions.

PROBLEMS OF ENTRANTS INTO THE OCCUPATIONAL WORLD

Despite the institutional facilities and efforts that are made to help persons get into occupations appropriate for them and for the economy, there are often practical problems attending the actual process of moving from school or college into work role. Decisions are taken at a time when, experience apart, young people are going through an emotional upheaval relating to biological development, social expectations, strivings for independence and relations with adults. Though he is protected to some extent by the school environment, the school-leaver may have his anxieties re-activated when he is trying to make a job choice or facing a prospective employer. The adolescent tends to be sensitive about making the adult grade. He may be facing not only a change in ways of spending his working hours but often of his way of life, possibly including geographical location and certainly many of his crucial primary group relationships. His position in the total social structure and the demands of other people upon him alter radically.

One facet of the adolescent crisis when it occurs can be a temporarily impaired capacity to see reality. Another facet is that the adolescent is likely to panic and not see the relation between his academic 'subjects' and practical tasks—he cannot divide the world (which comes all of a piece) into the same categories as academic disciplines. A third facet is the impulsiveness of choices he may make at this stage. It is difficult at this point to take care in one's choices and to tolerate not finding an immediate 'answer'.

The placement process has to do with more than a job, but with a whole person. In the course of seeking vocational advice or professional guidance the individual may raise a whole range of problems. This is often a socially acceptable way of raising personal difficulties, e.g. those connected with intellectual ability, academic achievement, capacity to make satisfactory relationships with contemporaries or with people in positions of authority. It may be that the vocational area is the main one in which the person is currently experiencing difficulty, that he has displaced other problems into this area, or that it is the one area where he feels it safe to seek help—in the hope that this will have a more general impact.

The young person may not have had adequate opportunities for voicing his wishes (some of which will probably be unrealistic) and testing his fantasies about careers. He may not have adequate information or contact with people doing the jobs he has in mind or enough first-hand observation of a variety of jobs to overcome his ignorance.

Considerable segregation of the educational system from other parts of the society exists before the age of occupational entry especially between the family and educational systems on one hand and the occupational system on the other, so the young person does not have a good knowledge of the opportunities offered by the economy and may make his choice of specialist field without realizing the implications. Parental guidance may be inadequate because of disparities between the educational levels and therefore the vocational potentialities of parent and child and because of rapid changes in the nature and range of occupations.

The young person may know one or a few requirements of a field—and make up his mind wholly on that basis. The information he commonly uses is what subjects he was good at in school—but this might lead him into a work context incompatible for him. In regard to the actual content of a job the young person can practise even less than he can see. There are few opportunities for 'job rehearsal'. He has no actual first-hand experience of the tasks that would be involved. He has limited opportunities for reality testing. Though people differ in different contexts he cannot usually try himself in several.

A good deal of his learning about himself may have to be through the destructive method of attending a succession of 'rejection' procedures. He may begin to ask, 'Is there anything at all for which I am fit?' Rejection experiences can give him a wrong idea of himself or damage his self-esteem. Our traditional intervening experiences, e.g. part-time work, vacation jobs, occasional help to parents and relatives, voluntary service overseas, function only partially (and in some cases unsuccessfully) to 'orient' the young person to the overall world of work. Inadequate induction procedures exist in many careers—seniors show impatience with the learner and with their own training function. There is often a lack of tolerance of problems of adolescence and of first adult relations, lack of appreciation of strangeness of the working world to an adolescent.

THREE CLASSICAL STUDIES IN THE THEORY OF OCCUPATIONAL CHOICE

E. Ginzberg and associates

In their book published in 1951,[1] E. Ginzberg and his associates identify three common approaches to, or theories about, occupational choice.

The first is that people make decisions about the future 'accidentally'. This is often the response of people asked directly about the choices they have themselves made, implying that they were affected by a factor or factors beyond their control—by an unplanned exposure to a powerful stimulus. But in the life of every person there are countless such occurrences, only a few of which so stimulate him that he responds in a way that has important consequences. The accident theory is correct to the extent that it stresses the importance of external factors in the choice process but wrong in that it neglects the fact that the way in which the person takes account of external factors depends on the way in which he perceives and reacts to them. The accident theory ignores the range of options available to the person.

A second contention, associated with psychoanalysis, is that occupational choice can be understood only through understanding the unconscious forces in individual behaviour. This may be called an 'impulse' theory of occupational choice. But a variety of occupations may permit expression of the same emotional impulses. The limitations of this type of explanation become further evident from the fact that there are profound differences in the emotional make-up of people in the same occupation. And it is obvious that, whatever his impulses, a person cannot enter an occupation unless the opportunities exist for him to do so.

A third approach, particularly associated with vocational guidance, is in terms primarily of aptitudes, interests and values. Vocational counsellors had long helped people to discover the relative strengths and weaknesses in their capacities so that they could have a firmer basis on which to make an occupational choice. Counsellors developed detailed inventories of the likes and dislikes (which they equated with interests) of successful people in different occupations and then sought to match the preferences of people still undecided about their occupations with these inventories, on the assumption that correspondence in interest patterns was a safe guide in making an occupational choice. Counsellors had also considered the reality factors in the environment of the person in advising him (such as the socio-economic position of his family, the economic pattern of the region, the conditions prevailing in the labour market). The role of values in occupational choice had, said Ginzberg, been less generally recognized. More recently counsellors had begun to consider choice of occupation as only an aspect of the broader field of personal guidance and were drawing more on psychodynamic personality theories.

It was the stated objective of Ginzberg and his colleagues to develop a theory so comprehensive that it would permit identification and analysis of the major factors in the vocational decision-making of the person. They were convinced that occupational decision-making could be delineated only as a result of understanding how internal and external factors act and react on each other.

The first part of the general theory of occupational choice associated with Ginzberg is contained in the same 1951 book. The book reports on an empirical study which it is important to describe. As Ginzberg and his colleagues acknowledge, and some of the contributors to this volume emphasize, the nature of the inquiry shaped, and in certain crucial senses, limited the general validity of the theory.

The main sample constituted 64 persons. The study consisted primarily of the conduct and intensive analysis of eight interviews of individuals at eight different stages in the educational process, starting in the sixth grades in high school; the freshman and senior years in college, first-year graduate students and advanced graduate students (total 64 persons). The age range was about 11–24 years. The boys in the sixth to the twelfth grades selected for interview were students of a school operating under the auspices of Teachers College, Columbia University. The collegiate and post-graduate students were enrolled in various divisions of Columbia University. The students in the college and graduate groups were equally divided between those who had an expressed choice in science or engineering and those whose preferences lay in the humanities or social sciences.

Respondents were white, Protestant or Catholic, of Anglo Saxon background and came mainly from families whose average income was about $10000 or $12000 per annum. As Ginzberg says, this was a highly favoured group having maximum freedom of choice (except insofar as their parents would probably have opposed attempts by them to enter lower-status occupations). In addition, the research team interviewed seventeen boys of lower socio-economic status, also urban white, Catholic or Protestant, contacted through a neighbourhood settlement house, and ten girls (sophomores and seniors) from Barnard College. Some were in the last year of grammar school (eighth grade) and the others were in the four years of high school, mainly in the second and third years, which represented the termination of formal schooling for the majority.

This brought the total of persons interviewed up to 91.

The research workers included the latter two groups as a subsidiary project because they wanted at least a preliminary insight into two sections of the population who are severely restricted in choice, boys who come from a deprived economic environment and girls who, even though they come from families with substantial incomes, approach their occupational choice within the framework of a primary desire to be married and raise a family.

The study attempted to gain some of the benefits of a 'genetic' form of research (which would include study of particular individuals' lives from infancy to adulthood) without involving the major disadvantages. The research workers therefore studied individuals from the same social category but

> 'of different ages and maturity, in order to identify the stages of a process accompanying individual maturation . . . the results from this method have relevance for the group as a whole but not necessarily for any individual within the group'.[2]

The theoretical conclusions[3] were the following:

> 'First, occupational choice is a process that takes place over a minimum of six or seven years, and more typically, over ten years or more. Second, since each decision during adolescence is related to one's experience up to that point, and in turn has an influence on the future, the process of decision-making is basically irreversible. Finally, since occupational choice involves the balancing of a series of subjective elements with the opportunities and limitations of reality, the crystallization of occupational choice inevitably has the quality of a compromise.'[4]

Ginzberg regards it as the outstanding conclusion from his findings that occupational choice is a developmental process, not a single decision but a series of decisions made over years, with each step in the process having a meaningful relation to those which preceded it and follow it.

> '. . . an individual never reaches the ultimate decision at a single moment in time, but through a series of decisions over a period of many years; the cumulative impact is the determining factor.'[5]

He argues that the process is largely irreversible because each decision made during the process is dependent on the chronological age and development of the individual. Time cannot be relived. Basic education and other exposures can be experienced only once. Although the person can shift even after he has tentatively committed himself to a particular choice, the entire process of decision-making cannot be repeated and later decisions are limited by previous decisions. Apart from the investment of time, psychological barriers stand in the way of a shift because a shift can easily take on the quality of failure and thereafter damage self-esteem.

Through the years of his development, the person has been trying to learn enough about his interests, capacities and values and about the opportunities and limitations in the real (external) world to make an occupational choice that will yield him maximum satisfaction. His choice would be simpler and more direct if he could make it without regard for the job market, income structure and prestige of different kinds of work. But he does not and cannot. He must compromise between interest, capacity and realistic opportunity. The process of occupational decision making could be analysed in terms of three periods or phases—those of fantasy, tentative and realistic choices.

In the fantasy period the young person cannot assess his capacities or the opportunities and limitations of reality. He believes he can be what-ever he wants to be. The choices are arbitrary and made without refer-ence to reality although the content differs according to the environment to which children are exposed.

The tentative period is characterised by recognition of the fact that the decision on a future occupation has a problematic element. The solution must be sought in terms of probable future satisfactions rather than in terms of current satisfaction.[6] During this period, however, emphasis remains mainly subjective, on interests, capacities and values. As persons reach the end of this period they realise that an effective resolution requires the incorporation of reality elements. (While Ginz-berg seems to mean here external reality, there is an undercurrent to his argument that implies that people have to become increasingly realistic in their assessment of their own capacities—as well as of opportunities in the external world.) They become

'aware more and more of the complex structure of reality with its job hier-archy, variety of working conditions, specific conditions of entrance into occupations, various income and security factors and the host of allied elements which are part of the working world.'[7]

During the realistic period the person recognizes that he must work out a compromise between what he wants and the opportunities that are available to him. The sex and educational status of the young adult become important and actual work experience ('the final test') has an impact on the definitive vocational decisions. Within this period three sub-phases can be distinguished: exploration (testing interest, values and presumably the reality of work experience), crystallization (involving the quality of acceptance) and specification (that is, specialization and planning within the area of choice).

Ginzberg mentions that among those studied some people became so dissatisfied with work in their chosen field that they found it necessary to return to the educational system and to seek a new field. It appeared that the choices of these people had never been really crystallized: it therefore required a relatively small amount of external pressure to upset the prior decision. However, he adds, some people respond to work experience by re-opening what had been a truly crystallized choice.

As mentioned above, Ginzberg first studied occupational decision-making among boys from upper income families. While he thought that systematic analysis of the way in which persons from one homogenous group dealt with their occupational choices would make it possible to identify regularities inherent in the decision-making process he recognized that the pattern discerned should be checked among other groups to see whether it appeared again. Accordingly, he made a supplementary selective appraisal of the occupational process among boys from lower-income families and among young women. This appraisal appears to be based partly on the work of other investigators but also on the small scale supplementary studies of lower-class boys and girls also conducted by the research team. Striking differences were found in the *content* of the choices of these two latter groups as compared with those of the boys in the upper income families. But it was also found that with respect to the *form* of the process of decision-making these three groups had much in common.

Ginzberg adds emphatically, however, that

'One of the important steps for future research should be controlled studies of different social groups: of boys and girls of different economic backgrounds living in urban centres; and of such radically different groups as sons of farmers or of the economically and socially handicapped, such as Negroes. Major environmental pressures will undoubtedly tend to distort not only the type of choices that are made but the form of the process of decision-making. Stunting in the development of the choice process, brought about by premature termination of schooling may have an important bearing on the later work adjustment of these groups.'[8]

Ginzberg notes that the school, with its emphasis on grades, helps the person to recognize his capacities and weaknesses although school-children themselves realize that effort, as well as endowment, control achievement.

An important addendum to this formulation is contained in a later book published by Ginzberg in 1964 with a different group of associates,[9] and which reported on a different group of respondents. The 1964 investigation was a questionnaire study of 345 men, each of whom had been awarded a fellowship for graduate or professional study in one or other department of Columbia University during the time period 1944–45 to 1950–51. The criterion for selection for these fellowships was academic achievement.

Ginzberg remarks that the research workers had originally included women fellowship winners. An early examination of their replies indicated, however, that

'many found the questionnaire unsuitable for reporting the patterning of their lives. Their occupational development was much less clearly structured than that of the men. In a great many cases the occupational development of the women was a derivative of their predominant life pattern in which husband and children took precedence.'[10]

Ginzberg and his associates concluded from this study that most people in their sample had determined on their occupational choice in their late teens when they were in college, and that the choice which they had then crystallized and later specified had provided a direction for their subsequent career decisions. It was not that they had come to like their work:

'They did not fall into their careers; they had selected them . . . they were content with the type of work they had selected . . . the satisfactions which these men derive from their work are primarily the result of their being in the fortunate position of realizing many, if not all, of their career objectives.'[11]

An individual's decisions transcend his concern about the present. More often than not he introduces into his calculations long-range considerations, considerations that appear to be guided by a projection of what he wants to be, or become, in the future. He engages in what might be described as a process of *self-realization*.

Ginzberg argued that

'Although "external" conditions such as existing market conditions or prior education may prove determining, the career development of our group cannot be adequately explained without taking account of an important internal factor, that is a desire to relate their present circumstances to a futuregoal.'[12]

Ginzberg underlines the importance of orientation towards the future in the shaping of a career:

'. . . career development is embedded in a time transcending process . . . the data concerned with work satisfaction contained an element of futurity.'[13]

As the future transformed into the present, the individual measured his present circumstances against his earlier expectations. As he progressed through life his expectations underwent varying degrees of transformation, affected by the congruence and the discrepancies between the goals that he had set for himself and his realization of them.

Discussing the role of expectations in the process of self-realization, Ginzberg states that to a high degree the work expectations of the respondents had been fulfilled. This would have been unlikely if their expectations had played a passive role in the process of their career determination and merely responded to external forces.

Ginzberg's notion of self-realization resembles Touraine's later concept of *projet*.[14] To Touraine a man's *projet* appears to be the intended trend of his life, what he wants to make of it and of himself in it. Tom Burns, to whom we owe this interpretation, points out that Touraine's concept of *projet* is an inversion of 'alienation'. Both the self-realization phenomenon and the *projet* may be upper-class phenomena, that is, people from lower social classes probably have fewer occupational alternatives and are more obliged to adapt themselves to what is realistically available to them. But surely even in the case of persons drawn from upper classes it may be common to have to adapt oneself to an occupational fate that is inferior to one's first theoretical preference.

Ginzberg considered that the research material provided additional understanding of the process of self-realization through the fact that two-thirds of the sample had never even considered the possibility of changing their lines of work: this indicated their satisfaction with the way in which their careers were unfolding.

However, he acknowledges that retroactive and prospective responses probably reveal more about the individual's present mood than about his past or future. That is, in trying to make sense of one's life one may represent one's past as a purposive set of steps towards the present. Most of the group were pursuing the type of careers and work that they preferred. Self realization presupposed some anticipating concept of oneself in the future . . . the *self* became the focal point.

'If the individual is able to conceptualise what he wants to be in the future, he acquires a major organizing principle which can give direction and provide continuity to what would otherwise be random and unrelated action.'[15]

Ginzberg says that the grown individual is able to review and revise his image of himself as a result of what he learns about himself and about reality. This is not easy for the young person. His interests, capacities and values become known to him only as he remains open and responds to the various influences that he encounters during the process of development.

'Each person must develop a strategy which will enable him to tie the present to the future so that the decisions which he makes today will enable him to move toward realizing what he hopes to be tomorrow.'[16]

D. E. Super

In a second major contribution to the understanding of occupational choice,[17] Super expressed the view that Ginzberg's (1951) theory had four important limitations.

1. It did not build adequately on previous work, for example the extensive literature on the nature, development and predictive value of inventoried interests.

2. Choice was defined as preference rather than as entry or some other implementation of choice, and hence means different things at different age levels. To the 14 year old it means nothing more than preference, because at that age the need for realism is reduced by the fact that the preference does not need to be acted on until the remote future. To the 21 year old student of engineering, by contrast, 'choice' means a preference which has already been acted upon in entering engineering school, although the final stage will come only with graduation and entry into a job. Reality plays a larger part in choice at age 21 when, unlike age 14, it is a reality-tested choice.

3. A false distinction was made between 'choice' and 'adjustment'. There is no sharp distinction: choice is a continuous process going on over a period of time, rather far removed from reality in early youth, but involving reality in increasing degrees with increasing age. Choice and adjustment blend in adolescence, 'with now the need to make a choice and now the need to make an adjustment predominating in the occupational or life situation.'

4. Although the Ginzberg team set out to study the process of occupational choice, and although they properly concluded that it is one of compromise between interests, capacities, values and opportunities, they did not study or describe the compromise process itself. This is the crux of the problem of occupational choice and adjustment: the nature of the compromise between self and reality, the degree to which and the conditions under which one yields to the other, and the way in which this compromise is effected.

Super goes on in his paper to review research findings and theories of occupational choice and organises these into 'a summary statement of a comprehensive theory' which he states in the following series of ten propositions.

(1) People differ in their abilities, interests and personalities.
(2) They are qualified, by virtue of these characteristics, each for a number of occupations.
(3) Each of these occupations require a characteristic pattern of abilities, interests and personality traits, with tolerances wide enough, however, to allow both some variety of occupations for each individual and some variety of individuals in each occupation.
(4) Vocational preferences and competencies, the situations in which people live and work, and hence their self concepts, change with time and experience (although self concepts are generally fairly stable from late adolescence until late maturity), making choice and adjustment a continuous process.
(5) This process may be summed up in a series of life stages characterized as those of growth, exploration, establishment, maintenance, and decline, and these stages may in turn be sub-divided into (a) the fantasy, tentative and realistic phases of the exploratory stage, and (b) the trial and stable phases of the establishment stage.
(6) The nature of the career pattern (that is, the occupational level attained and the sequence, frequency, and duration of trial and stable jobs) is determined by the individual's parental socio-economic level, mental ability, and personality characteristics, and by the opportunities to which he is exposed.
(7) Development through the life stages can be guided, partly by facilitating the process of maturation of abilities and interests and partly by aiding in reality testing and in the development of the self concept.
(8) The process of vocational development is essentially that of developing and implementing a self concept: it is a compromise process in which the self concept is a product of the interaction of inherited aptitudes, neural and endocrine make-up, opportunity to play various roles, and evaluations of the extent to which the results of role playing meet with the approval of superiors and fellows.
(9) The process of compromise between individual and social factors, between self concept and reality, is one of role playing, whether the role is played in fantasy, in the counselling interview, or in real life activities such as school classes, clubs, part-time work, and entry jobs.
(10) Work satisfactions and life satisfactions depend upon the extent to which the individual finds adequate outlets for his abilities, interests, personality traits, and values; they depend upon his establishment in the type of work, work situation, and way of life in which he can play the kind of role which his growth and exploratory experiences have led him to consider congenial and appropriate.

In a 1963 book Super starts from the position that:

'In expressing a vocational preference, a person puts into occupational terminology his idea of the kind of person he is; . . . in entering an occupation he seeks to implement a concept of himself: . . . in getting established in an occupation he achieves self-actualization. The occupation thus makes possible the playing of a role appropriate to the self concept.'

He goes on to review research on self concepts in vocational development and concludes with a systematic statement on 'the elements of a self-concept theory of vocational development, the processes by which the self concept affects vocational development'. He identifies these elements of the theory as the processes of formation, translation and implementation of the self concept.

Exploration, he says, appears to be the first phase of the evolution of the concept of self, though it is an essential and continuing process. The self is an object of exploration as it develops and changes; so, too, is the environment. The second phase is that of self differentiation, the realization that one is a separate entity from other persons and the learning of ways in which one resembles and is different from others. A process of identification with certain accessible adults and older persons, mainly of the same sex, occurs more or less simultaneously with differentiation. Role playing (emulation, trying on for size), either in imagination or attempts at actual imitation, accompanies or follows identification. From role playing stems reality testing, in the form of children's play, in school courses (in which one discovers the subjects in which one prospers or fails), in extra-curricular activities, in part-time or temporary employment. 'These reality testing experiences strengthen or modify self concepts and confirm or contradict the way in which they have been tentatively translated into an occupational role.'

Self concepts are translated into occupational terms. Identification with an adult sometimes seems to lead to a desire to play his occupational role; this global vocational self concept, assumed as a whole, may be just as totally discarded when subjected to reality testing. Experience in a role in which one is cast, perhaps more or less by chance, may lead to the discovering of a congenial and unexpected vocational translation of one's self concept. Awareness that one had attitudes that are said to be important in a certain field of work may lead one to look into that occupation and this may confirm one's idea that one will do well in it and enjoy it.

As education is completed or professional training entered and the young person moves into the world of work, he implements or actualizes his self concept. The young engineering graduate gets his first job as an engineer and rejoices in his new title. At the other extreme, the high school drop-out who never did well in his studies, who was never accepted by his classmates, who has faced a number of rejections for jobs, or dismissals, finds the occupational translation of his self concept as ne'er-do-well confirmed and implemented. 'With the population explosion in the labour market . . . the unfortunates who enter the market with poor self concepts and inadequate vocational translations of these self-concepts will have all too many opportunities to confirm them.'

Super, somewhat to my surprise, does not seem to be arguing entirely that the realization actualisation process is a satisfying, fulfilling one, supportive of one's self-concept. He says that entry into an occupation may confirm a negative self-image. It is an odd conception that one may be 'implementing' an unfavourable self-image.[18] Given the fact that most of us need to develop defensive beliefs to account for fates inferior to those we wish for ourselves, I would suggest that one is more likely to retain a moderately favourable self-concept and to develop notions about unfairness or luck in occupational placements.

P. M. Blau and associates

This well-known paper, published in 1956,[19] presents a framework for the understanding of occupational choice that constitutes an attempt to combine psychological, economic and sociological variables. In effect, the authors add the latter two categories of variables to the psycho-logically-centred theories of Ginzberg and Super, emphasising that the occupational preferences that come to crystallize do not finally determine occupational entry. Whether these preferences can be realized, must be modified or even set aside, depends on the decisions of persons selecting for education, training and occupations, and on the conditions affecting their choice.

In other words, to explain the occupations people are in, an examina-tion of the processes by which they choose one occupation in preference to another must be complemented by an analysis of the processes by which some individuals and not others come to be accepted for a given occupation. Understanding how people get into their occupations requires study of personality development (including the development and stabilization of occupational preferences) *together with* analysis of the development of the social and economic conditions of selection.

Social structure has a dual significance for occupational choice. On the one hand, it influences the personality developments of the choosers: on the other it defines the socio-economic conditions in which selection takes place. But the structural effects have their significance in different phases. At any choice point in his career, the individual's interests, skills, and preferences are affected by *past* social structure; but educational opportunities and the requirements for entry to occupations are deter-mined by the structure then current.

Blau and his colleagues provide conceptualizations of the analytically complementary processes of choices made on the one hand by persons seeking to enter particular occupations and, on the other, by educators and employers acting as gatekeepers or selectors. As they say, beginning with the person, if workers were completely indifferent between various occupations it would be only the selection process or pure chance that accounted for workers being in one occupation rather than another. But they are not indifferent. They possess, and attempt to implement, their preferences.

Choice is motivated by two sets of factors: (i) the individual's valuations of the rewards offered by different alternatives—his hierarchy of preferences; and (ii) his appraisal (expectations) of his chances of being able to realize each of the alternatives. (Such choices, these writers note, are restricted by lack of knowledge of alternatives and are not necessarily conscious and deliberate.)

The course of action on which a person decides will reflect a compromise between his preferences and expectations. His actual choice will not be identical with his first preference if his expectation of reaching the preferred goal is very low. The compromise is continually modified up to the time of actual entry, since each experience in the labour market (and in education) affects his preferences and expectations. Occupational choice is a process involving a series of decisions to present oneself to employers and other selectors as a candidate for a range of occupations. Each decision is governed by the way in which one compromises one's ideal preference with one's actual expectations of being able to enter a given occupation, the latter being conditioned by experience. Not everyone ends up in the first occupation for which he presents himself. Many are not accepted, quit or are dismissed after a time.

The process of choice involves a descent in a hierarchy of preferences (or the acquisition of new qualifications) which comes to an end, at least temporarily, by being selected for an occupation.

On the selection side, persons with certain characteristics, including relevant experience, have the greatest chances of being hired in a particular occupation. If fewer people with the optimal characteristics apply than are required, employers lower their standards of what is required (and try to remedy deficiencies later) *or* increase the rewards.

Occupational selection consists of successive decisions by employers (and other selectors) about applicants for jobs. The decision about each candidate is guided by the employer's ideal standards and by his estimate of the chances that a better qualified candidate than the one under consideration will present himself in the near future. The process involves a regression from ideal standards or an increase in rewards. As Blau and his colleagues say, their framework merely suggests the relevant variables to take into account; their relative weight can be determined only by empirical research on particular sectors of the population and of labour markets.

They remind us further of the need for an historical approach in this field of study. Prior personal experience affects range of choice and re-actions to new opportunities; the occupational experiences of parents transmit particular orientations to their children as well as influencing their preferences and their chances of implementing these; and know-ledge of past shifts in the labour market, alongside present labour demand conditions, is needed to help explain why people are distributed between occupations as they are and new prospective entrants develop the preferences that they do.

PAPERS REPRINTED IN THIS VOLUME

In this section I comment on certain points in the paper to which I feel special attention should be drawn. I do not provide a synopsis of each paper, as the authors have usually done this in a concluding section. In addition, several of the later papers summarize the main conclusions of those published earlier.

In some cases, it is a conceptual or theoretical contribution to which I draw attention. I have selected from the papers certain research findings on which social scientists are now converging, which take us appreciably forward in our substantive knowledge of the field, or which differ markedly from what most of us would assume to be true. In a few places I describe or point to sociological or social psychological work other than that referred to by the authors of the papers, where I feel that this sheds particular light on an issue that has been raised. At some points I suggest promising lines for further research.

It is, in the main, on the sociological rather than the psychological aspects of the papers that I comment. Some of the authors write as if they are trying to provide a complete or comprehensive theory of occupational choice. But the main overall contribution of the papers lies, I believe, in their analysis of the social arrangements that help shape early occupational preferences; of the structure and institutions that determine how people are, in fact, allocated between occupations; and of the effect of education and work environments on attitudes to work in general, and to the specific job in which the person finds himself.

Accuracy of appraisal of occupational chances

'The general picture that emerges from this study is one of startlingly accurate appraisal of life-chances by the children, and a shrewd appreciation of the social and economic implications of their placing within the educational system. They know at what age they will marry, the best type of job they can get, and the best wage they can hope to earn at that job. Having accepted the role they are to play in life, they rarely venture out of it even in fantasy.'

This is one of Liversidge's conclusions from his study of Grammar School and Modern School boys and girls at various stages of their schooling.[20] It is based mainly in his research findings that occupational aspirations and expectations are significantly higher among the Grammar School children who, in reality, do have substantially better chances of higher status and more rewarding occupations. The Grammar Schools appeared to elevate the expectations of those children who came to them from the lower social classes. Complementarily, in Modern Schools more than half of the upper class boys expected to get lower-class jobs. The pupils seem to be increasingly aware of the occupational implications of their educational selection: this became evident when Liversidge compared the aspirations of children at the primary and secondary school stages.

Liversidge quotes in support of his findings about children's realism a study by P. M. Freeston which found that only 6 per cent of 955 children expressed job choices which were rated 'impossible'. In Liversidge's study, perception of wages was also found to be 'extremely realistic'.

In the article by Keil and her colleagues, however, two important qualifications are made to this general proposition about realism concerning occupational prospects. One is that, while the mention of range of occupations may be realistic, several studies show that the mention of the favoured occupations within that range is less realistic. Within the limits of manual work, for instance, there is a concentration of aspirations toward skilled trades and, among these, toward certain favoured trades. The implication is that people are over-optimistic about the precise job they will get within an accurately specified overall range. The second proviso is that investigators agree that while knowledge of wages and hours is very accurate, knowledge of work content and training requirements is very slight.

In the paper by Timperley and Gregory, vagueness about the job one is likely to take up within a sector is interpreted as indifference to that sector, even if it is one which one realises one will probably enter. They do not mention whether there is a tendency to be over-optimistic in their case and they presumably are reporting mere vagueness. It is evidently a matter for further empirical research to discover what proportions of school leavers can be specific (and are subsequently proved correct) about the first jobs they will secure, what proportions are wrong and in what directions they err, and what proportions are simply unable to specify. Within this design one could test the various notions about the causes (or at least the obvious possible correlates) of accuracy, vagueness, pessimism and optimism.

Purposiveness and rationality in occupational decision making

Ford and Box interpret current discussions of occupational choice as implicitly stressing a purposive element in occupational choice. There is now, they feel, general agreement that the phenomenon of occupational choice is to be viewed as a rational process in which the person weighs certain ends he desires against the probability that he will attain them.[21] One of the authors, Ford, formulated with George Homans the following two propositions:

(1) In choosing between alternative occupations, a person will rank each occupation in terms of the relation between his values and the perceived characteristics of the occupation: the higher the coincidence between these characteristics and his values the higher the rank.

(2) The higher a person perceives the probability that he will obtain employment in the higher-ranked occupation, the more likely he is to choose that occupation.

Ford and Box describe in their paper a research project that yielded results roughly consistent with these two propositions.

Their argument is helpful in countering the view that occupational choices are adventitious or fortuitous, unique spontaneous behaviour explicable only by reference to the idiosyncracies of particular choice situations. The assertion in this argument is that because the person may be unconscious of his choice processes, and choices are often based on inadequate information, there are no sociological regularities to examine. As Ford and Box demonstrate, systematic reconciliations take place between values and expectations. Occupational choice is thereby seen as the culmination of a process in which hopes and desires come to terms with the realities of the occupational market situation. Ford and Box see occupational choice as purposive or rational in the sense that people try to realise their occupational values (or to minimize expected deprivations) in their choice of occupation. Occupational choice is not random.

A critic might justifiably express some reservations at this point, however, about the use of the terms 'purposive' and 'rational'. I would be happier with their argument if they had used the word 'understandable' or 'comprehensible'. As I see it, they are arguing essentially that if one sees the world from the point of view of the chooser his behaviour makes sense.

This would be consistent with the so-called 'action' frame of reference, popular today in sociology and a central tradition in social anthropology, emphasising that whether behaviour should be described as rational depends on the point of view of the describer. What makes sense to the person choosing his occupation in terms of his aspirations, his personal history, his personal values, his social acquaintanceships, his knowledge and perceptions of his opportunities might well seem strange to an external judge making a more 'objective' evaluation of his capacities in relation to the realities of the job market. It follows from this that a sociological analysis can be made of the social worlds of job seekers, of major categories of job values, and of attempts to realize these values in the occupational market. It does not follow that choice is rational, either from the chooser's point of view or from that of a hypothetical external observer, with respect to the outcome of the choice, that is, in regard to whether the choice has worked out as expected, whether the person has adapted to those parts of it he dislikes or that were unexpected, or whether he is satisfactory to his employer. The Ford and Box paper appears essentially to be a successful argument that systematic regularities can be identified in the expression of job preferences and in attempts during the course of job-seeking to implement those preferences.

A lead could have been taken here from H. A. Simon, who points out (in relation to administrative behaviour) that the concept of rationality poses multiple problems.[22] He suggested that the difficulties can be met by qualifying the concept in each case with the appropriate adverb. To adapt his reasoning to the particular case here, a decision could be 'objectively' rational if it maximised given values in a given situation, 'subjectively' rational if it maximised attainment relative to the actual knowledge of the subject, 'personally' rational if oriented to the individual's goals. Following Simon, one would argue that Ford and Box are demonstrating, so far as their research goes, that occupational decision making appears to be 'personally' and 'subjectively' rational.

A business-like contribution in a closely related area follows later from Haystead. Her style is highly reminiscent of Simon, whose approach has obviously influenced her considerably. She draws attention, like Ford and Box, to the chooser's definition of his situation and comments on the interplay between a person's awareness of different alternatives, and the objective facts regarding alternatives and possibilities of choice. As she says, this opens the way for study of how far people are aware, at various stages of their lives, of the possibilities and compulsions that face them. She is in effect suggesting repeated studies of a cohort of persons in regard to the 'subjective' rationality of their choices and the ways in which this might change with increased information and experience. Simon's work emphasises that people make choices within a range of alternatives more limited than the whole range objectively available to them. All alternatives are not evaluated before a decision is made. Alternatives are normally examined sequentially, with the important consequence that the first satisfactory alternative evaluated tends to be the one actually selected. The key to the simplification of the choice process is the replacement of the goal of maximizing (making the best possible choice) with the goal of 'satisficing', that is, finding a course of action that is good enough. Simon appears to see the central factor limiting rationality in human decision taking as the inability of the human mind to grasp more than a proportion of all knowable facts and possible consequences of action.[23] To this must be added the influence of emotional factors that structure perceptions of alternatives, sometimes distorting 'reality', sometimes resulting in the unconscious obliteration of what outside persons would regard as obvious facts.

These considerations, coupled with the work of Ford and Box, Haystead and certain other of our contributors, raise the question of the relation of personal and subjective rationality to objective rationality. 'Objective' rationality may be a mirage in occupational choice, because completeness of information is impossible and impractical and because one person cannot establish for another what is the 'correct' way for him to behave. But there is obviously a function for advisers to perform in pointing out to job-seekers ways of trying to obtain their objectives that may not have occurred to them, or in slowing them down when closure in job choice seems premature. As Dill, Hilton and Reitman remark,

'While a fair amount of rational effort may go into the final decision among a small number of definite job offers, less usually goes into the development of the set of offers from which this final choice is made. For most men, the alternatives that they consider depend as much on the haphazard structure of the information system to which they are exposed during the job hunt as on carefully spelled out career objectives.'[24]

They make this statement in discussing Business School graduates. It gains force when one applies it to the general population of school leavers, whom one can assume to be less systematic in attempts to generate job offers, less deliberately sought out by those offering jobs and less well informed about the possibilities.

Cyril Sofer

The role of school experience in adjustment to work

It is argued from time to time that the transition from school to work is stressful, particularly for young people whose first jobs are boring and monotonous, are closely supervised or are of a blind-alley character. This is said to lead to disappointment and to disillusion that can express itself in ill-health and social deviance. The experience has been described, in extreme terms, as a 'culture shock'. As Keil and her colleagues point out, in peasant societies without formal school systems the introduction to work is a gradual one, whereas in modern industrial societies a child is separated from the working world for a large part of his day and his formal contact with work is severely limited by legislation.

They cite Miller and Form as authors who have developed systematically the view that shock results from the confrontation of the realities of the work situation with expectations carried from the school situation. Main emphasis in the Miller and Form contrast between school and work is on the differences between the social situation and position of the young person in the two milieus, and, especially, on what they treat as the clash of values between these. As they put it, in school the ages of those with whom one interacts (apart from the teacher) are similar; at work ages vary widely. By his last year at school, a boy is very familiar with that institution, knows how it works, has some weight and possibly a formal position of authority in it: as a new entrant into a work situation he is a minor figure without experience or authority. At school he is a permanent member of a group: at work both he and his employer may terminate their relationship. Miller and Form then emphasise differences in the values which they suggest dominate school and work. School, they say, asserts the desirability of co-operation, work the primacy of self-interest. Schools attempt to implant an ethic of morally correct behaviour; work is characterized by amorality. Schools try to foster full self-development, i.e. encourage expression of many and diverse abilities and qualities: while work underlines the importance of persistence and mastery in one specialized sphere or other. Schools tend to accept and value individuality while work organizations deal with people more categorically. Apart from these suggested contrasts in situation, position and values, Miller and Form point out that stress is likely to result when aspirations do not correspond with the possibilities that the labour market offers: they cite American research indicating that school-children aspire to jobs above the level they achieve.

As Keil and her colleagues say, these sharp dichotomies (no doubt exaggerated by Miller and Form for expository and conceptualization purposes) under-represent the complexity and variety of actual late-schooling and early-work experiences; and the values listed for each context may correspond more with exhortations of educators (and they could have added the fantasies of academics) about industry than with real life. Many empirical studies of industrial work groups have described the existence of powerful group norms governing the cooperation expected from work group colleagues, including the maintenance of production within tolerable limits. Such studies demonstrate that it is inaccurate to characterize behaviour at work as expressing prominent values of self-interest and amorality.

These remarks convey that we should not be tempted to over-generalize about contrasts between school and work or to exaggerate the differences. Keil and colleagues make the further important point that certain informal aspects of school life perform positively socializing functions for work. Slum schools in city areas, with poor physical facilities and high turnover among teachers often place schoolchildren in conflict with their teachers and encourage the 'we-they' view of society. In these senses, as Keil says, these school situations can be seen as sources of experience that will help adjustment to the realities of industrial life in the lower ranks. The writers have an important point here, which deserves further study. One can think of many lessons of social life that are taught and underlined among schoolmates and practised at work. These include the setting of collective or average standards of performance that defy higher authority's attempts at influence; collusive practices of concealment of information that constitutes a group asset; techniques for getting by without effort or without attracting unwelcome attention; resistance to change; the introduction of distractions from boring routine tasks. All of these phenomena have been amply demonstrated in studies of industrial workers. A beginning has been made in certain studies of schools cited by Keil and also in studies of university students, such as the medical students in *Boys in White*[25], to document these phenomena.

A recent article by S. Millham, R. Bullock and P. Cherrett[26] implies that we should look for the causes of such resemblances in the behaviour of industrial workers and schoolchildren in the common mechanisms of social control used in such organizations.

In their rebuttal of the 'culture shock' hypothesis Keil and colleagues discuss the part said to be played by disappointed expectations when young people cannot get the jobs they want. They refer back at this point to the topic with which I opened my discussion of the contributed papers, i.e. the convergence of British studies on the finding that the vocational aspirations of British schoolchildren tend to be highly realistic. The more realistic clearly the less scope for shock. As several of the contributors indicate, for instance Musgrave in his earlier paper, school curricula shape occupational motives. The structure of the British schooling system (which is, of course, linked with type of home, neighbourhood and national social stratification) has the effect of directing a child's attention to the cluster of occupations characteristically followed by children from the type of school he attends. The British schooling system is highly stratified and, as Allen's article implies, pre-work social experience (including that gained at school, in the neighbourhood and in the family) correlates quite closely with subsequent position in the occupational structure. The school and subsequent work roles filled by a young person have a certain systematic connection and are not independently determined. Indeed one of the central conclusions from this collection of papers must be that particular types of school experience go together with particular types of occupation in unitary social worlds.

An interesting theoretical paper along these lines has been published by W. Watson[27] who pointed out that, in a local community of persons of roughly similar social status, superior educational achievement leading to a grammar-school education or its equivalent presages a discontinuity in occupational and social status between child and parent. Such children tend to leave the community and to become occupationally and physically mobile. They become 'spiralists' up the social system, sharing a distinct national culture with others similarly mobile, in contrast with their contemporaries (and families) who persist in the same residences with their distinguishing customs and local dialects.

Special abilities, special efforts and special social circumstances have to exist if people are to have occupational destinies other than those linked with their education. We can, and should, attempt to specify both the constraining factors and the combinations of circumstances that must exist for people to move out of closed social circles.

Frustration or potential frustration in the job

In the preceding discussion we mentioned, in connection with the 'culture shock' proposition, American evidence to the effect that in the U.S. a high proportion of young persons in the population may get jobs that they rate as inferior to those to which they aspired, and U.K. views regarding the negative implications for young workers when they realise that they are in blind alley occupations. These findings and assertions run counter to the proposition, already discussed, that schools, in Britain at any rate, probably go a long way to prepare (socialize) young people for the type of occupational experience they will actually have, in the sense that once one is in a particular type of school it is already fairly clear what sort of occupations are open or closed to one.

One of our papers does, however, suggest that young people in Britain are likely to feel frustrated in their jobs or have life experiences that doom them to disappointment and suffering in their jobs.

Timperley and Gregory examined the educational intentions, the aspirations and expectations of sixth form leavers, the information that appeared to influence their career perspectives and their images of industry and commerce. The research was carried out at 13 secondary schools in the Merseyside area. Five were boys' grammar schools, four were girls' grammar schools, one was a girls' direct grant school, and there were three mixed comprehensive schools. Questionnaires were sent out to these schools to be answered by students mid-way through their final sixth form year and who were about to take Advanced level subjects in the G.C.E. Examinations. Of the 431 replies received, 233 were from girls and 198 from boys.[28] Timperley and Gregory point to a sharp drop (difference) in proportions mentioning the 'more glamorous' areas (journalism, arts and entertainment) when aspirations and expectations are compared, and a corresponding rise in proportions mentioning industry, commerce and education. The authors assume that these changes come from those people who were 'unconvinced as to their abilities to obtain jobs in the areas of their choice'. While this differential response to questions on aspiration and expectation imply a realism in what will actually happen, the research workers emphasise that 15 per cent of their respondents may find themselves working in industry, commerce or education, which are not the areas in which they would ideally like to work. What is interpreted as further evidence on their indifference to these areas is their inability to specify the jobs in these sectors in which they would expect to work.[29] Timperley and Gregory note that expectations of being able to enter higher education are less certain among those who aspire to an industrial or commercial career and feel that this may mean that industry and commerce are recruiting people for whom an immediate industrial or commercial career is a second choice. Their data on expectations of entry to higher education imply more widely that, of sixth form leavers actually leaving to enter employment, half will regard immediate employment as second best. Further, they note from their data on images of industry that some 30 per cent even of those who wish to enter industry and commerce have a distinctly negative view of their proposed future occupation.

These results imply that quite considerable proportions of school leavers will enter sectors of the economy that are not their first choice and that those who enter industry and commerce are especially likely to be in occupations for which they do not have a high regard. While it is tempting to conclude from this that a high proportion of new entrants into jobs are likely to be disappointed or frustrated in those jobs, that temptation should be resisted. There are several reasons for this.

First, there is the fact that Timperley and Gregory are dealing particularly with the higher end of the British educational spectrum, that is, the smallest sector and that in which occupational aspirations are likely to be highest. As several of our contributors argue, the educational system of this country is so stratified that in general different types of schools steer their products to particular ranges of occupation. This is also true, of course, for educational level and here we have the highest level, the sixth form.

Second, there are strong indications from many sources in the literature, both in this book and elsewhere, that powerful adaptive mechanisms operate to reconcile persons with types of jobs that are not their first choice. The existence of a generic process, of which this can be regarded as an example, is suggested by psychological experiments on the formation and change of aspiration levels. These studies show that when performance falls short of level of aspiration, search behaviour, particularly search for new alternatives of action, is induced. At the same time, level of aspiration is adjusted downward until goals reach levels that are practically attainable. Many of our contributors, as well as the classic studies summarized, describe an evident passage from fantasy to greater realism in job preference. In effect this includes Timperley and Gregory, who distinguish between aspiration and expectation. As Roberts notes, although many school-leavers fail to enter their chosen jobs, few express dissatisfaction with the employment they actually attain: different investigations have found only about 50 per cent of school-leavers realizing their ambitions (presumably he means in the U.K.), but, once these 'thwarted school-leavers' are in employment, few want to leave their jobs. 'They claim to be satisfied with their work and adjust their ambitions to the occupations they have entered.' This statement is consistent with research on job satisfaction that indicates strongly that most people, when directly questioned, represent themselves as reasonably satisfied with their jobs. It appears that adult workers tend to become emotionally involved in whatever occupation they happen to be working at, or at least to adapt themselves to those social arrangements in which they are implicated.[30]

As Morse and Weiss put it, after finding, as many other U.S. investigators have done, that 80 per cent of the employed men in their study were either very satisfied or satisfied with their jobs, '. . . . most individuals accommodate themselves to their chances and possibilities in life and in general do not maintain, as aspirations chances and opportunities not within their scope to realize'.[31]

Since job fates differ from aspirations and vary enormously in material and non-material rewards, in interest, variety, autonomy and so on—all of which are known to be highly valued by most workers—the implication is strong that in Western industrial society at any rate, people reconcile themselves one way or another to occupational fates inferior to, or at any rate different from, those they would prefer. This phenomenon is usually discussed in terms of unconscious psychological defences, or, following Festinger, in terms of the reduction of dissonance in resolving post-decisional conflict. As Festinger puts it:

> 'There are two major ways in which the individual can reduce dissonance in this situation. He can persuade himself that the attractive features of the rejected alternative are not really so attractive as he had originally thought, and that the unattractive features of the chosen alternative are not really unattractive. He can also provide additional justification for his choice by exaggerating the attractive features of the rejected alternative. In other words, according to the theory the process of dissonance reduction should lead, after the decision, to an increase in the desirability of the chosen alternative and a decrease in the desirability of the rejected alternative.'[32]

There is also the fact that one's evaluation of one's fate depends closely on the persons with whom one compares oneself. If the school-leaver notices, as he will, that his peers land up in much the same type of occupation as himself, this will help him to reconcile himself to what has happened. As Stouffer and others have shown, deprivation is a relative matter and a key variable is with whom one is comparing oneself.[33] My own research has suggested, further, that occupational and organizational ideologies develop at all levels of work organisation which perform the function, *inter alia*, of providing a systematic theory that serves those who subscribe to it by protecting their self-esteem and warding off real, imagined or potential criticism from others. Colleagues and friends who share these ideologies play a key role in maintaining each other's self-esteem.[34]

In regard to 'unsatisfactory' or less preferable jobs, it has often been shown that meaning tends to be introduced into jobs and job contexts found unsatisfactory by those performing them.[35] This is done, for instance, by elaborating the movements required, by working to targets defined by the worker himself or by groups of workers, by introducing social rituals or games or by thwarting supervisors and managerial groups.

Finally, we must beware of the temptation endemic among intellectual workers to assign centrality to work in the life space of most people. Several research workers and writers on the theory of work have drawn attention in recent years to what appears to be a growing instrumental attitude to work and to an apparent trend toward 'privatization', i.e. a withdrawal into family and personal life from active participation in mass institutions, including the institutions of the work place and trade unions.[36] Whether or not there is such a trend, we must keep in mind the fact that work is only one of several life activities from which satisfactions are derived, or are potentially derivable, and that these can substitute or compensate for each other. One's work is not everything.

'Occupational choice' as process

Our contributors accept and elaborate the viewpoint of the classical studies described that occupational choices and occupational decisions are probably best regarded as largely continual processes in that they are often the result of interaction over a protracted period between aspiration, preference, self-discovery, influence, opportunity and experience.

As Keil and her colleagues put it

'. . . evidence from a wide range of research suggests that family, neighbourhood, peer groups, education received, influences from mass media, the extent of formal vocational guidance, all need to be considered, and that experience from these sources, as well as the nature of the work undertaken, are relevant to the development of any particular reaction toward working life. This implies that entering the world of work and adjusting to it is a *process*.

An indication of the nature of this process may be given in the following way: (*a*) *The socialization of the young person to the world of work*, together with (*b*) *Previous work experience*, and (*c*) *Wider social influences*, lead on the one hand to (*d*) *The formulation of a set of attitudes towards, and expectations about, work*. (*a*), (*b*) and (*c*) together, and (*d*) provide the explanation for (*e*) *The actual job entry*, and from this (*f*) *Experiences as a worker* lead to a situation of (*g*) *Adjustment/non-adjustment for the young worker* which can be expressed either by a measure of satisfaction, by a re-formulation of (*d*) above, by ritualized dissatisfaction, or by job change.'

Musgrave sees the process of the development of occupational preferences and of attempts to implement these[37] in terms of movement between a series of linked roles. He represents the (potential) life cycle as a large number of alternative pathways theoretically available to individual members of a given society. Choice (or direction by others) at each stage limits the possible pathways along which the individual may travel in the future. The pre-work stage of socialisation (in the sense of role preparation) for producer roles significantly shapes occupational preferences. In the pre-work stage the pathway of roles available to the child, and hence his occupational range, are narrowed by the experience he undergoes at the hands of family, school and peer group. He comes to realize what possible roles are available for him and develops a self-concept that narrows the range from which he will choose. The structure of the British schooling system directs the child's attention to the cluster of occupations in practice connected with the type of school he is attending. Peer group influence, including the dominant view of work—as a means to an end or an end in itself, as a central life interest or peripheral activity—will have an important bearing on the way in which he ultimately settles into the labour force. In the phase of entry into the labour force, preference must become choice and choice must match the selection processes of employers. The initial choice or first actual post may not be a final destination. The individual's personality may be grossly unsuited to the first job or jobs attempted, and technological changes and changes in the fates of organizations and of occupational groups may result in the person changing his job once or more often.

The subsequent critique of Musgrave by Coulson *et al.* does not reject the conceptualization of occupational choice as a process. It emphasises that the process of movement towards and into the world of work is not necessarily a smooth one and that the phases are not always neatly articulated with each other. As they say, anticipatory socialization may include rehearsal of roles that are anticipated wrongly and young people do not know the content of the work roles they may assume. Ford and Box are correct in summarizing a whole body of recent work as 'entailing the view that occupational choice represents the culmination of a process in which hopes and desires come to terms with the realities of the occupational market situation'. They agree with Keil and Musgrave that attention should be paid to socialization into work attitudes and say that 'It is clear that there is a need for the development of a theory to explain the process by which differential occupational values are acquired'.

Their next statement comes as a shock, that 'in order to derive and test a general theory of occupational choice it is sufficient to take value orientations as given and explore no longer the process by which they are acquired'. But this is a legitimate argument. Most writers in this area use the term 'occupational' choice very widely to refer to the development of preferences between occupations and attempts to implement those preferences. This is a different matter from the attempt of an individual to discriminate between alternatives concretely open to him, which is what Ford and Box are talking about. I think that this narrower use of the term occupational choice is more logical than its wider use and less likely to be misleading in its implications regarding the part played by deliberate personal selections in the distribution of people between occupations at any given time.

Most of our contributors concede or acknowledge that whether a person succeeds in implementing his earlier occupational preferences depends on his acceptability to employers in the jobs that might allow him to realize his values. The extent to which potential employers actively interest themselves in the process of opening and closing off routes to particular types of job and career could, however, do with more attention. In my own studies of executive careers I have described the highly formalised methods used by large organizations to induce potential management trainees to apply to them, to scrutinize their abilities and personalities in selection procedures, and subsequently to guide their experience, and to counsel them in a way that contributes to their usefulness to the employing organization and their progress up its hierarchy.[38] Similar efforts are made at national level by the Armed Services, by various other branches of government, by educational authorities and by the social services. The majority of new entrants to organizations are, however, most probably recruited more directly in local areas by neighbourhood organizations and analyses of their efforts to attract particular categories of worker would help to illuminate the processes by which young people get into their occupations.

Search for an appropriate occupation and settling into an occupation are closely linked with the process of developing and consolidating personal identity. Infants, children and adults learn, consolidate and to some extent alter over a period of time their conceptions of themselves. During adolescence the individual subordinates his childhood identifications to new kinds of identifications; he repudiates some and reinforces others. He must make gains by the end of adolescence in order to be ready for the tasks of adulthood. At adolescence or immediate post-adolescence the young person has ideas of some of his possibilities and tries them out on the people he meets. Some of these 'attempted identities' cannot be sustained. They will normally wither as a result of inner doubt and social rejection. Others have more reality in them, gain more external support and become consolidated.

The adolescent period has been described by Erikson as an institutionalized psycho-social moratorium, by which he means a period during which the person is entitled to experiment in his definitions of what he is and would like to become.[39] He need not feel obliged to stay within a line because he has entered it. He can fail without disgrace and without incurring the odium associated with failing to be what he has implied himself to be. Fluctuations in his beliefs, and ambitions are tolerated.

Each person needs to make the best of attributes that he really possesses and the value of which is recognized in his environment. His experiences of 'producing' and being rewarded help form his core of self-esteem and give him knowledge about the talents he has and those he lacks. He tends then to seek situations in which he can make the greatest use of himself. An important aspect of identity formation is the ability to recognize his own limitations, to abandon ambitions that require the exercise of talents and the development of potentialities that he lacks.

The young person searches for a 'true' personality, an internally consistent set of behaviours and attitudes that are maintained through time. Complementarily, he needs a social niche. As Rappaport has described it in discussing Erikson's theories the crucial co-ordination is between the developing individual and his human (social) environment, a cog-wheeling between person and society throughout his life cycle.[40] Jobs particularly confirm to oneself and to others that one is competent at a set of objective tasks and can maintain stable social relationships with people outside the family in a co-operative endeavour which is in social demand.

Although several students of occupational choice have argued that this involves a process rather than being a once and for all decision, attempts to describe the actual sequence of events are rare. Janis and Mann have, however, suggested five phases in a sequence through which a person goes in moving toward a decision, including an occupation decision.[41] The stages are:

Stage 1. *Appraisal of a challenge*: The individual is exposed to information, advice or influence that challenges his current action or inaction by calling attention to important losses that will ensue if he does not change. This produces personal tension because inconsistency between the new stimulus and the person's current plans and commitments generate conflict about continuing his present policy.

Stage 2. Appraisal of alternatives: He focuses his attention on a range of possible courses of action, which he initially evaluates to see whether one of them can meet the challenge. He also scans his memory for alternatives considered to have a good chance of averting or reducing the losses made salient by the challenge.

Stage 3. Selection of the best alternative: He proceeds to a more thorough evaluation of each of the surviving alternatives in an effort to select the best available policy. 'Satisficing' may occur when there is a large number of potential alternatives that seem almost equally attractive at the outset; a person may then simply choose the first which comes to his mind or is drawn to his attention and which meets his minimum requirements. This stage is characterized by a lack of commitment even after he has made his choice. He will remain responsive to new information and will find it relatively easy to change his mind.

Stage 4. Commitment to the new policy: The person announces or reveals his intended course of action to others, usually his friends first and potential critics last. There is a general tendency to avoid negative feedback at this point and to adduce new reasons that bolster the decision. He anticipates loss of self-esteem and social disapproval if he fails to carry out the new policy.

Stage 5. Adherence to the new policy despite negative feedback: This stage is parallel to Stage 1, except that, where adherence occurs, challenging information is discounted, resisted or minimised. In addition to refuting or ignoring arguments offered by opponents to his policy, the perservering decision-maker is likely to continue bolstering his decision. Other modes of resolution used to preserve the new policy include changing one's social network and emphasising to others the wisdom of the choice.

As Janis and Mann indicate, the five-stage sequence points up the continuity of past, current and future decisions.

Apart from the presentation of decisions as sequential, continuous and possibly protracted, the Janis–Mann statement conveys the view that decisions of the sort that interest us here are attended by internal conflict and involve social interaction as well as internal intellectual processes. It is also implicit in this viewpoint that the decisions are based partly on objectively ascertainable social facts and partly on ideas and feelings that are less immediately accessible to external checking or deliberate introspection, i.e. are pre-conscious (and recallable to memory) or unconscious.

Commitments in the decision process

Entry into an occupation is usually preceded by a number of educational steps that are difficult or impossible to retrieve. In a society where occupational fate depends largely on education, one of the major turning points in a person's life is that at which the decision is made as to what sort of school he enters; another is at the stage at which he decides (or has it decided for him) whether to go from school to university; another is at the stage of a completion of a first degree, at which he may have the choice between postgraduate work and immediate entry into a job. Similar crucial decisions have to be made later on with respect to choices between competing job offers, choices between technical and administrative work, choices between geographic locations and so on.

Initial entry into an occupation is often binding in regard to one's future work life. Initial entry into a particular occupation or organization sets an investment going, an irreplaceable amount of time is put into a particular job or career. Not following through entails a loss of the investment. A realized mis-investment and an attempt to correct it necessitates a new start. One is then handicapped in competing with others within our age-graded stratification and mobility structure.

As one continues in an occupation, one becomes committed to the title, technical function and ideology of the occupation (particularly those facets that underline its importance to the society). One is specifying implicitly in what sort of organization and position one sees one's future as lying. Through the commitment to the line of work the person has become committed to a particular social and personal identity.[42]

Becker has pointed out that these commitments to a line of work and to a personal identity are not necessarily made consciously and deliberately.[43] One may be precipitated by some one critical decision to identify with an occupation. But more usually one becomes committed by a series of small sequential acts in the job and connected with the job that together incline one in a particular direction.

Haystead's paper in this volume follows the same line of reasoning. She implies that one chooses jobs rather than occupations, but that the various job choices become systematically linked into an identifiable 'career'. These links and the process of crystallization of choice can be overlooked by a research worker when he breaks into a specific point in the overall choice process. Haystead refers helpfully to the 'decision tree' as a device for conceptualizing occupational choice: movements along some branches usually commit one to a point somewhere along that branch and render difficult transfer to other branches on the tree. And the 'actual' tree of decisional possibilities is, of course, something different from what the person perceives or has information about. His behaviour may be purposive or rational in the light of his personal awareness of the possibilities and in the light of his values and aspirations—though not necessarily to advisers or observers who specialise in the study of the occupational woods.

Again, there are illuminating parallels here between the conclusions of writers on occupational decision-taking and writers on organisational behaviour concerning the role of prior commitments in decision-taking.[44] Students of organizations have pointed out that in an established organization, scope for decision-making is constrained by prior decision, explicit or implicit, expressed in earlier investments, moral commitments and so on. This means that every fresh decision need not be made from scratch but also that the decision-maker's range of choice in new decisions is narrowed. Past decisions become an important part of the environment of new decisions.

One line of research that could be productive would be to examine attempts at what may be thought of as 'second chance' careers or attempts to reverse occupational decisions, that is, the efforts of persons well along a path into one type of work to establish themselves in something quite different. Several different kinds of case come to mind: young people who drop out of vocational courses, university students who change their subjects in mid-stream, science and engineering graduates who apply unsuccessfully for grants for postgraduate study; mid-career executives who have been made redundant; 'mature' students who enter universities after some years of employment. These would illuminate the problems involved in retrieving one's steps along a career line and starting off in a new direction, with all this entails in changed financial circumstances, changes in social relations, discrepancies in the customary age-status correspondence, together with internal adjustments in self-image and personal identity.

Structural aspects of occupational choice

Most of the papers in this volume have a predominantly social psychological thrust. I mean by social psychology the overlapping sectors of psychology and sociology which are particularly concerned with describing and explaining how selves are modified through interaction with others and how reciprocating behaviour is directed accordingly. Striking contributions of a more strictly sociological character come from Roberts and Allen: I am treating sociology here as more centrally concerned with the stable arrangements of specialized and mutually dependent institutions and the associated organizations of positions and categories of persons.[45]

Roberts questions the assumptions basic to the work of Ginzberg and Super (and to many other observers and writers on the subject) that occupational choice plays a key role in the employments young people take up. His own research and his careful consideration of the literature and its implications lead him to suggest that

'. . . amongst young people in Britain at any rate, occupational choice does not play the key role in the entry into employment that Super and Ginzberg ascribed to it. Popular commonsense conceives individuals as making up their minds about the sort of work they wish to do and then selecting appropriate jobs. Occupational roles are thought of as being chosen by their players. Popular commonsense, however, is not always consistent with social reality, and the idea that individuals choose jobs and then enter them is a proposition that requires supporting empirical evidence before it can be accepted. When the evidence on the interaction between the ambitions and the occupational behaviour of young people in Britain is carefully examined, the typical pattern of interaction seems not to be for jobs to be entered upon the basis of ambitions, but for ambitions to be adapted to the occupations that young people find themselves able to enter.'

He draws on three types of evidence to support his argument. First, most of the mobility that takes place in the adolescent labour force is not anticipated in their ambitions. Most young people who have been studied in Britain report ambitions consistent with their current jobs but the proportion who actually achieve permanent career stability at this stage is much smaller.

'When questioned, few young employees ever claim to want to move to a different type of work, yet in practice many do so. What seems to happen is that ambitions adjust to occupational changes, rather than change being planned in order to realize previously developed ambitions.'

Second, despite the fact that many school-leavers fail to enter their chosen jobs, few are dissatisfied with the employment that they do obtain. Once these 'thwarted' school-leavers are in employment few want to leave their jobs. They claim to be satisfied with their work and adjust their ambitions to the occupations they have actually entered.

Third, the ambitions of young people, as they describe them to research workers and try to realize them, appear to represent something other than their own 'true' (or original) aspirations. The school-leaver seems to make an effort to adopt realistic ambitions and to relegate to the realm of fantasy earlier aims that cannot be realized.

'To a large extent young people's ambitions appear to be based upon the occupations that they expect to enter rather than upon the vocations they would ideally choose to follow. Ambitions are anticipations of the direction

that careers are going to take. They are products of occupations that individuals are in the process of entering rather than determinants of the pattern
that careers take.'

So, according to Roberts, it is careers that determine ambitions. His
formulation is extremely close to that of Karl Mannheim in his discussion
of economic ambition, though Mannheim is not one of the writers whom
Roberts quotes.[46] Mannheim argues convincingly that our economic
system affects human personality and, especially, that it fosters particular
types of ambition. The actual structure of society, he says, has a direct
influence on the canalization of ambition.

'The economic system is an essential part of social life and a powerful forma-
tive force in man's environment, operating through the psychic mechanism
of ambition, of striving for success . . . an examination of the various social
groups in society and the process of production will give us a fairly comprehensive clue to the kind of incentive likely to characterize average behaviour
in them.'

He asserted what our own contributors later demonstrated, namely
that variability in ambition is closely related to the character of the social
structure of the country and where the person stands in this structure.

'. . . economic ambition is . . . socially differentiated . . . it appears
differently even in the same economic system accordingly the opportunities
for success afforded to the individual by his social position . . . striving for
success *even within the same economic system* and in the same historical period
is variable and elastic . . . work effort is motivated differently at different
points of the social structure . . . whether a man works, why he works,
whether he is ambitious, and if so, what kind of success he seeks, is to a very
large extent pre-determined by that customary range of motives and incentives
associated with his own social group.'

This line of reasoning implies a somewhat Marxist point of view, as
Mannheim acknowledges, that structural changes in the objective world
draw in their train changes in the subjective forms of human experience.
But in his conclusion to this chapter he qualifies what could otherwise
be regarded as an economic determinist argument by pointing out that he
has been arguing that the economic system forms men merely because
he wanted to work out systematically that aspect of the connection
between the two. That is, we are not helpless in the face of our economic
institutions. By this time, however, he has made a powerful case of
precisely the kind made in this volume by Roberts on more empirical
lines to the effect that the structure of the economic system in general,
and that of occupations in particular, moulds personal ambitions and that
differential access to occupations is one central 'causative' influence in
the differential distribution of ambition.

Mannheim's and Robert's arguments are borne out in my own research on career aspirations and satisfactions. This showed a close

similarity of ambition among two groups of industrial executives and technical specialists in different firms but at roughly the same salaries and levels in their organizations. These similarities existed even though one group consisted almost entirely of graduates who had entered industry as research workers or management trainees and the other of men who had left school as soon as they had legally been able and had entered industry on the shop floor or in the most junior positions in offices. The construction I put on my material was that these similarities had followed from similarities in the structure of the hierarchically-organized employing organizations and in the personnel institutions of those organizations, more especially in their management development programmes and evaluation practices. It is hard to see how anyone in such a situation, with even minimal chances of rising, would not develop ambitions to rise.[47]

The most radical paper in the book—radical in many senses—is that by Allen. For my present purpose, that of illustrating the relevance of 'structural' arguments and evidence to the general theme of the book, I wish to underline and support her contention that consideration of youth cannot be separated from the overall structure in which youth is located and is a consequence of structural conditions. She points out that

'In Britain the experience of a 19 year old working class youth is strikingly different from that of a middle or upper class person of the same age. This is not simply a difference of economic or social level, but a difference which permeates every aspect of life.'

As an example of such differences she cites Bernstein's work which shows dramatically the differences between the forms of language learning and thinking that are acquired in different social environments.

Allen argues convincingly that it is not deviant to be unemployed or to take up delinquent occupations if jobs do not exist for you or if rewards are higher in delinquent than in non-delinquent occupations, nor to leave school before completing a course if continuing your education makes only a marginal difference to your occupational chances as seems to be the case for working class youths in Britain and the U.S. As she says, the behaviour of young people, including the low aspirations of some working class school children in Britain, has to be assessed in terms of the realities of their socio-economic situations.

In concluding with and emphasizing structural effects on occupational choice and occupational entry I should like to return to Mannheim. With him, I

'. . . most certainly did not want to suggest that men must accept fatalistically everything that follows "inevitably" from the economic structure. On the contrary, we are of the opinion that under certain circumstances men can also form their own economic and social systems.'

The theories and empirical research reported in this book increase our understanding of the ways in which our present social institutions work and particularly the ways in which they impinge on young people entering the world of work. The reprinted papers together provide an analysis of the structure of constraints and opportunities within which young people and their advisers must at present move. They provide us with several leads as to the sorts of institutional modification that might be attempted to increase economic flexibility and personal choice. And they indicate the sort of empirical monitoring necessary to check how far our attempts at institutional mastery succeed.

[1] E. Ginzberg, S. W. Ginsberg, S. Axelrad and J. L. Herma: *Occupational Choice: an Approach to a General Theory*, New York, Columbia University Press, 1951.

[2] *Ibid.*, p. 40.

[3] *Ibid.*—these are stated mainly in Ch. 15.

[4] *Ibid.*, p. 198. Ginzberg at that stage represented the process of occupational choice as coming to a permanent closure when a person begins to work. He now sees the choice process as coextensive with a person's lifetime. In 1972 he described occupational choice as 'a lifelong process of decision-making in which the individual seeks to find the optimal fit between his career preparation and goals and the realities of the world of work.' E. Ginzberg, 'Toward a Theory of Occupational Choice: A Restatement', *Vocational Guidance Quarterly*, March 1972.

[5] *Ibid.*, p. 27.

[6] It would seem to follow from this that the person has to take into account the way in which he is likely to change.

[7] E. Ginzberg *et al.*, 1951, p. 196.

[8] *Ibid.*, p. 193.

[9] E. Ginzberg and J. L. Herma, with I. E. Berg, C. A. Brown, A. M. Yohalem, J. K. Anderson and L. Lipper: *Talent and Performance*, New York, Columbia University Press, 1964.

[10] *Ibid.*, p. 25.

[11] *Ibid.*, p. 154. The last sentence is rather unfortunate since it implies that satisfaction is not derived from current work. It is unlikely that the authors meant to convey this.

[12] *Ibid.*, pp. 155, 156.

[13] *Ibid.*, p. 157.

[14] *See* T. Burns: 'A Meaning in Everyday Life', *New Society*, May 1967; and Alan Touraine; *Sociologie de l'action*, Paris, Le Seuil, 1966.

[15] E. Ginzberg *et al.*: 1964, pp. 173 174.

[16] *Op. cit.*, p. 175.

[17] D. E. Super: 'A Theory of Vocational Development', *American Psychologist*, Vol. 8, 1953, pp. 185–90.

[18] This is, however, one of the standard meanings of the term (in the sense of understanding and accepting oneself), given in H. B. English and A. C. English: *A Comprehensive Dictionary of Psychological and Psychoanalytical Terms*, London, Longmans Green, 1958.

[19] P. M. Blau, J. W. Gustad, R. Jessor, H. S. Parnes and R. C. Wilcock: 'Occupational Choice: a Conceptual Framework', *Industrial and Labour Review*, Vol. 9, 1956, No. 4, pp. 531–43.

[20] It is not clear from Liversidge's paper whether he sampled whole classes (though one can infer that this is the case), and therefore exactly how his number of returned questionnaires relates to the number of people asked to complete them. I am assuming here that he did sample whole classes and that practically every member completed a questionnaire.

[21] A different view appears to be held by Keil and her colleagues, who say that 'rational assessment of abilities and opportunities . . . does not seem to be a general characteristic of those seeking work.' Unfortunately, they do not quote their evidence on this but refer to a book by them as yet unpublished. They appear primarily to have in mind 'objective rationality' in the sense used later in this section and, insofar as they do, the distance between them and Ford and Box is reduced. They also emphasise the play of influences from others on the prospective job entrant. Ford and Box treat such events as precedent to the individuals's own eventual act of opting between one concrete job alternative and another, on which they focus attention. (See section below on 'Occupational choice' as process.)

[22] H. A. Simon: *Administrative Behaviour: A Study of Decision Making Processes in Administrative Organization*, New York, Macmillan, 1948, pp. 76, 77.

[23] Apart from Simon: *Administrative Behaviour*, see also his *Models of Man, Social and Rational*, New York, Wiley, 1957; and his paper, 'Theories of Decision-making in Economics and Behavioural Science', *American Economic Review*, Vol. 49, June 1959.

[24] W. R. Dill, T. L. Hilton and W. R. Reitman: *The New Managers: Patterns of Behaviour and Development*, Englewood Cliffs, New Jersey, Prentice Hall, 1962.

[25] H. S. Becker, B. Geer, E. C. Hughes and A. L. Strauss: *Boys in White*, Chicago, 1963.

[26] 'Social Control in Organization', *British Journal of Sociology*, Vol. XXII, December 1972, No. 4.

[27] W. Watson: 'Social Mobility and Social Class in Industrial Communities', in M. Gluckman (Ed.): *Closed Systems and Open Minds*, London, Oliver and Boyd, 1964.

[28] Unfortunately the authors do not tell us the total numbers in the sixth forms of the schools so we are unable to judge how representative of those classes their findings are.

[29] See section headed 'Accuracy of appraisal of occupational chances' on whether vagueness on this topic should be interpreted as indifference or is associated with wishful thinking.

[30] This is not, of course, to say that level of satisfaction does not vary with occupation. Practically all studies, at any rate U.S. studies, show that higher proportions of satisfied workers are found among professionals and businessmen than others; among people with 'middle class' than manual working class occupations and within the manual levels, among skilled workers than unskilled labourers or those working on assembly lines. See review of work satisfaction studies by R. Blauner, 'Work Satisfaction and Industrial Trends in Modern Society', in W. Galenson and S. M. Lipset (Eds): *Labour and Trade Unionism: An Inter-disciplinary Reader*, New York, Wiley, 1960.

[31] N. C. Morse and R. S. Weiss: 'The Function and Meaning of the Job', *American Sociological Review*, Vol. 20, 1955.

[32] L. Festinger: 'Cognitive Dissonance', *Scientific American*, October 1962.

[33] S. A. Stouffer *et al.*: *The American Soldier*, Vol. 1, Princeton University Press, 1949.

[34] See C. Sofer: *Men in Mid-Career*, Cambridge University Press, 1970, Chapter 17.

[35] See, for example, D. Roy: 'Banana Time: Job Satisfaction and Informal Organization', *Human Organizations*, Winter 1959–60, Vol. 18, No. 4; and C. R. Walker: *The Man on the Assembly Line*, Cambridge, Mass., Harvard University Press, 1952.

[36] See extensive discussions in J. H. Goldthorpe, D. Lockwood, F. Bechhofer and J. Platt: *The Affluent Worker* series, Cambridge University Press, 1968 and 1969; and M. van de Vall, *Labour Organizations*, Cambridge University Press, 1970.

[37] This is my own phrasing rather than that of Musgrave, who speaks of 'occupational choice'.

[38] See C. Sofer: *Men in Mid-career*, especially Chs. 2 and 8.

[39] E. H. Erikson: 'Identity and Life Cycle', *Psychological Issues*, Vol. 1, No. 1, Monograph, 1959.

[40] D. Rappaport in Introduction to E. H. Erikson: 'Identity and the Life Cycle'.

[41] I. L. Janis and L. Mann: 'A Conflict-Theory Approach to Attitude Change and Decision Making', in A. Greenwald (Ed): *Psychological Foundations of Attitudes*, Academic Press, New York, 1968.

[42] H. S. Becker and J. Carper: 'The Elements of Identification with an Occupation', *American Sociological Review*, Vol. 2, June 1956.

[43] H. S. Becker: 'Notes on the Concept of Commitment', *American Journal of Sociology*, July 1960, pp. 32–40.

[44] See R. M. Cyert and J. G. March: *A Behavioural Theory of the Firm*, Englewood Cliffs, New Jersey, Prentice Hall, 1963; and C. I. Barnard: *The Functions of the Executive*, Cambridge Mass., Harvard University Press, 1958. Note also the relevance of Simon's work, discussed above.

[45] In these definitions I think I am following the fairly conventional usages described by J. Gould and W. L. Kolb (Eds): in *A Dictionary of the Social Sciences*, Tavistock Publications, London, 1964.

[46] K. Mannheim: *Essays on the Sociology of Knowledge*, Ch. VI. 'On the nature of economic ambition and its significance for the social education of man.' Routledge and Kegan Paul, London, 1952. I am indebted to my colleague, Peter Duncan in the Cambridge Management Studies Group for reminding me of the Mannheim essay in this connection, and to Simon Robinson, also of the Management Studies Group, for research assistance.

[47] See C. Sofer: *Men in Mid-career*.

Chapter Two
LIFE CHANCES*
William Liversidge

In these times, phrases such as 'parity of prestige' and 'equality of opportunity' occur frequently in discussions on the relative merits of the Grammar and Modern school systems and what they offer. The aim of this survey was to try to establish the relative influence of educational background and of social origin in determining the occupational expectations and aspirations of children, who, having been segregated at the age of eleven, have passed through two different school systems. Evidence is available that in a society where a 'comprehensive' school system is in use social class has a great effect, not only on their hopes for the future but on their normal school life. B. L. Neugarten[1] found that social-class differences in friendship and reputation are well established by the time children reach the fifth grade of a public school in the U.S.A. She shows that as the lower-class child grows older he drops out of school or takes on the values and behaviour of the middle-class child. Outwardly this may be so, but R. M. Stephenson's survey of 1,000 Ninth Graders[2] revealed that although 'aspirations are relatively unaffected by class, . . . plans or expectations are more definitely class based.' Moreover, E. Grant Youmans in a survey of Twelfth Grade Michigan boys[3] discovered 'a substantial and statistically significant association between social stratification and occupational expectations of the boys, using fathers' occupational levels as index.'

As the following survey is a comparative study of Grammar School and Modern School children, it may be thought that the differing levels of measured intelligence should have been taken into consideration. Similar criticism has been levelled at surveys carried out in America such as those quoted, and to meet such criticism W. H. Sewell, A. O. Haller, and M. A. Strauss conducted a survey[4] in which measured intelligence was controlled: they found

* The inquiry was designed and directed by Dr. F. Musgrove as an exercise in field work for a small group of students reading for the Diploma in the Social Psychology of Education at the Institute of Education, University of Leicester. The work was done as a group project. Mr. W. Liversidge, the author of the report in its present form was the group leader. Mr. R. L. Richer and Mr. J. D. Watson each prepared a section of the original report, other members of the team were Messrs. P. Burnham, and A. Sieuchand.

that despite this control status positions are 'important influences on levels of educational and occupational aspiration'. In short, in a society where a single school system is used 'class enters deeply into child acculturation . . . in school and outside the young learn rôles and statuses appropriate to their social position.'[5] Whether similar conclusions may be drawn of a two school system in this country is the purpose of this survey.

Scope of the Survey

The survey was made in the spring term 1961 and was confined to school leavers in parts of Leicestershire. Two Grammar Schools were used, one co-educational and serving an urban area and the other a City Girls' Grammar School. In the former, 67 sixth form pupils completed the questionnaire, 23 girls and 44 boys. In the city school the 135 girls came from both fifth and sixth forms. Three Modern Schools were used: one a boys' school serving a large city housing estate, the second a co-educational school covering a large rural and semi-rural area, and the third, also co-educational, is in the same town as the mixed Grammar School. In these three schools 253 children completed the questionnaire, 172 boys and 81 girls. Four Primary Schools, which feed the Modern and Grammar Schools in the urban area, were also included in the survey. Of the 158 Primary School children who completed the questionnaire, 72 were boys and 86 girls. In all 616 children returned usable forms. Ten were not used, eight being illegible and two incomplete. With the exception of the Girls' Grammar School all the questionnaires were completed under the supervision of the research team. Discussion of the questions was not allowed and no help was given in completing the answers.

The first section of the questionnaire concerned itself with the child's background, school, class, sex, age and parents' occupation. It was from this last question that the 'social class' of the child was determined (following other investigators, occupation was taken as the best single criterion of social class). Normally the father's occupation was used; if the father was not listed, because of death or other reasons, then the mother's occupation was used. Where parents had retired, their previous occupation was used. We based our grouping of occupations into social classes upon the categories used in the Registrar General's Occupation Tables.[6] This gave us a convenient index, classifying most known jobs into occupational groups. However, we wanted to distinguish between manual and non-manual occupations and this meant differentiating between various occupational groups in the Registrar General's Class III. Throughout this report 'upper class' refers to children whose parents are in the Registrar General's Class I (Professional) and Class II (Intermediate) together with those in Class III (skilled) who are in the Registrar General's Socio-Economic Groups 6 ('Clerical workers') and 7 ('shop assistants'). In the 'lower class' are the rest of Class III together with Class IV (Partly Skilled) and Class V (Unskilled). In making this division into two groups we felt, as did Willmott and Young in their classification of the residents of Woodford,[7] that we were doing what the people of the area would do themselves, although they would probably refer to the two groups as 'middle' and 'lower'. The class they would refer to as 'upper' is almost entirely absent in the schools we surveyed.

Of the total number of children in the survey—616—there were 232 (37 per cent) in the upper and 384 (63 per cent) in the lower class. Tables I and II show the proportions of the two classes within the three types of schools that were surveyed. It can be clearly seen from these figures that whilst two-thirds of the Grammar School children are upper class, within the survey as a whole only one third of the total belong to this group. This is consistent with the figures published by the Ministry of Education in 1954 which showed that 79 per cent of Grammar School children come from homes in Classes I, II, and III and 21 per cent from Classes IV and V. This effect of social origin on educational mobility is well known and, as B. L. Neugarten[8] shows, is not confined to this country.

TABLE I

Distribution of Subjects According to Social Class Position

BOYS

School	Total Number	Upper Class Number	Upper Class %	Lower Class Number	Lower Class %
Grammar ...	44	29	65.9	15	34.1
Modern ...	172	42	24.4	130	75.6
Primary ...	72	21	29.1	51	70.9
	288	92	31.9	196	68.1

TABLE II

GIRLS

School	Total Number	Upper Class Number	Upper Class %	Lower Class Number	Lower Class %
Grammar ...	161	100	62.5	61	37.5
Modern ...	81	12	13.5	69	86.5
Primary ...	86	28	32.5	58	67.5
	328	140	42.7	188	57.3

The Elevating Effect of the Grammar School

In the second part of the questionnaire the children were asked to state which kind of job they would most like to do if they could choose whatever they fancied. Their answers are referred to throughout the report as the 'fantasy aspirations' of the children. The next question asked what the children expected to do after leaving school, and their answers are referred to as the 'real expectations' of the children. The occupations given in the answers were classified in the same way as the parents' occupations, i.e. into upper and lower class.

Before making any comparison between schools we decided to determine the extent to which social origin affected the aspirations and expectations within the Grammar Schools. For convenience we dealt with the sexes separately. Comparison of the fantasy aspirations of the boys in the Grammar Schools according to their social origin (Table III) revealed no difference between them. When their real expectations were compared exactly the same results were obtained. In other words, their real expectations are as high as their fantasy aspirations; 93 per cent of both classes would not only like jobs in the 'upper class' but confidently expect to obtain work in this class.

TABLE III

Grading of Occupational and Expectation Choices according to Social Class Origin

GRAMMAR SCHOOLS

		Fantasy Aspirations				Real Expectations		
		% Choosing Upper Class	% Choosing Lower Class	Total %		% Choosing Upper Class	% Choosing Lower Class	Total %
Origin								
Boys	No.				No.			
Upper Class ...	29	93.1	6.9	100	29	93.1	6.9	100
Lower Class ...	15	93.3	6.7	100	15	93.3	6.7	100
All ...	44	93.2	6.8	100	44	93.2	6.8	100
Girls								
Upper Class ...	99	95.2	4.8	100	100	90	10	100
Lower Class ...	58	89.6	10.4	100	61	86.9	13.1	100
All ...	157	93	7	100	161	88.8	11.2	100

A similar picture is seen when comparison is made of the girls' choices, which show that the aspirations and expectations are little influenced by their social origin. The class choices are in fact almost identical.

It was now established that within the Grammar Schools social origin had no effect upon the choices of the children. The lower-class child's fantasy hopes and expectations were on the same level as those of the upper-class child. Before asserting that this elevation is due to the Grammar School itself, we had to make sure that children who had not benefited from a Grammar School education were not so elevated. Comparison between the Grammar and Modern School boys (Table IV) shows a significant difference between the choices of the lower-class boys, even in fantasy. While 93 per cent of the Grammar School boys would like jobs in the upper class, only 46 per cent of the Modern School boys aspire to them. A test of significance gave Chi-Square = 10.35 with a level of probability (P) less than .01. Even more striking is the fact that 93 per cent of the Grammar School boys expect to move into a higher class of employment than their parents, while only 17.7 per cent of the Modern School boys have such high hopes. There is a high significant difference between these choices—Chi-Square = 84.89 and the value of P less than .001.

TABLE IV

SECONDARY MODERN SCHOOLS

		Fantasy Aspirations				Real Expectations		
Origin		% Choosing Upper Class	% Choosing Lower Class	Total %		% Choosing Upper Class	% Choosing Lower Class	Total %
Boys	No.				No.			
Upper Class ...	42	62	38	100	42	43	57	100
Lower Class ...	130	46	54	100	130	17.7	82.3	100
All ...	172	50	50	100	171	23.9	76.1	100
Girls								
Upper Class ...	11	90.9	9.1	100	11	72.7	27.3	100
Lower Class ...	70	90	10	100	70	54.3	45.7	100
All ...	81	90.1	9.9	100	81	56.8	43.2	100

The position is not the same with the lower class girls in the two schools. Comparison of the fantasy aspirations showed the choices of Modern School girls to be virtually the same as those of the Grammar Schools. While 89.6 per cent of the latter chose occupations in the upper class, 90 per cent of the Modern School girls made choices in the same category. In the real expectations of the girls, 86.9 per cent of the lower-class girls in the Grammar Schools expect to obtain higher class employment, and 54.3 per cent of lower-class Modern School girls. The difference between these figures is significant—Chi-Square = 16.33 and the value of P is less than .001.

It is worth noting at this point that the aspirations and expectations of the girls in the Grammar Schools are slightly lower than those of the boys. The girls in the Modern Schools not only aspire higher, but expect to work in a higher class than their male counterparts. This may partly be explained by the higher social grading of the clerical and office work sought by these girls. In our opinion, their higher fantasy aspirations may be due to their different curricular activities and also the traditionally different treatment they receive throughout the educative process.

TABLE V

PRIMARY SCHOOLS

		Fantasy Aspirations				Real Expectations		
Origin		% Choosing Upper Class	% Choosing Lower Class	Total %		% Choosing Upper Class	% Choosing Lower Class	Total %
Boys	No.				No.			
Upper Class ...	21	71.4	28.6	100	16	50	50	100
Lower Class ...	51	60.8	39.2	100	50	38	62	100
All ...	72	64	36	100	66	59	41	100
Girls								
Upper Class ...	28	96.4	3.6	100	28	81.9	18.1	100
Lower Class ...	58	70.7	29.3	100	57	68.4	31.6	100
All ...	86	79.1	20.9	100	85	73	27	100

The elevating effect of the Grammar Schools is further demonstrated by comparing their lower-class figures with those of the lower-class in the Primary Schools (Table V). Comparison of the fantasy aspirations of boys of this class in the two schools, with 93.3 per cent of the Grammar School boys choosing upper-class, and 60.8 per cent of the Primary boys so doing, shows a significant difference between the two groups; Chi-Square = 4.504 with the value of P less than .05. The difference is even more significant when the real expectations of the two groups are compared. Only 38 per cent of the Primary lower-class boys expect promotion in the social scale, compared with 93.3 per cent of those in the Grammar School. A test of the degree of significance of this difference gave us Chi-Square $= 12.48$ and a value of P of less than .001.

Comparison between the lower-class girls in the Grammar and Primary schools further emphasises the effect of the Grammar School milieu. It is not surprising that the Grammar School girls expect higher class work than the Primary School girls. With 86.9 per cent of the former choosing upper class work and only 68.4 of the latter doing so, the difference between them is significant; Chi-Square $= 5.846$, value of P less than .02. What is surprising is that there should be such a significant difference between their choices in the realms of fantasy. In the Grammar School, 89.6 per cent chose jobs in the upper class, against 70.7 per cent of the Primary School girls; Chi-Square $= 6.24$, value of P is less than .02.

We have shown that a Grammar School education does raise the aspirations of its pupils—which is to be expected. The selective system aims at training the more academic child for work which will be high in the social scale we have used. Pupils are fully aware of the social implications of their educational selection. The figures we have quoted show that the Grammar School boys' real choices are as high as their fantasy aspirations. It can only be conjecture at this stage, but we are led to think that many of these boys may suffer disappointment and frustration if these very high expectations are not fulfilled. These findings are at variance with those of J. W. Campbell,[9] who concluded from his enquiry among 200 secondary-school children in London that 'In spite of the different types of education that are being provided . . . occupational choices cannot be clearly grouped according to type of school.' He was surprised at the high proportion of Grammar School boys who stated a preference for technical and commercial occupations, for which intermediate schools of the area provided a more obvious and appropriate preparation. He concedes 'It is true that very few of the modern school children aspire to enter a profession', but states 'neither do many from the grammar school, although this latter is popularly believed to be the source of the University population.'[10] Neither the design nor the scope of Campbell's inquiry is sufficient to support this generalisation. The total population involved in the inquiry was only 200 and were aged 12 to 14 years. Half of the children were in the first or second year only and the two Grammar

School groups were 14-year old children in academically inferior streams. The total number of Grammar School pupils was only 50. It is probable that the full social implications of the Grammar School are seen by pupils in the fifth, and particularly the sixth forms. It was among pupils at this level that the present inquiry was conducted.

The Depressing Effect of the Modern School

It is still widely assumed that the increased status according to the non-selective schools since the 1944 Education Act has done much to give them parity of prestige with the Grammar Schools. Previously we have demonstrated that the Grammar School has an elevating effect upon the occupational aspirations and expectations of its pupils. Comparisons drawn between children of the Grammar and Modern Schools have shown the extent of this elevation and have also indicated a marked difference between the two groups. In this respect, then, it cannot be said that there is parity of prestige. Knowing that the Modern School does not have an elevating effect on the occupational aspirations of its pupils, our next concern was to establish what effect it did have, if any. We could well expect their choices to be influenced by their social origin, as were the choices of the Michigan boys in Youmans' study.[11]

We compared first the choices of the children within the Modern Schools to test this hypothesis. In the fantasy choices of the boys there is no significant difference when comparison is made according to their social origin. It is worth drawing attention to the surprisingly high percentage of boys from both classes who chose lower class jobs when given absolutely free choice (38 per cent of the upper class and 54 per cent of the lower class). Indeed the fantasy choices of these boys are at a distressingly mundane and realistic level; the majority rarely leave their immediate world. We had expected that in their flights of fancy they would select the more exciting occupations such as pilot, professional footballer, explorer, 'pop' singer, or even the old-fashioned engine-driver. Instead, we have the boy who expects to be a labourer at the brick-yard choosing the very same job in fantasy, and the potential rubber moulder who, when offered the whole world from which to choose, still wants to be a rubber moulder.

Looking at the occupational expectations of these children, one is struck by their utter realism. This is supported by P. M. Freeston's survey,[12] which found only 6 per cent of 955 children giving job choices which were rated 'impossible'. Comparison of the real expectations of the boys in the Modern Schools reveals a significant difference between the choices of the two classes: 43 per cent of the upper-class boys expected upper-class work and only 17.7 per cent of the lower class; Chi-Square = 10.89, the value of P less than .001. However, it can be seen that more than half of the upper-class boys expect to get lower-class jobs, so that the influence of their background is not as great as one might have thought.

The social origin of girls in the Modern School has even less effect upon their choices, and comparison revealed no significant difference in either their aspirations or their expectations. The fantasy choices are high in both classes: 90 per cent in each group choose occupations in the upper class. In their real choice 54 per cent of the lower class and 72.7 per cent of the upper class expect to obtain 'upper-class' jobs, most of which can be classified as office or secretarial work. Whatever the nature of these high choices it must be stated that they are still not determined by the social origin of the girls.

The disparity between the social origin and the occupational aspirations and expectations of the children attending Modern Schools is further emphasized when comparison is made between the choices of the upper-class groups in both schools. There is a significant difference in both fantasy and reality choices among the boys. In fantasy aspirations with 93.1 per cent of the Grammar School boys and 62 per cent of the Modern School boys choosing upper class, we have Chi-Square = 8.824 and the value of P less than .01. With 57 per cent of the upper-class boys in the Modern Schools and only 6.9 per cent of the same group in the Grammar School expecting lower-class work, the high significance of the difference is shown by a Chi-Square = 18.66 and the value of P less than .001.

Mention has already been made of the high aspirations and expectations of the Modern School girl, and this is further substantiated when comparison is made between the upper-class choices of these girls and those of the same group in the Grammar School. It can be seen from Tables III and IV that the fantasy aspiration figures are practically the same. In real expectations, although 90 per cent of the Grammar School girls expect upper-class work and only 72.7 per cent of the Modern School girls, the difference between them is not significant. Further comment will be made later about this difference between the boys and girls in the Modern Schools.

It was appreciated at this stage that the difference between the choices of the Modern Schools and the Grammar Schools might be attributed more to the elevating effect of the Grammar School than to any change caused by the Modern School. With this in mind we compared the Modern School choices with those who are still at the primary stage of education. As there is little difference in the social class distribution in the two types of school (Tables I and II) we were able to compare the total figures for both boys and girls. Of the boys, 50 per cent in the Modern Schools and 64 per cent in the Primary Schools aspired to upper-class jobs; the difference is significant, Chi-Square = 3.943, value of P less than .05. While 59 per cent of the Primary School boys expect upper-class work, only 23.9 per cent of the Modern School boys do so. Again the difference is significant, Chi-Square = 6.671, value of P less than .01.

In our opinion the results of the comparisons we have made clearly illustrate that the occupational hopes and expectations of many non-selected boys are considerably depressed by the time they have completed their secondary school education. Moreover, our findings do not in any way support the hypothesis that social origin is the all-important factor in occupational preference.

The impression we received from comparisons between the fantasy aspirations of girls at the Modern Schools and at the Primary Schools is not quite the same as that given by comparing the boys. The older girls aspire higher than the younger; 90.1 per cent of the Modern School and 79.1 per cent of the Primary Schools chose the higher class jobs. The difference between them is significant; Chi-Square = 3.877, value of P less than .05. The depressing effect of the Modern School is again seen when the real expectations of the girls in the two schools are compared. While 73 per cent of the Primary School girls chose upper-class work, only 56.8 per cent of the Modern School girls did so. The difference between the two groups is significant; Chi-Square = 4.76, value of P less than .05.

So far, all direct comparisons have been made between groups of the same sex, either in the same schools, or in different schools. In order to examine further the depressing effect at the non-selective secondary stage of education, and to substantiate our earlier statement that girls aspire higher than boys, we next compared the fantasy and real choices of the two sexes from the Modern Schools. In fantasy only 50 per cent of the boys chose upper-class jobs, against 90.1 per cent of the girls. This difference is significant; Chi-Square

=37.96, value of P less than .001. In the real expectation, with 23.9 per cent of the boys expecting upper-class work, and 56.8 per cent of the girls, the difference is again significant; Chi-Square=26.17 value of P less than .001.

In short, while the girls in the Modern Schools do not expect the same degree of upper-class work as their sisters in the Grammar and Primary schools, their expectations are higher than those of the boys working alongside them. Their fantasy aspirations seem to be relatively unaffected, and compare favourably with the girls in the other schools, being much higher than their male fellow pupils. Nevertheless these aspirations are not socially conditioned, for as we have seen, both upper and lower groups of girls aspire equally high.

It would seem, then, that the secondary educational system has a greater influence upon the occupational aspirations and expectations of the child than his or her social background. This agrees substantially with one of the conclusions drawn by Mary D. Wilson[13] who said: 'The general impression left from this study of vocational choice is . . . that children tend to aim at the highest levels available to the group to which they belong. If this hypothesis is correct it follows that the segregation of children into different types of secondary schools will have a profound effect on their attitudes to vocations.'

The Realism of Children's Appraisal of their Social Position

The realism of children's views of the social framework and of their place and life chances in it was assessed: (a) by asking them to grade various occupations and comparing the results with adult rankings, (b) by asking them what earnings they expected in the jobs of their choice and checking their estimates against wage rates actually prevailing, and (c) by asking them their preferred age of marriage and comparing the ages given with current trends. Differences between Grammar School and Modern School children were examined on all three counts, and also differences between children in different ability streams within the same school.

(a) The grading of occupations

The views of adolescents on aspects of the social class structure have been previously investigated and discussed by Himmelweit, Halsey and Oppenheim.[14] Despite the fact that a preliminary survey had shown that 60 per cent of their experimental group attached no precise meaning to the term 'social class', it was concluded that 'the boys had already acquired (at 13/14 years) a very thorough understanding of the social class system'.

Amongst other evidence this statement was supported by an investigation which served as a model for our investigation. The boys in the earlier study were asked to grade eight occupations, seven being the equivalent of the Hall-Jones' gradings,[15] whilst the eighth, 'Member of Parliament', was selected 'as an example of an occupation with a very high prestige level to provide an upper reference point'. It was found that rank orders were almost identical with those of adults. The items of greatest variability were newsagent and tobacconist and carpenter, i.e. the 4th and 5th grades respectively. These are in any case the points of greatest variability on the Hall-Jones scale. Within this general pattern of unanimity there were indications of the influence of the social class of the respondents. Thus while working-class boys up-graded, middle-class boys depressed occupations of similar prestige level to that of their fathers. Further, working class boys in Secondary Modern Schools tended to depress the social grade of the teacher whilst elevating that of the carpenter.

In our investigation the children's assessment of the relative standing and prestige of different occupations was done by asking them to place nine different occupations in the order in which 'they were most looked up to'. Some of the Hall-Jones terms were altered to suit the child's understanding. Subsequently in the marking of the scale factory worker and coal-face worker were deleted, and the order of grading of each occupation was adjusted to a seven point scale, providing direct equivalence to the seven Hall-Jones categories.

It was decided that the median ranking of each occupation would give the most appropriate measure of central tendency and facilitate comparison with other research. Table VI gives these median rankings by school and again the sexes have been dealt with separately. It will be seen that in general the conclusions of Himmelweit, Halsey and Oppenheim[16] are maintained. Clearly, both primary and secondary children agree in their placing of the upper and lower grades. Nevertheless it would seem that primary age children are less sure of their ranking of the middle range of occupations than their seniors. We may conclude that some of the refinements of our social class system are learned in the intervening years.

TABLE VI
Median Ranking of Occupations

Occupations	Hall-Jones Rank	BOYS			GIRLS		
		P.S.	M.S.	G.S.	P.S.	M.S.	G.S.
Doctor	1	1.9	2.0	1.6	2.0	1.7	1.5
Mine Manager ...	2	4.0	3.8	3.5	4.8	4.0	3.4
School Teacher ...	3	3.2	3.5	2.7	2.4	3.5	2.7
Small Shopkeeper...	4	4.8	5.2	5.3	4.5	5.5	5.3
Clerk	5	4.4	3.0	4.9	4.7	3.2	4.7
Farm Labourer ...	6	5.5	6.0	6.4	5.8	5.8	6.4
Dustman	7	7.3	7.4	7.3	7.4	6.5	7.4
N =		77	30	44	86	34	23

P.S. = Primary Schools. M.S. = Secondary Modern Schools.
G.S. = Grammar Schools.

The Secondary Modern group tend to elevate the status of the clerk and depress that of the mine manager. In view of the frequent reiterations of social leaders that technical knowledge is prestige knowledge, and of black-coated workers' complaints of the depression of their socal status, it is interesting to note that the association of high status with clerical work persists amongst Secondary Modern children. It is the same group who most depress the status of the mine manager, though only slightly so, placing him without exception below the schoolteacher, who in turn is demoted a little by this group of children. All the adolescents in this survey tended to elevate the status of the white-collar workers relative to the adult scale, this being most marked in the Secondary Modern School. Despite these minor deviations, it would seem clear that these children, even from the primary school age, have a pretty clear idea of the social structure of the community in which they live, and of the position they will occupy in that community when they leave school. As we have shown earlier, this position is dependent upon the type of secondary school they attend.

(b) Wage and Salary Structure

In order to pursue our study of the child's perception of social realities we included the following questions on the expected wage and salary structure. 'How much do you think you will earn a week when you start?' What do you think you are likely to be earning a week by the time you are thirty?'

Each answer was classified as: Very Low, Low, Normal, High, Very High, when compared to the actual wage rate or salary being paid currently in the various trades or professions. These wage rates were extracted from Ministry of Labour publications,[17] from Youth Employment brochures and from the National Union of Students' pamphlet 'Choosing a Career'. Care was taken to ensure that all wage rates were accurate but some difficulty was experienced in gaining the relevant data for professional workers at the upper reference point. However a fairly wide tolerance was given, it being decided that for our purpose the following standard of classification would suffice:

Rank 1. Very Low ......100 per cent below actual wage rate.

Rank 2. Low ....25—100 percent below actual wage rate.

Rank 3. Normal ....+ or - 25 per cent of actual wage rate.

Rank 4. High ....25—100 per cent above actual wage rate.

Rank 5. Very High ......100 per cent above actual wage rate.

Thus a median ranking of 3.5 indicated a high degree of realism in wage expectation.

TABLE VII

Median Rank of Wage Realism by School and Sex

School Group		N.	Median Rank of Realism School Leaving	Median Rank of Realism Age 30
Primary School, Boys	...	70	4.5	4.1
Primary School, Girls	...	82	3.9	3.9
Modern School, Boys	...	171	3.75	4.3
Modern School, Girls	...	79	3.4	3.7
Grammar School, Boys	...	44	3.5	3.5
Grammar School, Girls	...	150	3.5	3.5

It will be seen from Table VII that, in general, children have an extremely realistic perception of the adult wage and salary structure. This is particularly so with the Grammar School group, though this is hardly surprising in view of the present-day career advertising and advice available in these schools. The Secondary Modern girls are also very realistic in their estimates, but the boys in the same schools may tend to over-estimate their adult earning capacity, particularly at the age of 30. Though the Primary School group as a whole has more elevated sights, 27 of the 70 boys making estimates classified as 'Very High', yet the eleven year old girl seems to have made a fairly shrewd judgment of her future earning power.

It was decided to examine the influence of social class on the median rankings of Grammar School boys, and of those Secondary Modern boys who were taking the College of Preceptors examination.

The ranking of the Grammar School upper class group was 3.6, the same class in the modern school giving a median rank of 4.0. This shows a slight tendency for all upper class boys to be over-optimistic, the high median ranking of the upper class Secondary Modern school boys probably reflecting the incentive value of the examination. Although, as we have demonstrated, the lower class boys in the Grammar Schools have high occupational expectations, there is no evidence here of unrealistically high wage expectations. The Grammar School lower .class group has a median rank of 3.5 and the same group in the Modern School has 3.6.

TABLE VIII

School Group		N.	Arithmetic Mean of Median Salaries					
			S.L. Age			Age 30		
Primary School, Boys	...	70	£6	13	9	£15	18	0
Primary School, Girls	...	82	£5	3	2	£11	19	0
Modern School, Boys	...	171	£3	15	7	£16	0	4
Modern School, Girls	...	79	£3	9	4	£10	11	5
Grammar School, Boys	...	44	£10	10	0	£22	0	0
Grammar School, Girls	...	70	£8	8	10	£15	17	3

Table VIII shows the arithmetic means of the median salaries for each school class, offering further evidence of the realism of these children's expectations. Both Secondary Modern boys and girls give substantially lower estimates than Grammar School pupils of their initial earnings and earnings at age 30. Grammar School girls realistically estimated their future incomes appreciably below those of Grammar School boys; Secondary Modern girls did not expect wages appreciably below the boys initially, but substantially below at age 30.

Among the Secondary Modern School boys the level of expectation at age 30 declined with the level of the ability stream: within the three Secondary Modern Schools the expected median income in the A-stream was £17, in the B-stream £17, in the C-stream £14. 13s. and in the D-stream £12. In other words, the children have accepted the fact that their position in the school is an indication of their earning capacity in the future.

(c) *Expected Age of Marriage*

The child's perception of his or her social rôle was further considered in relation to the preferred age of marriage. Boys and girls were asked the question 'At what age do you wish to marry?' Median ages were calculated, and in Table IX these are set out according to the social origin and school of the subjects.

It will be seen that boys and girls in the Grammar School envisage marriage two years later than their opposite numbers in the Secondary Modern School, and that the lower-class children in each case give an earlier age than the upper-class children. Further it will be seen that there is an interval of approximately two years between the preferred age of marriage of the sexes. This reflects the present national trend in that in 1959 the mean age of marriage for all bachelors was 25.77 years and for spinsters 23.37 years.[18]

TABLE IX

Child's Preferred Age of Marriage

	Median Ages	
	Secondary Modern	Grammar School
Boys		
Upper Class	24.0 Years	24.9 Years
Lower Class	22.5 Years	24.2 Years
All	22.7 Years	24.8 Years
Girls		
Upper Class	21.0 Years	23.5 Years
Lower Class	20.8 Years	21.5 Years
All	20.9 Years	22.9 Years

A more direct comparison to the figures given by the children can be seen by abstracting the median age of marriage for the area of this survey from the Registrar General's report. These are (North Midland Area), below 55 years: 23.4 years for males and 21.5 years for females.

Plainly there are substantial reasons for the Vth and VIth form Grammar School children marrying later than those children who leave Secondary Modern School at fifteen. These reasons need not be related to social class and could simply reflect the longer school life and/or anticipated periods of professional training. The Grammar School children do not see delayed marriage as the concomitant of higher education as they almost certainly did before 1939. Further, when the preferred age of marriage of the Secondary Modern School group is compared with the median age of all those who marry below 35 years (93 per cent of all marriages in this area) a very close correspondence is observed: boys, 22.7 years for this survey and 23.1 in the area; girls, 20.9 years in this survey, 21.2 years in the area. Such a degree of correspondence between the preferred age of marriage at fifteen years and the actual age of marriage within the local community further emphasises the clarity of the child's perception of the social situation.

Conclusion

The general picture that emerges from this study is one of startlingly accurate appraisal of life chances by the children, and a shrewd appreciation of the social and economic implications of their placing within the educational system. They know at what age they will marry, the best type of job they can get, and the best wage they can hope to earn at that job. Having accepted the rôle they are to play in life, they rarely venture out of it even in fantasy.

The main conclusion of this study is that while previous experience may be of great importance in shaping the school-child's expectations of the future, the most potent force operating is undoubtedly the experience through which the child passes during his involvement in that part of the educational system to which he has been assigned.

[1] Bernice L. Neugarten: 'Social Class and Friendship Among School Children,' *American Journal of Sociology*, Vol. 51, 1945-46.

[2] Richard M. Stephenson: 'Mobility Orientation and Stratification of 1,000 Ninth Graders,' *American Sociological Review*, Vol. 22, 1957, pp. 204-211.

[3] E. Grant Youmans: 'Occupational Expectations of Twelfth Grade Michigan Boys,' *The Journal of Experimental Education*, June 1956.

[4] W. H. Sewell, A. O. Haller, and M. A. Straus: 'Social Status and Educational and Occupational Aspiration,' *American Sociological Review*, Vol. 22, 1957, pp. 67-73.

[5] L. A. Cook and E. F. Cook: *A Sociological Approach to Education*, New York, 1960, p. 206.

[6] *Classification of Occupations*, H.M.S.O., Census 1951, p. xi and Table I.

[7] P. Willmott and M. Young: *Family and Class in a London Suburb*, London, 1960.

[8] Bernice L. Neugarten: *op. cit.*, p. 307

[9] J. W. Campbell: *The Influence of the Socio-Cultural Environment upon the Educational Progress of Children at Secondary School Level*, unpublished Ph. D. thesis, London, 1951.

[10] *Ibid.*, p. 145.

[11] E. Grant Youmans: *op. cit.*

[12] P. M. Freeston: *Children's Conception of Adult Life*, unpublished M.A. Thesis, London, 1945.

[13] Mary D. Wilson: 'Vocational Preferences of Secondary School-children,' *The British Journal of Educational Psychology*, June 1953, p.112.

[14] H. T. Himmelweit, A. H. Halsey, and A. N. Oppenheim: 'The views of adolescents on some aspects of the social class structure,' *British Journal of Sociology*, Vol. III, No. 2, June, 1952.

[15] John Hall and D. Caradog Jones: 'Social Grading of Occupations,' *British Journal of Sociology*, Vol. I, No. 1, March, 1950.

[16] Himmelweit, Halsey & Oppenheim: *op. cit.*

[17] Ministry of Labour: *Time, Rates and Hours of Work*, 1960.

[18] Registrar General: *Statistical Review of England and Wales*, 1959, Table L.

Chapter Three

YOUTH AND WORK: PROBLEMS AND PERSPECTIVES

E. Teresa Keil, C. Riddell, B. S. R. Green

Introduction

Т he literature on the adjustment of young people to working life is large, but lacks coherence.[1] Although the subject has become a popular research topic, there have been no thorough surveys of the field. This chapter, in the light of an extensive survey of the literature, develops a method of approach which differs from those adopted by the small number of previous writers who have found any theoretical interest in the topic.

It should not be forgotten that the provision of full-time education for the whole of the population of Great Britain is less than a hundred years old. While the period of compulsory school attendance has increased, the minimum age of leaving has been fifteen years only since 1947, and fourteen only since 1922. Six out of every ten boys and girls leave school at the minimum age. The same proportion complete their education at secondary modern schools.[2] Of fifteen year old male leavers 60 per cent go into unskilled and semi-skilled work, and 35 per cent into apprenticeships. Proportions going into unskilled work decline steeply as the age of leaving increases, but even among seventeen year old leavers, about one out of four goes into unskilled work.[3] Because of the large numbers in the age group (the 'bulge'), there has been a slight decrease in the proportion entering apprenticeships in the last year or two, although the total number of apprentice entrants has gone up.

Educationalists and administrators have argued for a long time that the transition from school to work involves stress. A departmental committee was set up in 1916 by the President of the Board of Education, which, in its report emphasised the difficulties of the period between leaving school and taking up apprenticeships, as well as those for young workers going into stop-gap and unskilled employment, remarking that,

© E. T. Keil, C. Riddell, B. S. R. Green 1966 (This article was first published in *The Sociological Review*, Vol. 14, No. 2, July 1966.)

'The effect in discouragement, disillusionment and disappointment on the morale and on the health of young people on the threshold of adult life is one of the gravest menaces of the times, and a contributory cause to permanent and intermittent unemployment, and to juvenile delinquency.'[4]

The proposals of this committee were to set up compulsory, one day a week, day continuation schools until the age of sixteen; to provide better vocational education; and thus to alleviate the sudden transition. For various reasons they were largely still-born.[5] However, such proposals have been continually revived, on the same grounds, and re-appear in the 1944 Education Act, and in the *Crowther Report*, which gives its recommendation for setting up county colleges—the modern version of day continuation schools—a priority second only to that of raising the leaving age to sixteen.[6]

Previous Theoretical Approaches

Apart from the recent studies by Carter, Veness, and *Crowther Report* itself,[7] few areas of the general subject of moving from school to work have been carefully investigated, and the material as a whole shows a remarkable lack of systematization, and a failure to consider previous work. With the exception of the topic of occupational choice,[8] which is not considered here, there have been few organized surveys, and much of the literature consists of the impressions of teachers, personnel managers, youth employment officers, etc., which, although valuable in themselves, give only a partial insight into the problems of young people at this period of their lives, and are loaded with moral judgements and evaluations.[9] Some of this material is reconsidered in the later sections of the chapter.

The literature on adjustment to work is even less helpful. One of the major features of any adjustment to a worker's rôle or position, however defined, must be the preparation received in school. In peasant societies without formal school systems the introduction to work is a gradual one,[10] whereas in modern industrial societies, a child is separated from the working world for a large part of his day, and his formal contact with work is severely limited by legislation. Noticing this contrast, some writers have been led to suggest that entering work after being a schoolboy involves some sort of a shock, often termed a 'culture shock', creating problems of adjustment.[11]

This view has been most fully developed in a long section of Miller and Form's text, *Industrial Sociology*, which is one of the most systematic approaches to the subject.[12] They argue that for the young person entering industry there are two sets of problems—those arising from differences of situation and position; and those arising from differences in orientations.

	School	*Work*
(a) *Situation*	Ages are all very similar, apart from teachers.	Ages vary over a wide range.
(b) *Position*	A boy in his last year is very familiar with the institution, knows how it works, has some weight in it, if not a formal authority position.	A new entrant is a very minor figure, with no experience and no authority.

(c) *Value Orientations*

1. Enforced permanent group membership.	Freedom of employer and employee to terminate employment.
2. Co-operation	Self-interest.
3. Morally correct behaviour.	Amorality.
4. Full self-development.	Learning persistence at a job.
5. Valuation by individual characteristics.	Valuation by characteristics of group and class membership.[13]

Furthermore, Miller and Form cite some evidence to show that in the United States, aspirations do not correspond with the possibilities that the labour market offers. 91 per cent of the respondents in a pre-war survey wanted white collar jobs—only one in five got them.[14] The shock which the authors suggest occurs from going to work results from the confrontation of the realities of the work situation with the expectations carried from the school situation.

Some criticism of this approach is fairly self-evident. While it is true that age structures vary in schools and in industry, the implications of this for the psychology of the new entrant are not known. The above list of school value orientations may correspond more to the exhortations of educational philosophy than to the realities of school situations. The list of work values does not correspond in many respects with the findings of industrial sociologists and psychologists who have made systematic studies of worker behaviour in industry. In addition, the presentation of these differences in such a dichotomous fashion does injustice to the actual complexity of the experiences young people undergo in their last years at school and in their first years of work. Miller and Form tend to assume that all school situations and all work situations are the same. There is evidence to suggest that they differ very much according to broad differences in social class, type of school, occupational level and type of work situation, etc.

For instance, work on aspiration suggests that for groups of school children with similar social backgrounds, there are national differences. Among children of broadly working class origin, in France wishes incline to handicrafts and small farming,[15] in the United States they tend to reflect mobility aspirations,[16] in this country, Germany and parts of Poland, they are directed towards a skilled trade—a 'trade in one's hands', to use the stereotyped phrase summing up the vocational aspirations of this section of British youth.[17] Additionally, investigators have noted, and sometimes been dismayed by, the realism of the aspirations of some young people in this country:

> 'Indeed the fantasy choices of these boys are at a distressingly mundane and realistic level; the majority rarely leave their immediate world. We had expected that in their flights of fancy they would select the more exciting occupations such as pilot, professional footballer, explorer, 'pop' singer, or even the old-fashioned engine driver. Instead we have the boy who expects to be a labourer at the brick yard choosing the very same job in fantasy, and the potential rubber moulder, who, when offered the whole world from which to choose, still wants to be a rubber moulder.'[18]

However, investigations agree that while knowledge of wages and hours is very accurate, knowledge of work content and training requirements is very slight. Within the limits of manual work, there is a concentration of aspiration towards skilled trades, and, within them, towards certain favoured trades such as printing, hairdressing, which must mean that a considerable proportion of young people are going to be frustrated. There are several studies showing that young people choose unrealistically but within a realistic range, and, in general, it seems that the poorer the school performance, the lower the realism of aspiration.[19]

An alternative approach is that of the French sociologist, de Maupeou. This relates the adjustment of young workers to the conceptions possessed by them of industrial society in its broadest sense.[20] If these conceptions are inadequate—i.e. do not correspond to the present or future realities of the situation, tension will be built up, and frustration or dissatisfaction will occur. De Maupeou outlines the different conceptions young workers have, and the type of response they will make to industrial situations. There are two difficulties about this approach. The first is the virtual impossibility of defining an 'accurate' conception of industrial society in its entirety. Thus, various views which de Maupeou characterizes as 'unrealistic' may correspond closely to the immediate future of the industry which a young person is in, even if not to that of industrial society as a whole. Secondly, these conceptions, where they are coherently held at all, and the responses inferred from them may, in fact, develop out of general features of upbringing and experience, and it is to this possibility that we should turn if we wish to understand adjustment problems of different social groups.

An Alternative Approach

The above approaches offer many valuable insights. However, evidence from a wide range of research suggests that family, neighbourhood, peer groups, education received, influences from mass media, the extent of formal vocational guidance, all need to be considered, and that experience from these sources, as well as the nature of the work undertaken, are relevant to the development of any particular reaction towards working life. This implies that entering the world of work and adjusting to it is a *process*.

An indication of the nature of this process may be given in the following way: (a) *The socialization of the young person to the world of work,* together with (b) *Previous work experience,* and (c) *Wider social influences,* lead on the one hand to (d) *The formulation of a set of attitudes towards, and expectations about, work.* (a), (b) and (c) together, and (d) provide the explanation for (e) *The actual job entry,* and from this, (f) *Experiences as a worker* lead to a situation of (g) *Adjustment/non-adjustment for the young worker* which can be expressed either by a measure of satisfaction, by a re-formulation of (d) above, by ritualized dissatisfaction, or by job change.

The research already done indicates the sorts of factors which may be considered significant in the process, in more detail. They may be sub-categorized as 'informal' and 'formal' influences in the adjustment process, and grouped as follows:

1. *Informal influences on* (a) (Examples of differentiating variables that research has shown to be significant are given in brackets.)
   Family. (Economic level; social class; sibling pressure; family tradition; degree of parental aspiration for young people.)
   Neighbourhood. (Type of residential area and house; stability of residence.)

School. (Type; area; attitude of teaching staff to pupils as individuals and as group members; school culture.)
Peer Group. (Ages; occupations if any; social backgrounds;
    activities.)

2. *Informal influences on* (*b*)
Part-time jobs.
Industrial visits.
Observations of industrial life.

3. *Informal influences on* (*c*)
Communications media.
Political/religious affiliation.

4. *Dimensions of attitudes and expectations* (*d*)
Expectations of life as a worker. (Positive/negative; hopeful/pessimistic; realistic/unrealistic aspirations.)
Attitude to old life as school pupil. (positive/negative.)
'Core' attitude. (Intrinsic—work valued for itself; extrinsic—
    work valued as a means to an end; career—work as a status provider.)

5. *Informal influences on* (*f*)
Work situation. (Content of work done; conditions; payment;
    hours; training; relations with authority; relations with
    other workers.)
Home situation. (Relations with parents; saving; possessions.)
Leisure situation. (Friendship patterns and activities; spending;
    relations with opposite sex.)

Formal influences may be more briefly listed. Complementary to
(a) *The socialization of the young person, through* (c) *Wider social
influences,* affecting (d) *The formulation of a set of attitudes towards,
and expectations about, work* are the school Careers Master with the
provision of careers literature, and the Youth Employment Service in
its placement function. Affecting (f) *Experiences as a worker* are the
firm's personnel department, the trade union, and the Youth Employment Service in its follow-up function. In the broadest terms, the
whole process takes place within the context of the labour market,
taking account of the number and variety of jobs available and also of
the numbers in and qualifications of the youth labour force.[21]
To set out the factors involved in this way gives the impression of
a time scale, but it should be remembered that one set of factors

does not necessarily cease to operate at a later period. Thus, the influence of, for example, the neighbourhood does not cease when young people actually start work. The continuing influence of the home will be illustrated below.

The influence of the factors in Group 1 affects the amount and nature of previous work experience and access to wider social influences. The interaction of all these factors produces attitudes towards, and expectations about, work, which may or may not influence actual job entry. For example, a young person might derive from previous social influences, the mass media say, a strong desire for a particular satisfaction in work. It does not follow that he will possess the necessary skills to set about translating his desire into reality, in which case his job entry will conform to the usual pattern of the social group from which he comes. The use of the term job 'entry' rather than the more usual job 'choice' is intentional. The latter has connotations of rational assessment of abilities and opportunities which do not seem to be a general characteristic of those seeking work.[22] Experiences as a worker test the predispositions and attitudes of the new entrant and in turn interact with home and leisure behaviour, resulting in adjustment or non-adjustment, however it is measured. Additionally, this adjustment process takes place in the context of a labour market situation which differs markedly from area to area and at different periods in time, a situation in which the young person may be in competition with other young people and sometimes with adults. Even such a brief discussion of the process of job adjustment indicates how over-simplified it is to consider only the nature of the work undertaken.[23]

It is not intended, nor would it be possible within the scope of a chapter to justify in detail all the factors given significance. The identification of such factors is easier than measuring the effects in actual work situations, a problem which is rooted in general difficulties of methodology in the social sciences, nor does it suggest that all are equally important. There is too much research which asks informants to rank money, friends, or a chance to get on, in order of relevance to job satisfaction or depends on questions such as, 'Do you like your job?'. Such research has the advantage of presenting easily measured indicators of 'satisfaction' but it does not do justice to the complexity of the influences and experiences involved; many of the problem areas indicated by the present approach are as yet hardly investigated. Nevertheless it is of value to consider some of them. The examples chosen are, the influence of the home, the school, the formal vocational guidance institutions, attitudes to work, and the general work situation for the new entrant.

The Influence of the Home (Groups 1 and 5)

The importance of the home environment in discussing the process of adjustment cannot be over-estimated. In general terms, the recent study by Douglas demonstrates the marked effects of different types of social background on the school performance and the socio-medical histories of individuals.[24] This national sample is being followed through into working life. The work of Bernstein has shown that there is a relationship between the forms of language learning and thinking, and the different methods of upbringing of working and middle class groups, so that it is no surprise to find that the social class of parents influences the type and length of education open to and received by their children.[25] It follows from this that, since education and occupation are linked, such characteristics as social class and economic level of the family will have a marked influence on the attitudes to and expectations about work, as well as on the type of job entered.[26] It is more difficult to identify and describe the processes which result in such attitudes and expectations.

Carter gives the clearest picture of the way in which the process happens for some working class children: visits to the father's place of work, the talk at home about wages and hours, the relief that the working day is over, all convey to the young person the way in which his parents, siblings and relatives—often the people he admires and relies upon most—regard the world of work. From this he will accumulate general impressions of 'good' and 'bad' jobs, and work which is appropriate for him when the time comes to leave school.[27] Reynolds and Shister, in a study of adult workers, suggest that home and neighbourhood experiences make for the development of job 'horizons' beyond which few individuals look. As a result, actual job selection often seems casual; it is not an assessment of the market possibilities but an apparently unthinking acceptance of the suggestions and recommendations of relatives and friends.[28] However, job horizons may be defined broadly as well as narrowly; there are homes where work is discussed more formally, where parents explore with their children the full range of possibilities and instil career aspirations. It would be valuable to have a more precise analysis of these processes, particularly as it seems that social class divisions are too broad to be more than general predictors of their occurrence. The work of Kahl in the United States and of Swift in this country are important reminders of the complexity of the development of value systems which result in various educational and occupational aspirations.[29]

This qualification apart, parental occupation has a general importance both for aspirations and for job entry. There is some evidence to suggest that before taking a job the occupational goals of many young people are higher than their father's occupational level, for example, more boys want skilled manual work than have fathers in skilled manual work, and fewer whose fathers are unskilled want unskilled work for themselves.[30] These aspirations are still connected with parental occupation though; the more ambitious sons of semi-skilled or unskilled workers aspire, not to professional jobs, but to skilled trades.[31] Although there is not an absolute relationship between the occupational status of fathers and sons, there is an association, stronger in some groups than others. And even where there are changes in occupation level between father and son, the sons tend to be fairly close to their fathers' level in the occupational hierarchy.[32]

The home background provides continuity when the young person enters work, and again the work of Carter, and of Ferguson and Cunnison, describes its influence. Some families disapprove of job changing, for example, others rarely discuss such decisions; both attitudes are likely to influence the young person's approach to his work. In some circumstances the features of the home influence job performance, particularly in terms of job change, work lost and extent of unemployment.[33] It is also at this time that the long term effects of home background become evident, as Venables has shown in her demonstration of the depressant effect of working class and secondary modern school background on the verbal intelligence of day-release apprentices.[34] However, the continuity of the home influence does not mean that the young person's position within it remains unchanged. A full discussion of the interaction of the young worker and the family group is beyond the scope of this chapter, but some brief comments may be made. The young persons' wages bring benefits to the family,[35] but economic independence may also be a way of achieving emancipation from the authority of home and family.[36] This may lead to more or less overt parent/child conflict, expressed in disputes about use of money and leisure time, conflict which some research suggests is more frequent in middle class than working class homes.[37] Within working class groups, work in educational sociology would lead us to predict that conflict is more likely where parental and filial aspirations are at variance.[38] But on the whole, even in financial terms, the changes in the home appear to be gradual.[39] Where a home breaks up, however, the effect on working life may be very marked. Ferguson and Cunnison's study indicates a high correlation between broken homes and job change.[40]

The Influence of the School (Group 1)

While schools obviously differ from most work situations in their age composition, there may be other important respects in which they are not dissimilar. Current discussions of the educational system have tended to stress its importance as an avenue of social mobility and the barriers impeding the achievement of this. It is also necessary to consider schools as, in many cases, reinforcing the informal patterns of home and neighbourhood. Carter, studying Sheffield school leavers, relates the attitudes found in the five schools he investigated to the predominant attitudes of the populations from which they drew their pupils, a finding reinforced by Coleman's study in the Chicago area.[41] This latter draws attention to the importance of the informal social groupings which develop among school children. Webb, in an impressionistic study of his experiences in a British secondary modern school, argues that the classroom situation contains many elements of informal co-operation among the children, who are as a group in conflict with the teacher. Many industrial situations are similar.[42] Sociologists have stressed the importance of informal groupings in some industrial situations, and such schools are likely to provide good preparation for this aspect of industrial life. This kind of school, usually in slum buildings in decaying city centres, with inadequate facilities and high teacher turnover, is still very common in this country.[43] The dichotomous 'us'—'them' view of society characteristic of industrial workers is strengthened by such situations.[44] In addition, both Carter and Webb stress that for this group of young people, which must make up a significant proportion of the urban population, the last year at school is seen as a waste of time, imposed by impersonal social forces, interfering with what the young people feel is the real continuity in their lives—moving from home to work.

In contrast to the implication of Miller and Form's approach, and whatever the children themselves may feel, the school situation can be seen not only as the antithesis of the industrial situation, but also as one where experience helping the adjustment to working life may be gained, and where attitudes easing the transition to industry are developed. Much more research on the inter-relationship between home, school and industry is required.

The Influence of Formal Institutions (Groups 6 and 7)

The formal aid given to young people in the process of adjustment to working life by the schools and the Youth Employment Service should be briefly considered. The range and content of vocational instruction in schools varies, but suffers from a view held by many school teachers that their job is to provide a 'general education', an aim absolving them from any responsibility for the details of the mundane problems of their children's vocational prospects; from the fact that few teachers have had any experience of work either in factory, office or shop, and often disparage such work; and from the fact that few have any knowledge of the occupational range of the local community. Literature about schools' career services is slight. Some schools have a careers' master who has a stock, large or small, of pamphlets; in others the Headmaster gives a talk to leavers. In a few, various representatives of firms are asked to visit, and take the opportunity of recruiting. There are organized works visits in some schools, which give a general impression of factory atmosphere, but it is not clear whether these do more than reinforce the attitudes, positive or negative, which young people already have towards industrial life.[45]

The Youth Employment Officer visits the school at least twice, once for a general discussion with leavers, and the second time in the term before leaving, for an interview with each child. In theory he has for this meeting all the details of the child's career to hand, but some schools do not co-operate.[46] In others, teachers are present at the interview and inhibit the child's responses.[47] In theory, the function of the Youth Employment Service is three-fold:- to ascertain a child's abilities and inclinations; to provide the child with a knowledge of a range of occupations compatible with these, and to give some idea of the content of and prospects in the work that would be done; finally, to offer some suggestions for placement.[48] However, Carter's and Jahoda's work has shown that, for many young people, regardless of social background, only the latter function is considered. The Youth Employment Service is seen merely as a means of getting a job if one has not already been fixed up. The follow-up procedures seem to be even less effective. The structural problems of the Youth Employment Service are discussed elsewhere.[49] As part of the process of adjustment to working life, these formal agencies are relatively ineffective in comparison with informal influences.

Attitudes towards Work (Group 4)

Informal and formal background features of the types described above create general attitudes towards, and expectations of work, and some studies of these attitudes, both among schoolchildren and adult workers have been undertaken, mainly in the United States. In these studies, three basic or 'core' attitudes to work are distinguishable, each itself capable of subdivision :- an 'intrinsic' or vocational attitude, in which work, and/or elements of the work situation are valued in themselves; an 'extrinsic' or instrumental one in which work is seen as a means of providing external satisfaction, whether financial, or in terms of status, such as adultness; and a 'career-orientated' one, in which work is seen in terms of social mobility for the individual.[50] Since the range of experience in socialization is so broad, it is likely that elements of all three attitudes are to be found in the majority of people, but certain types of background experience will tend to reinforce some at the expense of others. It is clear that any discussion of work satisfaction which ignores these variations in attitude is inadequate.[51] It is also probably important to distinguish another 'core' attitude which cannot really be subsumed under the other three—a desire for security. This manifests itself particularly in conditions of unemployment.[52] Some sociologists have also argued that it is a feature of bureaucratization.[53] It appears among young people in Britain today in expressions such as 'having something to fall back on' and 'having a trade in one's hands'. Such an attitude is partly instrumental, in that it springs from a fear of not being able to maintain accepted living standards, but it may be useful to treat it separately.[54]

Irrespective of parental occupational background, there is some evidence that most young people enter working life with elements of an intrinsic orientation.[55] Thus the Eppels remark in their article, 'Moral Beliefs of Young Workers' :-

'There is at this stage a considerable amount of potential personal

87

identification with work, and a fairly strong feeling of personal responsibility to complete what has been undertaken. The current stereotypes of adolescents tend to under-estimate the extent to which this is true, and unfortunately the conditions in industry often facilitate the dissipation of this potential sentiment, and its substitution by apathy or discontent.'[56]

Their evidence is based on studies of day-release apprentices. A study of those in unskilled occupations might lead to a modification of the generalization. If the view presented here, of work adjustment as a process, is correct, a great deal of social selection had occurred prior to the entry into apprenticeship. Ginzberg also found the same attitudes, which he says, change with age, tending towards a greater instrumentality, both in young workers, and in those still at school. The same qualification applies, as his samples were weighted in favour of middle class groups.[57]

The relevance of this conceptualization of attitudes towards work lies in the possibility of conflict between the attitudes developed in the young person, and the work situation he enters, either in the terms of attitudes of other workers or of the nature of the job. To take a hypothetical example, a boy who has developed an intrinsic attitude towards work as a result of influences from, say, school and peer groups, but whose home persuaded him to take a piece-rate job with the possibility of high pay, might find himself in a work situation in which his desires were continually thwarted by his experience. On the other hand, the attitudes of the young person may coincide more or less completely with those of his fellow workers. Much more work on the distribution of attitudes between different social groups needs to be done.

The General Work Situation for the New Entrant; Adjustment (Group 5 and (g))

Detailed information about the general conditions in which the adjustment takes place is not given here. The numbers and distribution of young people can be obtained from *Census Reports* and the occupational level and types of jobs entered are described in the annual article in the May issue of the *Ministry of Labour Gazette*. There is also some transfer during the first years of working life from small to large firms, a feature applying more to boys than to girls, and most especially to boy apprentices.[58] Such features set limits to the range of possibilities open and may even underlie what appears to be an individual decision to change a job.

As mentioned above, the majority of fifteen year old male leavers either go into apprenticeships or some form of unskilled work; almost all male clerks have at least one year's further schooling. For girls there are few apprenticeships, so that most go into clerical or unskilled work in factories or shops. Some girls classified as unskilled do have several months' training in some firms in the hosiery and shoe industries. But for the majority of unskilled boys and girls, induction consists of a brief interview, being taken to the place of work, and handed over to the chargehand or foreman, who either shows what is to be done, or assigns the entrant to another worker for the same purpose. Many of these young people will remain in that job, or type of job, for the remainder of their working lives, and will have no further training.[59] Many young entrants do not even get shown over their firm.[60]

Among other groups of employees, opportunities for formal training are not uniform. Apprentices fall into two groups—those who go into firms willing and able to give them formal training, and those who do not receive such training. Actual procedure has grown up as a response to pressures from craft unions to maintain the exclusiveness of their craft, from employers for cheap labour, and from technological demand.[61] Apprenticeships last five years for the most part, and have no certification other than the right to hold a union card on the completion of time, in some cases.

Boys who enter large-scale modern engineering works often get at least one year's formal training of a very high standard, coupled with at least three years' day or block release at technical college, which is semi-compulsory. Many of these firms are now demanding 'O' levels, i.e. an extra year at school, from their recruits. Some other industries such as printing make large scale use of day-release facilities. But those who enter small firms often have neither any formal training from the firm, nor are they allowed or encouraged to take day or block release. Their apprenticeship is as mate to another worker, who 'shows them the ropes'. An in-between group struggles—with marked lack of success as the *Crowther Report* shows—at evening courses.[62] Among clerical and shop workers the situation in respect of induction and particularly training is, if anything, worse—a situation documented in a recent book on commercial apprenticeships.[63]

Thus the multiplicity of training procedures, the variations in their standard, and their uneven availability are all potential sources of dissatisfaction. Many more can be postulated from the examples given in the scheme, such as payment, hours worked, and relations with authority, but the above suffices to indicate the range of variables within the work situation. It is in the light of this discussion that some studies of adjustment to work should be considered. At first it seems working life is very attractive compared with school. Young people mention especially the lack of formal discipline and the fact of earning. The demands made by the job are not too arduous. There is a general feeling of satisfaction.[64] In terms of the whole process of adjustment to working life, the negative attitudes of young people towards their last year at school assume importance as a possible explanation.

But for those whose aspirations are not fulfilled, or whose grasp of the demand their work will make is inaccurate, the feeling of satisfaction may be ephemeral. Also for some it may be that further experience gained at work induces consideration of a range of alternative occupations now closed to the young person because of the work he has entered.[65] In confirmation of this, where there is dissatisfaction, it appears to increase with length of work experience. In Tenen's study of unskilled young workers:-

'It soon became evident that the most prevalent attitude to work and the work authority among the adolescents in these factories was that of dissatisfaction, even resentment. Neither youth nor sex was found to be the decisive factor in shaping these attitudes. On the contrary, among both sexes the average number of complaints increased with age.'[66]

In a Glasgow study of day-release apprentices, the Eppels also found that dissatisfaction as measured by dislike of jobs, and frequency of changes, increased with age.[67] Kelchner, in pre-war Germany, found that it was after two years of work experience that worries about unemployment and complaints about jobs reached their peak.[68] In Austria, Lazarsfeld found in a pioneer study that dissatisfaction with work was expressed by one quarter of the group studied in the year after leaving school, but by three-fifths after seven years' work experience.[69] Vollmer and Kinney report an increase of dissatisfaction in an all age sample in U.S. ordnance factories until the age of thirty, after which it declines.[70]

It is clear then, that while there is no evidence that the transition between the institutions of school and work leads to any kind of sudden traumatic experience, some evidence exists that for a minority at least there is a delayed realization that work may have more frustrations than were expected by the school leaver. This only begins the explanation. It is essential to be able to specify which social groups and which work situations are in conflict and, equally importantly, which coincide.

Conclusion

The above examples, tentative and partial as they are, reveal the gaps in our knowledge of the process of moving into working life. On the one hand much of the literature is concerned with the aspirations of schoolchildren, who are, of course, much easier to contact. On the other, general studies of adolescence are over-whelmingly concerned with biological and sexual development, and the major social changes of the adolescent period are either ignored or discussed quite briefly and speculatively.[71] The theories of Miller and Form and de Maupeou have certain defects as approaches to the problem of working life. It is hoped that the present approach will serve students of the field both by establishing a framework for the interpretation of previous work, and by generating problems for solution. The complexity of the interrelationships involved is apparent, but a recognition of their existence as opposed to the accumulation of more or less *ad hoc* correlations must contribute to more fruitful research. The subject like most in industrial sociology is a very open one. Whatever the specific value of the approach outlined, the authors are convinced that it is only by attempting to integrate on-going and future research within some such general framework that the fragmentary state of existing work can be superceded.

The University of Aston in Birmingham.

[1] The expressions 'adjustment' and 'non-adjustment' refer to the variety of attitudes and behaviour of young people in the work situation. This may be measured in many ways, indices ranging, for example, from expressions of satisfaction and dissatisfaction, through absenteeism, to job change. By the use of the term 'adjustment', the authors in no way wish to imply that there should be any one-way adaptation of the young worker to whatever situation he may find himself in.

[2] *Statistics of Education*, 1964, part 1, Table 2, H.M.S.O.

[3] *Ministry of Labour Gazette*, May 1965, p. 208. Unskilled and semi-skilled includes some jobs with unspecified 'planned training'.

[4] A paraphrase of the Report of the Departmental Committee of the Board of Education, 1916, 'Juvenile Education in Relation to Employment after the War', by P. I. Kitchen, in *From Learning to Earning*, Faber, 1944, p. 12. German literature on the subject is more extensive than British, and much more thorough. Studies date back even earlier, e.g. K. Frankenstein:

'Die Lage der Fabrikarbeiterinnen in der Deutsche Grossstadten', *Schmollers Jahrbuch*, 1888, cited in G. Wurzbacher, *et. al.*: *Die Junge Arbeiterin*, Munich, Juventa, 1960.

[5] For a discussion, see Kitchen: *op. cit.*, pp. 51-58.

[6] Central Advisory Council for Education—England. (*The Crowther Report*) '*15-18*', Vol. 1. p. 143, H.M.S.O., 1959.

[7] M. P. Carter: *Home School and Work*, Pergamon, 1962; *Crowther Report; op. cit.*; T. Veness: *School Leavers*, Methuen, 1962.

[8] The approach developed here is relevant to the study of occupational choice. Theories of occupational choice have been developed by: E. Ginzberg, *et. al.*: *Occupational Choice*, London, 1951, and W. Jaide: *Die Berufswahl*, Munich, Juventa, 1961.

[9] As examples of a general type, see: L. D. Crow and A. Crow: *Adolescent Development and Adjustment*, McGraw-Hill, 1956, Ch. 16, 'Vocational Adjustment', and W. Lean: 'Work Problems of Young Factory Employees', *Personnel Practice Bulletin*, Vol. 16, 1960, pp. 26-30.

[10] For a general comparison of the problems of the adolescent in advanced as opposed to undeveloped societies, see: K. Davis: 'Adolescence and the Social Structure', *Annals of the American Academy of Political and Social Science*, Vol. 236, 1944, pp. 8-16, and M. Mead: *Coming of Age in Samoa* Pelican, 1944.

[11] For example: H. Dansereau: 'Work and the Teenager', *Annals of the American Academy of Political and Social Sciences*, 338, Nov. 1961, pp. 44-52; D. Harris: 'Psychological Aspects of the Rôle of Work in Adolescent Development' *The American Child*, Vol. 39, March 1957; Kitchen: *op. cit*, p. 10; J. MacAlistair Brew: *Youth and Youth Groups*, Faber, 1957, p. 15f. For a similar French view see: J. Rousselet: *L'Adòlescent en Apprentissage*, Paris, Presses Universitaires de France, 1961.

[12] D. C. Miller & W. H. Form: *Industrial Sociology*, New York, Harper, 1951 ed., Chs. XV—XVIII.

[13] Miller & Form: *op. cit.*, p. 622. Miller and Form do consider adjustment to work as part of a socialization process. But their main emphasis is on the clash of values between pre-work and work experience. They devote only six out of almost 200 pages to socialization within the home and school (pp. 523-529).

[14] H. M. Bell: *Youth Tell their Story*, American Council on Education, Washington D. C., 1938. Cited in Miller and Form: *op. cit.*, p. 592.

[15] N. de Maupeou: 'Le Jeune Ouvrier dans l'Industrie—Une Situation de Minorité', *Sociologie du Travail*, Vol. 2, 1960, pp. 39-51.

[16] Among others: R. Stephenson: 'Mobility Orientation and Stratification of 1000 Ninth Graders', *Am. Soc. Rev.*, Vol. 22, 1957, pp. 204-212.

[17] P. Lazarsfield: 'Jugend Und Beruf', *Quellen und Studien zur Jugendkunde*, Vol. 8, Jena, Gustav Fischer, 1931; Veness: *op. cit.*, p. 93f.

[18] See Chapter Two.

[19] Among many studies the following are particularly interesting: H. B. Hood: 'Occupational Preferences of Secondary Modern School-children', *Educational Rev.*, Vol. 4, 1951-2, p. 55f; G. Jahoda: 'Social Class Attitudes and Levels of Occupational Aspiration in Secondary Modern School Leavers',

Br. J. Psy., Vol. 44, 1953, pp. 95-107; H. Pallister: 'Vocational Preferences of School Leavers in a Scottish Industrial Area', *Br. J. Psy.*, Vol. 29, 1938, pp. 144-166; Veness: *op. cit*; M. D. Wilson: 'The Vocational Preferences of Secondary Modern School-children', *Br. J. Ed. Psy.*, Vol. 23, 1953, pp. 97-113, and pp. 163-179. See also: J. K. Morland: 'Educational and Occupational Aspirations of Mill and Town Schoolchildren in a Southern Community', *Social Forces*, Vol. 39, 1960. p. 169f.

[20] This is based on a memorandum, *Young Workers in Modern Industrial Society. Types of Behaviour: an Interpretation.* (Unpublished), which Madame de Maupeou has sent us, but see also: N. de Maupeou: 'Le Jeune Ouvrier . . .' *op. cit*; and her 'Pour Une Sociologie des Jeunes dans La Societé Industrielle', *Annales Economies-Societes-Civilisations*, Vol. 1, 1961; 'Niveau d'Aspiration, Statut Professionel et Revenue', *Sociologie du Travail*, Vol. 4, 1962, pp. 15-33.

[21] For examples of similar approaches, see: C. W. Gordon: *The Social System of the High School*, Glencoe, Ill. Free Press, 1957; A. Campbell, et. al.: *The American Voter*, New York, Wiley, 1960.

[22] B. Green, T. Keil, and D. Riddell: *Occupational Choice—the Social Setting*, forcoming.

[23] Friedmann might be criticised on this score, See G. Friedmann: *Industrial Society*, Glencoe, Ill., Free Press, 1955.

[24] J. W. B. Douglas: *The Home and the School*, McGibbon and Kee, 1964.

[25] B. Bernstein: 'Social Class and Linguistic Development: A Theory of Social Learning', in A. H. Halsey *et. al.* (Eds.): *Education, Economy and Society*, Glencoe, Ill., Free Press, 1961, pp. 288-314.

[26] Central Advisory Council for Education (England): *Early Leaving*, H.M.S.O., 1954; *Crowther Report*: *op. cit*; Carter: *op. cit.*

[27] Carter: *op. cit*, pp. 45, 53.

[28] L. Reynolds and J. Shister: *Job Horizons*, New York, Harper, 1949, Ch. 6.

[29] J. Kahl: 'Common Man Boys', in *Education, Economy and Society*, *op. cit.*, pp. 348-366. The whole of part 4, on social factors in educational achievement, is relevant. D. Swift: 'Who Passes the 11 + ?', *New Society*, 5/3/64, pp. 6-10.

[30] T. Ferguson & J. Cunnison: *The Young Wage Earner*, O.U.P., 1951. p. 110.

[31] See footnote 19, and N. F. Dufty: 'The Relationship Between Paternal Occupation and Occupational Choice', *Int. J. Comp. Soc.*, Vol. 2, 1961, pp. 81-87; R. Samson & B. Stefflre: 'Like Father . . . Like Son', *Personnel Guidance J.*, Vol. 31, No. 1, October 1952; P. Jenson & W. Kirchner: 'A National Answer to the Question, "Do Sons Follow their Fathers' Occupations?"', *J. App. Psy.*, Vol. 39, 1955, pp. 419-421.

[32] D. Glass & J. Hall: 'Social Mobility in Britain: A Study of Intergeneration Change in Status', in D. Glass (Ed.): *Social Mobility in Britain*, Routledge, 1954, p. 177.

[33] Carter: *op. cit.*, p. 190; Ferguson & Cunnison: *op. cit.* pp. 25, 30.

[34] E. Venables: 'The Reserve of Ability in Part-time Technical Courses', *Universities Quarterly*, Vol. 17, 1962, pp. 60-75.

[35] F. Zweig: *Labour, Life and Poverty*, Gollancz, 1949.

[36] W. F. Connel, *et. al.*: *Growing Up in an Australian City*, Melbourne, 1957.

[37] E. Eppel and M. Eppel: 'Young Workers at a County College', *Br. J. Ed. Psy.*, Vol. 23, 1953, pp. 29-44, 87-96, especially the second part; R. Koskas: 'L'Adolescent et sa Famille', *Enfance*, Vol. 2, 1949, pp. 68-71; J. Pitts: 'The Family and Peer Groups', in N. Bell & E. Vogel: *A Reader on the Family*, Routledge, 1961, Ch. 21.

[38] For example, R. Hoggart: *The Uses of Literacy*, Pelican, 1958; B. Jackson and D. Marsden: *Education and the Working Class*, Routledge, 1962.

[39] There are few studies of the actual amounts earned and money spent amongst young wage earners. Mark Abrams in his study, *The Teenage Consumer*, Press Exchange Papers, 1959, defines the teenage group in such a way as to include unmarried people up to 25 years old, giving a very distorted impression of the amount of money available to the young person between 15 and 18. See the tables in Carter: *op. cit.*, p. 152, and Ferguson and Cunnison: *op. cit.*, p. 100.

[40] Ferguson and Cunnison: *op. cit.*, p. 31. See also the interesting table in E. Schulz, *Elternhaus und Lehrling*, Institut fur Berufserziehung an der Universität Köln, 1960, p. 19, showing that a father's death has a noticeable effect on occupational choice, and J. G. Friend: 'Work Adjustment in Relation to Family Background', *J. Social Casework*, Vol. 29, 1948, pp. 89-93.

[41] Carter: *op. cit.*, Ch. 3, and J. S. Coleman: *The Adolescent Society*, Glencoe, Ill., Free Press, 1961.

[42] J. Webb: 'The Sociology of a School', *Br. J. Soc.*, Vol. 13, 1962, pp. 264-272. See also Carter: *op. cit.* Ch. 4.

[43] Central Advisory Council for Education (England). *The Newsom Report; Half Our Future*, H.M.S.O., 1963; National Union of Teachers, *The State of our Schools*, 1964; Government White Paper, *The School Building Survey*, 1962, H.M.S.O., 1965.

[44] See J. Goldthorpe and D. Lockwood: 'Affluence and the British Class Structure', *Soc. Rev.*, Vol. 11, 1963, pp. 133-163.

[45] A study of Lancashire school leavers makes some comment about these topics; G. Jahoda: 'Job Attitudes and Job Choice among Secondary Modern School Leavers', *Occup. Psy.*, Vol. 26, 1952, pp. 125-140, 206-224, especially the latter part.

[46] G. Jahoda and A. Chalmers: 'The Youth Employment Service, A Consumer Perspective', *Occup. Psy.*, Vol. 37, 1964, p. 20f.

[47] Carter: *op. cit.*, pp. 117-118.

[48] G. France: 'The Youth Employment Service: A look from Within', *Technical Education*, Vol. 4, 1962, No. 3, pp. 20-23 and No. 5, pp. 37-40.

[49] See the latter part of Green, Keil and Riddell: *op. cit.*

[50] The authors have drawn, among others, on the work of G. Friedmann: *op. cit.*; F. Herzberg, *et al.*, *The Motivation to Work*, Chapman Hall, 1959; Reynolds and Shister: *op. cit.*; S. Boggs: 'The Values of Laboratory Workers', *Human Organization*, Vol. 22, 1963, pp. 207-215.

[51] For example, L. Klein: *Meaning in Work*, Fabian Pamphlet, 1963.

[52] There were no systematic studies in Britain in the 1930's, but much interesting work was done in Germany, e.g. L. Franzen-Hellersberg: *Die Jugendliche Arbeiterin*, Tübingen, Mohr, 1932; M. Kelchner: 'Kummer und Trost Jugendliche Arbeiterinnen', *Forschungen zur Volkspsychologie und Soziologie*, Band 6, Leipzig, Hirschfeld, 1929. A good bibliography, especially of work relating to young female workers is contained in Wurzbacher: *op. cit.*

[53] C.f. R. Merton: *Social Theory and Social Structure*, Glencoe, Ill., Free Press, 1957, Ch. 6; W. H. Whyte: *The Organization Man*, Jonathan Cape, 1957.

[54] Other researchers have posited a 'service' oriented attitude. In our terms, this would be a sub-category of 'intrinsic' orientation. See H. D. Schwarzkeller: 'Values and Occupational Choice', *Social Forces*, Vol. 39, 1960-61, pp. 126-135.

[55] G. Jahoda: 'Job Attitudes and Job Choice . . .', *op. cit.* Part I; N. F. Dufty. 'Vocational Choices of 13 to 14 year old Males', *Australian Journal of Education*, 1960, Vol. 4, No. 1, pp. 38-56.

[56] E. M. Eppel: Moral Beliefs of Young Workers', *Br. J. Sociol.*, Vol. 14, 1963, p. 215.

[57] Ginzberg, *et. al.; op. cit.*

[58] E. T. Kiel, C. Riddell and C. Tipton: 'The Size of Firms Entered by Young Workers', *Br. J. Ind. Rel.*, Vol. 1, 1963, pp. 408-411. The same situation has been reported for West Germany; see F. Gegler and R. Ferber: 'Berufsnachwuchs und Berufswechsel', *Das Arbeitsamt*, Band 2, March 1951, No. 3.

[59] In the United States, only 25 per cent of young entrants get any training, according to A. Bartleman: 'Teenagers—Industry's Hidden Asset', *Business*, Vol. 91, 1961, No. 8, pp. 58-60.

[60] J. A. Paquin: 'An Examination of 14 Employee Induction Programmes', *Personnel Practice Bulletin*, Vol. 17, 1961, No. 3, pp. 38-42.

[61] G. Williams: *Recruitment to Skilled Trades*, Routledge, 1957.

[62] *Crowther Report*: *op. cit.*, p. 354f. See also G. Ashton: 'Enrolment and Examination Success of Day Release Students by Size of Firm', *Br. J. Ind. Rel.*, Vol. 3, 1965, pp. 90-94.

[63] E. Tonkinson, et. al. : *Commercial Apprenticeships*, University of London Press, 1962.

[64] Carter: *op. cit.*, ch. 9.

[65] Lipset and Malm show that first job is the best predictor of subsequent career; S. Lipset and F. Malm: 'First Jobs and Career Patterns', *Am. J. of Econ. & Sociol.*, Vol. 14, pp. 247-261.

[66] C. Tenen: 'The Adolescent in the Factory', *Br. J. Ed. Psy.*, Vol. 17, 1947, p. 76.

E. Teresa Keil, C. Riddell, B. S. R. Green

67 Eppel & Eppel: *op. cit.*

68 Kelchner: *op. cit.*

69 Lazarsfeld: *op. cit.*

70 H. Vollmer and J. Kinney: 'Age, Education and Job Satisfaction', *Personnel*, Vol. 32, 1955, No. 1, pp. 38-43.

71 A good review of such studies is that by R. E. Muuss: *Theories of Adolescence*, New York, Random House, 1962. The authors looked through eighteen general textbooks of adolescence without discovering one that emphasized the new adjustments necessary to the rôle of worker.

96

Chapter Four
TOWARDS A SOCIOLOGICAL THEORY OF OCCUPATIONAL CHOICE[1]
P. W. Musgrave

In the previous chapter, Keil, Riddell and Green comment that:

> 'The literature on the adjustment of young people to working life is large, but lacks coherence.'[2]

These authors suggest a new approach based on the view that starting work and adjusting to this new situation is a process;[3] they analyse the influences operating on youths at the point of movement from school into work. The purpose of this chapter is to suggest that their new approach, whilst worth while in itself, is limited and would be much more valuable if it were set in the framework of a general theory of occupational choice. Such a theory should cover the whole process of first choice of occupation and take account of influences operating on any individual from birth onwards. Furthermore, if the theory is to be a general one, it should be applicable to choice of job other than the first that is made at later stages of the life cycle.

There is at present no sociological theory of occupational choice. Two major attempts by psychologists, Ginzberg *et al.* and Super,[4] have resulted in descriptive, developmental theories. This pioneering work misses much of sociological relevance and, as Chown[5] has shown, Ginzberg's work at least seems more applicable to the U.S.A. than to Britain. Both Bordin's[6] monograph on the development of vocational interests and H. D. Carter's[7] on the development of vocational attitudes are important in that their work can be rephrased in rôle theory terms. This, together with Schwarzweller's recent paper on values and occupational choice,[8] reinforces the suggestion made by Keil *et al.* that an approach to occupational choice through the concept of socialisation could be fruitful. The only other relevant work of a theoretical sociological nature is that by an inter-disciplinary team led by Blau[9] which, unlike the work so far mentioned, specifically allows for the structure of the labour force, but because of this

© P. W. Musgrave 1967 (This article was first published in *The Sociological Review*, Vol. 15, No. 1, March 1967.)

structural approach misses the lead into rôle theory that a sociologist can find in some of the psychological work.

I. Development of a Sociological Theory

(i) *Socialisation*. In addition to the theoretical arguments for making socialisation the conceptual focus for developing a theory of occupational choice there are three other reasons of a more practical nature. Firstly, socialisation is now seen by sociologists not just as a tool for examining the way children take on new rôles, but as applicable to rôle-taking in adult life. Furthermore, the concept of socialisation directs attention to the central sociological concept of rôle. Secondly, work by Brim and Wheeler and by Myerhoff and Larson[10] ties socialisation to another emerging field, the theory of organisations. This emphasis is very relevant to choice of occupation, a process that takes place largely within such organisations as schools and factories. Finally, work on political socialisation by Almond and Verba and Greenstein[11] has reactivated the concept of 'secondary socialisation'.

The problem is raised at this point of how to differentiate between 'primary' and 'secondary' socialisation in a way that is realistic and suggestive of research issues. Parsons uses as his criterion the manner in which the particular new rôle is learnt; primary socialisation takes place mainly through identification and secondary socialisation through imitation. Thus primary socialisation would relate to the basic structure of the personality, whilst secondary would cover such rôles as profit-seeking, which is, in fact, the example analysed in theoretical terms by Parsons.[12] In an analysis of socialisation throughout the life cycle Brim compares childhood with adult socialisation, but despite a Meadian approach the criterion used to distinguish 'primary' from 'secondary' seems to be somewhat psychologistic.[13]

Central to any sociological analysis of socialisation is the nature of the rôles available to those undergoing the process. From the point of view of any child the life cycle can be seen as a large number of alternative pathways consisting of the series of rôles that are available for choice by the individual or by surrogates, such as parents or teachers, on his behalf. Choice at each stage limits the possible pathways along which the individual may travel in the future. One of the major problems of rôle theory is the mode of articulation of such a system of rôles. Up to this point the problem has been stated from a societal point of view, but it can also be rephrased from the individual's point of view as follows: what is the mode of summation of all the rôles any individual plays?[14] Both ways of stating the problem have analytical uses, but the latter will be used here for the purpose of developing a theory of occupational choice.

Rôles will be categorised according to the number of settings in which the rôle under consideration is played. Primary socialisation will refer to rôles played in all settings, secondary socialisation to rôles played in some settings, and tertiary socialisation will cover those rôles only played in one setting. Many rôles learnt in the process of primary socialisation are 'latent' in the taking and playing of rôles learnt in secondary socialisation, and likewise secondary rôles are 'latent' at the tertiary stage.[15] One type of secondary socialisation which has as yet not received specific attention in the literature is economic socialisation.

(ii) *Economic Socialisation.* The term 'economic socialisation' has now been introduced. In scope it covers that important cluster of rôles that relate to the economic institutions of any culture. The exact nature of these rôles will vary by culture. The dominant values that govern the particular social system will specify the content and importance of the rôle system to be learnt. The need to get a living, or, more specifically in a money economy, to earn a living, imposes a rôle pattern with differences by sex and by nation or region. Social class is a very important influence on the particular economic rôle taken since it largely determines the life-chances or future pathway of the individual. In addition, as Centers has indicated, membership of a social class imposes upon the individual

'certain attitudes, values and interests relating to his rôle and status in the political and economic sphere'.[16]

Economic socialisation can be subdivided conceptually into the learning of producer and of consumer rôles. This division follows the practice in economic analysis of considering both supply and demand. Consumer rôles have been studied little by sociologists, though much attention has been given to this field by commercial market researchers. However, studies of the styles of life of members of different social classes with the same or different incomes are of relevance.[17] The study of producer rôles would cover all the behaviour, values and attitudes relating to economic production. An important area of concern here would be occupational choice, since some explanation of such points as the following is relevant: how and when the individual learns the stereotypes of the various occupations in the labour force, how he comes to see which occupations are available to him and how he learns the behaviour, values and attitudes needed in the various work situations of his culture or subculture.

Before considering occupational choice in more detail one further point must be made for the sake of completeness. Deviance and delinquency are as possible in the field of economic socialisation as in any other type of socialisation. Economic delinquents are those who are caught breaking the laws particularly relating to economic rôles. Deviance in producer rôles raises the issues of deviant occupations that recruit for the most part individuals who either are unable to play 'normal' economic rôles because of personality problems or who exhibit what Fromm has called 'socially patterned defect'.[18] In this latter category may be put all those who through primary socialisation come to have personalities such that they are willing or able to play occupational rôles of a certain type, namely those that are either looked down upon or that cater for individuals who are slightly unusual. An example of the first type of occupational rôle is that of prison-warder and an instance of the second might be a long-distance lorry-driver or night watchman, on the grounds that recruits to these last two occupations wish to work alone rather than in the more usual work groups.

(iii) *Occupational Choice.* It is now possible to locate occupational choice firmly in sociological theory, more specifically in that part of secondary socialisation that deals with producer rôles, though primary, tertiary and other types of secondary socialisation may have latent relevance. Analysis of occupational choice from this perspective has been brief and rare. For instance, in his examination of rôle passage from adolescence to adulthood Parsons introduces a brief consideration of occupational rôles by saying,

> 'The case of occupational rôles for the male as the goal of this stage of socialisation in our society is so clear as to need relatively little comment.'[19]

The occupational rôles of girls are not mentioned.

The child has to build up a rôle map of his society so that he can locate occupational names on it and can know the rôle prescriptions associated with these names.[20] From such a map the child learns something of the way that rôles are articulated in the occupational structure so that he knows near and complementary rôles. This knowledge eases his task at the point of entry to the labour force of choosing an occupation that more or less matches his wishes from amongst the limited range locally available to him.

Socialisation is a *process*. There is, therefore, the possibility that there are stages to the process. Certainly the commonest method of analysis is to split the process into stages. Parsons uses Freudian stages possibly because his stress is on the development of personality.[21] Since factual knowledge and the appreciation of relationships are important in such second degree socialisation as economic or political socialisation, it is at least arguable that the Piagetian stages are more apposite. These are marked by the progressive ability to perform mental operations. One sociological framework exists; Form and Miller[22] have proposed three developmental phases:

(1) the initial work period which covers jobs held while still at school,
(2) the trial work period while a young worker 'shops around' for a job,
(3) the stable work period which 'some workers may never experience'.

This framework omits any consideration of the relevant latent parts of primary socialisation and seems unrealistic in that the final stage may never be reached.

Here it is proposed to use stages based on the structural and organisational framework within which the whole process of economic socialisation takes place. Four stages will be considered: (1) pre-work socialisation, (2) entry to the labour force, (3) socialisation into the labour force, (4) job changes. These stages are chosen so that despite the prominance given to the first choice of occupation the framework can be applied to all choices of occupation that an individual makes throughout his working life.

(iv) *Anticipatory Socialisation.* Before giving some consideration to each of these stages a further analytical tool must be introduced. This is the concept of anticipatory socialisation. The process of moving through the various positions involved in the four stages will be easier and less lacking in continuity if the individual has prior knowledge of what is involved in filling these positions. Prior rôle rehearsal is an important element in preparing to move to the next stage in the process of socialisation whether primary, secondary or tertiary.

Much anticipatory secondary socialisation occurs in the family. Thus an important part of economic socialisation at the pre-work stage is the move from viewing one's future occupation in a spirit of fantasy and idealism to taking a realistic view of one's potentialities.[23] The individual in anticipation practises taking the values and behaviour prescribed for an occupational rôle in which he sees himself.

Adequate anticipatory socialisation will ease the later taking of the rôle. It is important to know the reference groups to which the child is referring since these may be either functional or dysfunctional for the ultimate choice of occupation. An example of dysfunction for the economy is where able working class children refer to their families rather than to the school and therefore refuse to aim for high status occupations.[24]

The field of anticipatory economic socialisation is an important one in practice. Knowledge as to how far it has gone for different social groups will reveal the extent of the reversability of occupational choice at the point of entry to work, since prior rehearsal of the rôles that an individual believes he is going to play will, at least in his own expectations, narrow the area of choice available to him.

II. *A Brief Consideration of the Stages*

(i) *Pre-work socialisation.* During this period there occurs the relevant primary socialisation that will be latent to subsequent secondary and tertiary socialisation. The pathway of rôles available to the child, and hence his choice of occupation, is narrowed by the experiences that he undergoes, more particularly at the hands of three of the main agents of socialisation, namely, the family, the school and the peer group.[25] Gradually the child either comes to realise what possible rôles are available to him or is restricted by the socialisation process so that he adopts a self-concept of his own ability that narrows the range of rôles from which he will choose.

(a) The Family. For the child his parents are the main point of juncture between two important systems—the family and the economy. Each system has its own particular rôle system, but the father, and often the mother, will hold positions in both systems, so that the child has a chance of learning about his parents' economic rôles. Parents may act as conscious rôle models, but very often they perform this function unconsciously, transmitting the behaviour, values and attitudes essential for playing some economic rôle without themselves being aware that they are so doing.[26] A very important set of values that influences economic behaviour and that is learnt to a large extent unconsciously at this stage is that relating to authority. In the family the child starts to learn the rôle of one who obeys and co-operates. Practice in such rôles ensures that a child is able to behave functionally when he starts work. Many other rôles played in the family increase the ability to take successfully subsequent economic rôles. Thus children learn their sex rôles at home and come to see themselves as males or females with particular work expectations. Boys may come to think of themselves as future bread-winners and girls to consider work as a prelude or supplement to marriage.

Play is a very important form of rôle rehearsal that gives children knowledge of the values and behaviour of occupational rôles. Crucial here is the visibility of the rôles to be imitated. The occupational rôle of his father may be more easily seen by the boy living in the country than in a city; there may be differences in visibility between the social classes or the sexes. Such distinctive signs as dress may be important; the young child will easily learn of postmen and bus con-ductors or of blue- and white-collar jobs.[27] From such experiences the child will learn occupational names and start to build up his rôle-map of the occupational structure and, as he plays shops or schools, the child will learn something of the complexity and the interrelationships of the rôles in the occupational structure.

(b) The School. The school is an important agent at this stage. In any culture one important dimension of the system of alternative rôle opportunities is the occupational structure and in a modern economy the paths that an individual can take through this structure are influenced greatly by the path that he takes through the educa-tional system. The curriculum of a school can shape the goals of the children in it; these goals play a great part in motivating occupational choice. Allocation to a particular type of either secondary school or course within a secondary school, or again a choice of one particular option can restrict the future occupational rôle open to the child. The tripartite structure of the British schools plays an important part in directing children's attention to the cluster of occupations usually connected with their particular secondary school. This tends to direct their anticipatory socialisation in very definite directions. A very clear example of anticipatory socialisation can be found at the level of higher vocational education, where medical students come to see themselves as doctors whilst still in training.[28]

(c) The Peer Group. Inasmuch as the peer group is often the escape from the values of family and school it may be an important source of dysfunctional anticipatory economic socialisation. Able children may leave school because their friends have started work. One of the most important sets of attitudes that may be influenced by the peer group prior to a child's leaving school is that towards work itself. The way in which a boy or girl, regardless of social class, views work, whether as a means or an end in itself, whether as a 'central life interest'[29] or as merely peripheral, will have an important bearing on how he ultimately settles into the labour force.

(ii) *Entry to the Labour Force.* So far this chapter has described the development of occupational preferences. At entry to the labour force preference must become choice, though this process may have been well rehearsed by anticipatory economic socialisation. Furthermore, choice must match the selection process of industry and commerce. For the majority of school leavers this means that choice is constrained by local opportunities. The wider the range of occupations in the local labour force, the greater the chance seems to be that young people will find the first job that they want. Children will by this stage have learnt a rôle map, representative in some measure of the occupations available to them either locally or nationally. The public images of the jobs upon which this map is based may vary through time due, perhaps, to technical change. The presence of immigrants or low status ethnic groups could also alter stereotypes. In addition there is some evidence that the stereotypes of occupations vary by social class.[30]

It is against this background that the vocational guidance service of a country operates for that proportion of the population that asks its help. Various techniques are used to ensure that young people do not commit themselves too deeply to definite occupational rôles in anticipation of leaving school. Visits to work places whilst still at school and trial work periods both prior to and after leaving school are becoming more common. Similar arrangements are normal for those entering higher level occupations from university. The Youth Employment Officer (and the University Appointments Board to a lesser extent and on a national scale) has to match the outcomes of the pre-work socialisation period to local needs by placing the young person either in the job he wants or one that will satisfy 'psychological contiguous values'.[31] Choice of occupation can be seen as a focus where the outcomes of much secondary socialisation and perhaps even anticipatory tertiary socialisation are manifestly at work. In addition such outcomes of primary socialisation as the need to achieve will play a latent part here.

(iii) *Socialisation into the Job.* This is a vital part of any theory of occupational choice for three reasons. Firstly, the initial choice may not be the final choice even assuming that the best possible advice is given; some hidden quirks of personality or some unknown demand of the specific job may prevent an individual from settling into a position. The individual may succeed in meeting the rôle prescriptions of the position into which he has been recruited, or he may suffer conflict which is bearable or he may fail to meet the requirements of his present occupation.[32] In the first two cases he may stay in this occupation for some time or for his working life; in the last case he will change his job. Secondly, since the process of moving into the initial job is not at the moment particularly efficient, some subsequent change is inevitable. Lastly, even if the working of occupational guidance at every level of the labour force were improved, the accelerating rate of technical change ensures that many individuals will have to change jobs at least once, if not more often, during their working life. On these three grounds the way people are socialised into their jobs is important.

Even in the case of a first job much of this process will be the learning of rôle behaviour particular to one occupation or even position, namely what has been termed tertiary socialisation. Certainly, compared with the socialisation undergone at school, the process will be much more specific, though in the early years of work, some more diffuse secondary economic socialisation will still be learnt. One can differentiate between 'the British working man' and 'the British ironworker'; the junior operative in an iron and steel works must learn much of the former rôle in his early days at work that will later stand him in good stead in other occupational rôles. Inasmuch as the private sphere of life is totally separated from the work sphere a worker may have to operate two codes of morality, the public one which must be learnt at work and which may contradict the private one learnt at home.[33] Since there is low visibility between these two spheres, socialisation into the separate codes should be easy and their coexistence supported.

When a new recruit joins any organisation he must have the new situation defined to him. As he becomes socialised into his occupational rôle the self-image that he constructs must meet the demands of new significant others, more particularly of managers and work mates. The extent of prior anticipatory socialisation may be crucial in the adjustment to this process. The definition of the situation that is learnt will allow for some tolerance in the behaviour prescribed; some compromise between self and others will be possible. Such adjustment seems to be rapid; Hollingshead has commented on the rapidity with which lower class youths already at work adjusted to their lower chances of upward social mobility when compared with their age mates who were still at school.[34]

In Britain where the majority of children still leave school at fifteen, many problems of unsatisfactory choice of job have to be worked out in the labour force and a large proportion of young workers change jobs in their first year after school. In M. P. Carter's sample of secondary modern school children just over a third of both boys and girls left their first job during the year after leaving school.[35] As Goffman has pointed out, failure is permitted to the young since they are considered as 'not-yet-persons', but adults are not allowed to fail and so must not change jobs too often.[36] From the point of view of the employer the young worker may be 'a not-yet worker' and some floundering permitted, yet frequent job changes do not lead to an efficient economy or the growth of a stable personality.

(iv) *Job Changes*. Even those who settle easily into their first job may want or have to change their job or occupation in later life. All such changes are not the result of idiosyncratic whims, but may be due to changes in the occupational structure because of, for example, technical change. Such changes can result in occupational mobility for adults who have to choose a new job and be socialised into it in somewhat the same way as is the case for adolescents. This process may be hidden because the job is still called by the same name despite a radical alteration in the work done. This resocialisation is normally of the tertiary type since it is only relevant to one social setting, namely the work situation.

For non-manual workers who form a slowly growing proportion of all workers it is feasible to talk of 'a career', but as Wilensky has said, 'most men do not have careers'.[37] Wilensky has calculated that even in the U.S.A. today two-thirds to three-quarters of the labour force do not follow 'an ordered, predictable sequence' of jobs. A general theory of occupational choice has to account for the direction of such moves; one focus for investigation would seem to be the balancing of satisfaction in the present job against current job vacancies, whether nearby or at some distance. Job turnover seems to be higher in a state of full employment than at times when jobs are hard to find and, therefore, the degree of dissatisfaction that will drive a worker to try to change his job would appear to change with the level of employment.

III. *Conclusion*

In this paper a conceptual framework has been constructed as a first approach to a sociological theory of occupational choice. The central focus has been on socialisation seen strictly as learning to take rôles. Economic socialisation to which occupational choice is mainly related has been seen here as an important instance of secondary socialisation, certainly up to adolescence, though the concept of tertiary socialisation grows in importance with the age at which the occupational rôle must be learnt. The criterion by which the degree of socialisation is judged has been taken as the number of settings in which the rôle is played.

Anticipatory socialisation is important. At each stage of economic socialisation rôles may be rehearsed in such a way that transition to the next stage is more easily accomplished. This is particularly the case in the movement from the pre-work period through the first choice of occupation into the labour force. During this process certain elements of primary socialisation will also have latent importance for economic socialisation.

The conceptual framework has been backed at relevant points by findings from the British and American literature. If this approach to a theory of occupational choice is a valid one, it should be possible both to order the literature[38] and to indicate a number of problems about which little or nothing is known either in Britain or, in some cases, in either country. Relevant problems would seem to be:

(i) What primary socialisation has latent importance for such subsequent secondary socialisation as economic socialisation? (This question can equally be phrased in terms of secondary and tertiary socialisation).

(ii) How do parents act as economic rôle-models, either consciously or unconsciously, for their children?

(iii) What are the occupational stereotypes that influence young people's choice of occupation?[39]

(iv) What is the nature of anticipatory socialisation that is relevant to economic socialisation and how far has it proceeded in the case of young people at various ages?

(v) What are the important agents of secondary and tertiary economic socialisation and what weight should be given to these various agents?

Work at these points would be important for a deeper theoretical understanding of the process of socialisation and would also have an

P. W. Musgrave

important practical application to the work of 'vocational guidance', thereby, perhaps, both minimising the loss of talent and maximising individual satisfaction from the jobs that a person has throughout his working life.

University of Aberdeen.

[1] I am indebted to Professor M. Banton for some comments on an earlier version of this chapter.

[2] *Op. cit.*, p. 76.

[3] *Op. cit.*, p. 80.

[4] E. Ginzberg, S. W. Ginsburg, S. Axelrad, J. L. Herma: *Occupational Choice: An Approach to a General Theory'*, New York, 1951; D. E. Super: *The Psychology of Occupations*, New York, 1957.

[5] S. M. Chown: 'The Formation of Occupational Choice Among Grammar School Pupils', *Occup. Psychol.*, July 1958, pp. 175-6.

[6] E. S. Bordin: 'A Theory of Vocational Interests as Dynamic Phenomenon', *Educ. Psychol. Measurement*, 1943, pp. 49-66.

[7] H. D. Carter: 'Vocational Interests and Job Orientation', *Applied Psychol. Monog.*, No. 2, 1944.

[8] H. K. Schwarzweller: 'Values and Occupational Choice', *Soc. Forces*, Dec. 1960, pp. 126-135.

[9] P. M. Blau, J. W. Gustad, R. Jessor, H. S. Parnes, R. C. Wilcock: 'Occupational Choice: A Conceptual Framework', *Ind. & Lab. R.*, 1956, pp. 531-543.

[10] O. G. Brim & S. Wheeler: *Socialisation After Childhood*, New York, 1966; B. G. Myerhoff & W. R. Larson: 'Primary and Formal Aspects of Family Organisation: Group Consensus, Problem Perception and Adolescent School Success', *J. Marr. Fam.*, May 1965, pp. 213-217.

[11] G. S. Almond & S. Verba: *The Civic Culture*, Princeton, 1963 (espec. Chapter 12); F. I. Greenstein: *Children and Politics*, Newhaven, 1965.

[12] T. Parsons: *The Social System*, London, 1951, p. 211, pp. 236-7 and pp. 243-248.

[13] O. G. Brim, in Brim and Wheeler: *op. cit.*, pp. 26-7. Here childhood socialisation is connected with 'control (of) . . . the qualification of primary drive systems' (p. 26) and adult socialisation is seen as making 'little attempt to influence motivation of a fundamental kind' (p. 27).

[14] See S. F. Nadel: *The Theory of Social Structure*, London, 1957, espec. Chap. IV ('The Coherence of Rôle Systems') and M. Banton: *Rôles*, London, 1965, espec. Chap. 2, pp. 29-36 ('The Classification of Rôles').

[15] For 'latent rôles' see A. W. Gouldner: 'Cosmopolitans and Locals: Toward an Analysis of Latent Social Rôles—I', *Admin. Sci. Quarterly*, 2, 1957, espec. pp. 282-7; H. S. Becker & B. Geer: 'Latent Culture: A Note on the Theory of Latent Social Rôles', *Admin. Sci. Quarterly*, 5, 1960, pp. 304-313.

[16] R. Centers: *The Psychology of Social Classes*, Princeton, 1949, p. 28.

[17] See, for example, R. F. Hamilton: 'Affluence and the Worker: The West German Case', *Amer. J. Sociol.*, Sept. 1965, pp. 144-152.

[18] E. Fromm: 'Individual and Social Origins of Neurosis', *Amer. Sociol. R.*, Aug. 1944, p. 383.

[19] T. Parsons: *Family, Socialisation and Interaction Process*, London, 1956, p. 128.

[20] M. Reeb: 'How People See Jobs: A Multidimensional Analysis', *Occupational Psychol.*, Jan. 1965, pp. 1-17.

[21] *Op. cit*, particularly Chap. II.

[22] W. H. Form & D. C. Miller: 'Occupational Career Pattern as a Sociological Instrument', *Amer. J. Sociol.*, Jan. 1949, pp. 317-329.

[23] A. L. Strauss: *Mirrors and Masks*, New York, 1959, p. 67, points out that ' "daydreaming" . . . is important for the conservation and change of identities'.

[24] See, for example, J. A. Kahl: ' "Common Man" Boys', *Harvard Educ. R.*, Summer, 1953.

[25] It is a matter for research to determine the weight these different agents have and also which other agents (e.g. the mass media) may be influential in the process of occupational choice.

[26] A very clear example of unconscious rôle modelling can be found in D. F. Aberle & K. D. Naegele: 'Middle-Class Father's Occupational Rôle and Attitudes toward Children', *Amer. J. Orthopsychiatry*, April 1952, pp. 366-278.

[27] See S. M. Wood: 'Uniform—Its Significance as a Factor in Rôle-Relationships', *Sociol. Rev.*, July 1966, espec. pp. 142-7.

[28] See H. S. Becker, B. Geer, E. C. Hughes, A. L. Strauss: *Boys in White*, Chicago, 1961. Also relevant is M. Janowitz: *The Professional Soldier*, New York, 1960, Chap. 7 ('Career Development').

[29] R. Dubin: 'Industrial Worker's Worlds: A Study of the Central Life Interests of Industrial Workers', *Soc. Probl.*, Jan. 1956; for a study of a middle-class female occupation see L. H. Orzack: 'Work as a "Central Life Interest" of Professionals', *Soc. Probl.*, Fall 1959, pp. 125-132.

[30] W. H. Form: 'Toward an Occupational Social Psychology', *J. Soc. Psychol.*, May 1946, pp. 85-99.

[31] M. Rosenberg: *Occupations and Values*, New York, 1957, pp. 13-15.

[32] S. Box & S. Cotgrove: 'Social Identity, Occupational Selection and Rôle Strain', *Brit. J. Sociol.*, March 1966, pp. 20-28.

[33] P. L. Berger: 'Some Observations on the Problem of Work', in P. L. Berger (Ed.): *The Human Shape of Work*, New York, 1964, pp. 217-8.

[34] A. B. Hollingshead: *Elmtown's Youth*, New York, 1949, pp. 382-3.

[35] M. P. Carter: *Home, School and Work*, Oxford, 1962, p. 178.

[36] E. Goffman: 'On Cooling the Mark Out', *Psychiatry*, November 1952, pp. 451-463.

[37] H. L. Wilensky: 'Work, Careers and Social Integration', *Int. Soc. Sci. Bulletin*, December 1960, pp. 553-5. Because of this increase in the rate of job-changing this paper has been couched in terms of *'occupational* choice' rather than 'vocational choice'. The latter term hardly seems to apply except to that small proportion of youths who plan life-long commitment to a career.

[38] The present author has made a preliminary attempt at this and hopes to publish such an article in the near future.

[39] For some work on this problem see T. Veness: *School Leavers*, London, 1962, pp. 81-87.

Chapter Five

SOCIOLOGICAL THEORY AND OCCUPATIONAL CHOICE*

Julienne Ford and Steven Box

I n his discussion, 'Towards a Sociological Theory of Occupational Choice', Musgrave states that 'There is at present no sociological theory of occupational choice'.[1] It is our aim in this chapter to demonstrate that, despite the fact that the explicit propositions of such a theory have not yet been stated formally, there is at present considerable consensus among sociologists on an implicit theory of occupational choice. We shall first show how the various discussions of the process of occupational choice have been converging around one major theme, then we shall make explicit the propositions involved in a sociological theory arising from this theme. Finally we shall present data from a sample of chemistry undergraduates to support hypotheses derived from the theory.

If we ignore the more descriptive work of psychologists[2] then the previous studies of occupational choice can be meaningfully divided into two main approaches: those stressing the *adventitious* nature of such choices and those stressing the *purposive* element.[3] The studies comprising the first group can be readily dismissed as having no relevance to the development of a *sociological theory* of occupational choice. For characterisation of such choices as unique spontaneous behaviours explicable only by reference to the idiocyncracies of particular choice situations is essentially atheoretical and of no interest to the sociologist.[4] In any case those who have been described as adhering to this view do not in practice maintain it. Neither Katz and Martin[5] nor Caplow[6] argue that *all* career choice behaviour is determined by situational contingencies, but merely that such behaviour is sometimes fortuitous and that a *conscious* decision is not always made. Yet even if choices are not always conscious, even if they are often based on inadequate information,[7] 'even if an individual has not made a deliberate occupational choice

---

*The authors are indebted to George C. Homans for his valuable contribution to this chapter.

© Julienne Ford and Steven Box 1967 (This article was first published in *The Sociological Review*, Vol. 15, No. 3, November 1967.)

and is not aware of the factors that induced him to look for one kind of job instead of others, these factors are subject to scientific inquiry, and the conception of a compromise between values and expectations suggests one method by which such inquiry can proceed.'[8]

It is just this focus on the process of reconciliation of values and expectations which provides the common theme around which the discussions making up the second main approach have been tending to converge.[9] This whole body of work can be summarised as entailing the view that occupational choice represents the culmination of a process in which hopes and desires come to terms with the realities of the occupational market situation.[10] The individual is seen as attempting to realise his occupational values (or alternatively to minimise the expected deprivation of those values[11]) in his choice of employment location. Thus his actual choice is a function of his values and his perception of the chances of realising them in the alternative occupations.

It is clear that there is a need for the development of a theory to explain the process by which differential occupational values are acquired. Thus Kiel *et al*[12] and Musgrave[13] urge that attention be paid to socialisation into work attitudes.[14] Yet, in order to derive and test a general theory of occupational choice it is sufficient to take value orientations as given and explore no further the process by which they are acquired. Indeed, even if it were our aim to develop procedures to enable practitioners to predict the occupational choices of specific individuals it would still be adequate to treat values as an independent variable.[15]

In sum, apart from those studies which are idiographic in implication on the one hand, and those, on the other hand, which are concerned with the correlates of differential socialisation into occupational orientations, most sociological discussions of occupational choice have converged. There is now general agreement that this phenomenon is to be viewed as a *rational process*[16] by which certain desired ends are weighed against the perceived probability of their attainment. It remains only to make explicit the propositions of this hitherto implicit theory.

The Theory

Following Homans we intend to restrict the use of the term theory to those bodies of propositions which meet the requirements of the classical definition.[17] Thus it is required of a theory that it consists

(i) of a set of concepts, (ii) of a set of propositions forming a deductive system, and that (iii) some of the propositions are contingent.

Let us first consider the rationality proposition from which the present theory is deduced: In choosing between alternative actions, a person will choose the one for which, as perceived by him, the (mathematical) value of $p \times v$ is the greater, where p is the probability of the action's being successful in getting a given reward, and v is the value of the reward.

Now, in applying this proposition to a person's choice of occupation let us consider first the value of the reward. In this case the reward is entry into the occupation and its value is the degree to which the characteristics of the occupation, as the person perceives them, measure up to what he wants to get from an occupation (i.e. his values). In studies of occupational choice absolute values of v can never be measured, thus in the present research all that can be obtained is the person's ranking of occupations in terms of his values.

Let us consider next the probability of success. This consists in the probability, as the person perceives it, of his obtaining employment in a given occupation. These two considerations lead to the following two propositions which comprise the present theory:

1. *In choosing between alternative occupations, a person will rank the occupations in terms of the relation between his values and the perceived characteristics of the occupation; the higher the coincidence between the characteristics and his values the higher the rank.*

2. *The higher a person perceives the probability that he will obtain employment in the higher-ranked occupation, the more likely he is to choose that occupation.*[18]

A Test of the Theory

Data obtained by postal questionnaire from a sample of final year chemistry undergraduates in three English universities[19] were used to test the following hypotheses derived from the theory:

1. Chemistry students will have differing values.
2. They will have differing evaluations of the perceived characteristics of the various employment locations available to them.
3. They will have differing perceptions of the probabilities that they will obtain employment in their preferred locations.
4. They will tend to choose to work in those locations which, while falling within the range which they perceive to be realistically avail-

able to them, are most favourable to the maintenance of their particular values.

We chose this sample for two reasons. In the first place, they were so near to leaving university and starting work that they would probably have given the matter some serious consideration. Secondly, they had been exposed to the socialising influence of the university for nearly three years—long enough for this to have affected their values and perceptions.

Commitment to Professional Values

A meaningful classification of students in the natural sciences according to their values can be produced by considering their differential commitment to the values and norms of the 'scientific community'. For an important part of the professional training of these undergraduates consists in their being exposed to and exhorted to accept the value of extension of certified knowledge as it is expressed in the organising norms of communality, disinterestedness and organised scepticism.[20] The norm of communality has as an imperative the publication of academic work, thus ideas and findings are shared with other members of the scientific community; the norm of disinterestedness directs the scientist to seek a position in which rewards such as power, income and other material benefits are secondary to the intrinsic rewards of scientific research and recognition; the norm of organised scepticism orients the scientist to accept no claims on trust but to examine each, including his own, in a diligent attempt to falsify it.

These norms of science are mediated to students at university in at least three ways. Firstly, in the books and journals which they read, particularly in those which are about, rather than on, the subject. Secondly, they are mediated by the university academic staff who are themselves likely to exemplify conformity to these norms, and to extol students to accept them as a means of securing their involvement in the subject. Thirdly, these norms are likely to form the core of the culture of some of the university peer groups, and membership in these groups is likely to reinforce the socialising influence of the academics, both at the university and in print.

In these ways it is open to students to learn that the social institution of science consists of a social control system centred around the process of 'gift-exchange-recognition'.[21] The scientific community recognises the worth of scientists according not only to the amount and frequency of gifts to the community in the form of academic papers, but also the quality of the scholarship contained in these papers.

Now this process of professional socialisation obviously affects different students in different ways. Why students should respond differentially to this training has already been reported in part by the authors elsewhere.[22] Here we are content to take differential orientation to science as an independent variable, classifying types of science students according to their patterned internalisation of the norms of science.[23] Briefly, our first type, the *'public scientist'*, accepts all three norms,[24] our second type, the *'private scientist'*, has internalised the norms of disinterestedness and organised scepticism but does not take the norm of communalism as a personal imperative in that he is not interested in publishing his academic work,[25] whilst our third type, the *'instrumental scientist'* attaches little importance to any of the norms. These three types of norm clusters can be seen as representing different rôle-identities[26] *qua* scientist, that is to say different idealised self-conceptions as performers of the scientist rôle.

We classified students into these groups by dichotomising acceptance of each norm into high or low in relation to the median point for the distribution. In this way, of the one hundred and seventy seven third year students who completed all the questions relevant to the present analysis,[27] sixty (34%) were classified as public scientists, sixty three (36%) as private scientists and fifty four (30%) as instrumental.

Perception of Different Employment Locations

The respondents were required to rate the provision of certain conditions, such as salaries, freedom to choose research projects and freedom to publish research, on a five point scale for both industrial and university employment. In this way a direct measure of their perception of the relative conditions in the two major employment locations for scientists was obtained.

It was found that differential perception of conditions in industry and higher education was not strongly related to scientific rôle-identity as described above. Although comparatively more public scientists perceived the provision of freedom for research and publication to be better in university than in industry this was not a statistically significant difference.[28] In general, regardless of professional values, the students tended to share a common image of the relative features of the two employment locales. The majority saw industry as providing higher salaries and better technical equipment, while universities were perceived as providing greater freedom for research and publication, more pleasant geographical locations and longer holidays. No differences were perceived between the two with regard to the provision of 'social and welfare facilities'.

Now it is not simply the facts about the various places of employment as perceived by the student that will affect his occupational decision making. Rather it is the meaning which he attaches to these facts. In other words for different students different features of the competing locales will assume importance.

It follows from our conception of the public scientist that the factors which assume the most critical importance in his assessment of the alternative modes of employment are publication freedom, freedom to choose research projects and freedom to choose work colleagues. The private scientist also attaches importance to freedom of choice of projects and colleagues but is not concerned with publication freedom, while the instrumental scientist is primarily interested in the extrinsic rewards of which the most important is, of course, salary.

For public scientists we compared their relative conceptions of university and industry on all three features and divided them into two groups: those who perceived these freedoms to be better in university than in industry and those who perceived there to be little difference between the two. No public scientists perceived there to be better professional freedoms in industry. We followed the same procedure for private scientists but considered only freedom of project choice and choice of colleagues. For instrumental scientists we considered salaries alone but here the procedure was reversed: the group was divided into those who considered industry to provide higher salaries and those who perceived no difference (none of these perceived university to provide higher salaries than industry).

Perceived opportunity of obtaining the desired employment

In order to obtain an index of the students' perceived chances of obtaining employment in university as opposed to industry we measured their expectations about their subsequent academic performance. Responses to open-ended questions had indicated that the students were aware that the type of work they could realistically hope to do depended largely on their degree results. Thus students were asked what class of degree they expected to obtain. Naturally we are not suggesting that a suitable degree result is the only factor which a student considers to be the essential key to academic life, but it is unlikely that many students expecting to obtain a degree lower than an upper second class honours would view their chances of an academic career favourably. Since industry is currently experiencing a shortage of scientists,[29] we do not think that students would consider a poor degree performance a barrier to industrial employment.

Now it could, of course, be argued that expected results are a poor indicator of actual results. Yet this does not invalidate the present analysis, for our hypothesis concerns the individual's *assessment* of his chances of success; at this stage such an assessment will be made on the basis of the only information he has. Of course, at a later stage when he knows his results these will become part of the information about himself which he incorporates into his plans for the future. Thus many students expecting to qualify for academic employment may subsequently have their hopes dashed by falling the wrong side of the upper second class honours division. On the other hand there will be those who, obtaining better results than they had imagined and experiencing the consequent transformations of their market situations, may alter their employment preferences in the opposite direction.

Occupational Choice

Having discussed the operationalisation and measurement of our three independent variables we will now consider the dependent variable—actual occupational choice. Students were asked to say which of a list of post-graduate options they preferred to pursue. These included immediate research or development work in an industrial or government laboratory, remaining at university to undertake research or study with the ultimate aim of industrial or government employment, embarking immediately on an academic career, teaching in an organisation other than one of higher education, and any other employment specified by the respondent. For the sake of brevity and simplicity of analysis only those choosing university or industrial employment are considered below. Of the remainder, thirty seven students (17%) chose teaching, ten (4%)

chose work in a government laboratory and forty (18%) chose other modes of employment (these included sales, industrial management, advertising, etc.). All those who said that they would at some stage prefer to work in industry were collapsed into a group and these were compared with those choosing an academic career, while control was simultaneously made for all three independent variables: professional rôle-identity, perception of employment conditions and expected degree results. The results are shown in the table.

TABLE I

Type of Scientist, Comparative Perception of Conditions in University and Industrial Laboratories, Expected Degree Result, and Future Employment Preference.

Type of Scientist	Favourable Employment Conditions	Expected Degree Result	Future Employment Preference:*		n= (100%)
			University	Industry	
PUBLIC	Better Professional Freedom in University	High**	15 (79)	4 (21)	19
		Low	2 (11)	16 (89)	18
	Professional Freedoms More or Less Equal	High	2 (50)	2 (50)	4
		Low	1 (17)	5 (83)	6
			20 (42)	27 (58)	47
PRIVATE	Better Professional Freedom in University	High	6 (43)	8 (57)	14
		Low	3 (19)	13 (81)	16
	Professional Freedoms More or Less Equal	High	2 (28)	5 (72)	7
		Low	1 (25)	3 (75)	4
			12 (29)	29 (71)	41
INSTRUMENTAL	Extrinsic Rewards More or Less Equal	High	2 (28)	5 (72)	7
		Low	1 (20)	5 (80)	6
	Extrinsic Rewards Better in Industry	High	3 (19)	13 (81)	16
		Low	1 (8)	12 (92)	13
			7 (17)	35 (83)	42

* This does not include 10 students who preferred to work in government laboratories, 37 who preferred to teach, and 40 students who preferred to work outside the range of research/development/teaching.

** High means First or Upper Second, Low means any other response.

It can be seen from the table that each independent variable is separately related to occupational choice. Thus forty two per cent of the public scientists preferred academic employment compared with twenty nine per cent of the private scientists and seventeen per cent of the instrumental scientists ($\chi^2 = 7.17$, d.f. $= 2$, p $= .02$). When only perception of employment conditions is considered, thirty six per cent of those who perceive university as more favourable (that is providing better professional freedom and at least equal salaries) prefer to work in a university. This compares with only twenty per cent of those who perceive industry as more favourable (that is as providing better salaries and more or less the same professional freedoms), ($\chi^2 = 3.71$, d.f. $= 1$, p $= .1$). Turning to expected degree results we see that forty five per cent of those expecting an upper second class degree or better choose university employment compared with only fourteen per cent of those expecting a lower class of degree ($\chi^2 = 14.68$, d.f. $= 1$, p $= .001$).

When all three variables are considered together, however, our ability to predict occupational choice is much improved. Thus four out of five public scientists perceiving university as providing better professional freedom and expecting good degrees chose academic employment, while less than one in ten instrumental scientists perceiving industry as providing higher salaries than universities and expecting degrees of lower second class standard or less chose such employment.

Summary and Discussion

In our account we have set out in explicit propositional form the general sociological theory which, we believe, has been implied in the vast majority of previous sociological studies of occupational choice. However the particular test of the theory presented here has been a very limited one, and has not therefore brought out the full scope of the theory.

Our empirical analysis was limited in two ways. In the first place we have only considered in detail here those students preferring industrial or university employment. Our original questionnaire did not, unfortunately, contain items measuring perception of schools as places of employment, so those students who chose teaching as a career could not be analysed in the same manner.[30] Furthermore, since this was an exploratory study and the full range of job choices that might have been made by chemistry students could not be anticipated, the relatively small number (18%) intending to work outside of research, development or teaching were· not included. In addition the number of students choosing to work in government laboratories (ten) was too small for these to be considered, even though all the relevant information was available.

In the second place our empirical study is an example of analysis of the more limited phenomenon of secondary choice. Our sample comprised individuals who had already made one basic decision—to read chemistry at university—and therefore were left with a narrowed spectrum of occupations from which they reasonably could choose. Unfortunately the majority of the available literature covering specific types of choice processes is concentrated into the small area of secondary choice, especially that of individuals who have undergone some kind of higher education.[31] The more difficult and, because this type of choice is far more frequent, more important problem of predicting the occupational choices of potential manual and lower white collar workers has scarcely been touched upon.[32] Yet if the theory is, as we claim, a general one then it can be operationalised and tested in these areas too.

Now when we consider the process of occupational choice of the less privileged, the boys and girls leaving school at fifteen and considering their first jobs, it at first appears as if the assumption of rationality contained in the theory is unrealistic. Surely, one might argue, the transition from school to work in most cases cannot be described as *choice* at all? These children do not know the full range of jobs open to them and have no efficient criteria for differentiating one job from another. Yet, for an individual's behaviour to be *Wertrational* and hence to fall within the scope of the theory, it is not necessary for him to have a complete knowledge of all the available ends. However the school leaver has acquired his particular values, however inadequate his perception of the available jobs and the conditions within them, and however faulty his perception of his own chance of attaining employment in any of these jobs, it is still possible to determine the extent to which he attempts to gain employment in that job which he considers both available to him and consistent with his particular values.[33]

University of Kent at Canterbury.

[1] See Chapter Four.

[2] A fairly comprehensive bibliography of such studies is to be found in P. A. Perrone: 'Vocational Development', *Review of Education Research*, 36, 1966, pp. 298-307.

[3] This classification was suggested by B. Sherlock and A. Cohen: 'A Strategy of Occupational Choice: Recruitment to Dentistry', *Soc. Forces*, 44, 1966, pp. 303-313.

[4] If sociology is a nomothetic discipline then to state that any phenomenon defies generalisation is to state that it lies outside the scope of sociology. For one of the most comprehensive modern statements of this view see J. C. McKinney: 'Methodology, Procedures, and Techniques in Sociology', in H. Becker and A. Boskoff (eds.): *Modern Sociological Theory*, New York, Holt, Rinehart and Winston, 1957, pp. 186-235.

[5] F. E. Katz and H. W. Martin: 'Career Choice Processes', *Soc. Forces*, 41, 1962, pp. 149-154.

[6] T. Caplow: *The Sociology of Work*, New York, McGraw-Hill, 1954.

[7] L. G. Reynolds: *The Structure of Labour Markets*, New York, Harper, 1951. He suggests that 'rational' choice is often precluded, for many workers do not have sufficient knowledge of the market to assess the relative values of employment loci.

[8] P. M. Blau *et al*: 'Occupational Choice; A Conceptual Framework', *Ind. & Lab. R.*, 9, 1956, p. 535.

[9] See for examples E. Ginzberg *et al*: *Occupational Choice: An Approach to a General Theory*, New York, Columbia U.P., 1951; *Blau*: *op. cit.* pp. 531-543; M. Rosenberg: *Occupations and Values*, New York, Free Press, 1957; D. E. Super: *The Psychology of Careers*, New York, Harper, 1957; D. V. Tiedeman and R. T. O'Hara: *Career Development: Choice and Adjustment*, Princeton, College Entrance Examination Board, 1963; B. S. Phillips: 'Expected Value Deprivation and Occupational Preference', *Sociometry*, 27, 1964, pp. 151-160; A. Pavalko *et al*: 'Vocational Choice as a Focus of the Identity Search', *Brit. J. Counselling Psychol.*, 13, 1966, pp. 89-92. Other studies give rise, though less directly, to the same implications. Thus for example F. G. Caro and C. T. Philblad: 'Aspirations and Expectations: A Re-examination of the Bases for Social Class Differences in the Occupational Orientations of Male High School Students', *Sociol. & Soc. Research.*, 49, 1965, pp. 465-475. They argue that class differentials in occupational choice derive not from different conceptions of the occupations but differing assessments of the chances of achieving them.

[10] For a further discussion of this process see S. Box and J. Ford: 'Commitment to Science: A Solution to Student Marginality?', *Sociology*, 1, Sept. 1967.

[11] See Phillips: *op. cit.*

[12] See Chapter Three.

[13] In Chapter Four.

[14] There is quite a large body of literature on the process of socialisation into work attitudes, see for examples of this process at the level of higher education H. S. Becker and J. Carper: 'Elements of Identification with an Occupation', *Amer. Sociol. Rev.*, 21, 1956, pp. 341-348; Box and Ford: *op. cit.* For studies of this socialisation at the level of the school see especially M. Carter: *Into Work*, London, Penguin, 1966.

[15] The theory presented here could provide a basis for the development of prediction methods similar to those used, for an entirely different purpose, by Wilkins and his colleagues. See L. Wilkins: 'Problems in Prediction Methods; in W. E. Wolfgang *et al*: *The Sociology of Crime and Delinquency*, New York, Wiley, 1962.

[16] We are not suggesting that this is necessarily a *Zweckrational* process, more usually it will be *Wertrational*.

[17] G. C. Homans: 'Contemporary Theory in Sociology' in R. E. L. Faris (ed.): *Handbook of Modern Sociology*, Chicago; Rand McNally, 1964, pp. 951-977, and *The Nature of Social Science*, New York, Harcourt Brace and World, forthcoming.

[18] These propositions were formulated by G. C. Homans and the first author.

[19] These did not include any London, Oxford or Cambridge College or any of the new universities. The data was collected in the Summer/Autumn of 1965.

[20] See on the norms of science N. Storer: *The Social System of Science*, New York, Holt, Rinehart and Winston, 1966, especially chapters 5 and 6; W. O. Hagstrom: *The Scientific Community*, New York, Basic Books, 1965, chapter 1; B. Glaser: *Organizational Scientists*, Indianapolis, Bobbs Merril, 1964, chapter 1., all of whom draw heavily on the original work of R. K. Merton in his *Social Theory and Social Structure* 2nd ed., New York, Free Press, 1957, pp. 550-562.

[21] W. O. Hagstrom: *op. cit.*

[22] Box and Ford: *op. cit.*

[23] S. Box and S. Cotgrove: 'Scientific Identity, Occupational Selection and Rôle Strain', *Brit. J. Sociol.*, 17, 1966, pp. 20-28.

[24] This is the type labelled 'Cosmopolitan' by Gouldner: see A. W. Gouldner, 'Cosmopolitans and Locals' *Admin. Sci. Quarterly*, 2, 1957-8, pp. 281-306, 444-480. For a recent critical summary of typologies of scientists and professionals see L. C. Goldberg *et al* 'Local-Cosmopolitan: Unidimensional or Multidimensional?', *Amer. J. Sociol.*, 70, 1965, pp. 704-717.

[25] This use of the concept of privatisation is similar to that of J. H. Goldthorpe and D. Lockwood: 'Affluence and the British Class Structure', *Sociol Rev.*, 11, 1963, pp. 133-163. These individuals are normatively integrated within, but physically isolated from, the scientific community.

[26] 'Rôle-identity may be defined as the character and the rôle that an individual devises for himself as an occupant of a particular social position . . . more intuitively it is his imaginative view of himself *as he likes to think of himself being and acting* as an occupant of a position.' G. L. McCall and J. L. Simmons: *Identities and Interactions*, New York, Free Press, 1966, p. 67.

[27] Of the initial sample forty students who did not intend working in any kind of research, development or teaching, did not complete the professional identity items and could not therefore be included in the analysis.

[28] For example 86% of public scientists saw provision of freedom to publish research as excellent in universities compared with 71% of instrumental scientists ($\chi^2 = 2.70, \mathrm{d.f.} = 1, p = \mathrm{n.s.}$).

[29] See for evidence and reasons for this, Committee on Manpower Resources for Science and Technology: *Interim Report of the Working Group on Manpower Parameters for Scientific Growth*, Cmnd. 3102, London, H.M.S.O., 1966; S. Box: 'Why They Don't Choose Industry', *Twentieth Century*, Autumn, 1966, pp. 52-3.

[30] It is interesting to note that 41% of those preferring teaching were women, whereas women constituted only 15% of the total sample. An *ex post factum* explanation of the preference for teaching among women can be put forward in the light of the theory. One major rôle-identity which women can adopt is that attaching to their sex rôle. For those girls who intend ultimately to marry and be mothers, a job in teaching may be seen as a more suitable 'stop-gap' than a 'blue-stocking' career.

[31] See for examples, K. W. Back *et al*: 'Public Health as a Career in Medicine: Secondary Choice Within a Profession', *Amer. Sociol. Rev.*, 23, 1958, pp. 533-541; W. L. Wallace 'Peer Influences and Undergraduates' Aspirations for Graduate Study', *Sociol. of Educ.*, 38, 1965, pp. 377-392; I. D. Currie *et al* 'Images of the Professor and Interest in the Academic Profession', *Sociol. of Educ.*, 39, 1966, pp. 301-322.

[32] See for one of the very few examples N. J. Dufty: 'The Characteristics of Thirteen to Fourteen Year Old Males Choosing Skilled Trades as Occupations', *Aust. J. Educ.*, 10, 1961, pp. 49-66. However the relationship between such choice and social class has been very well documented and this literature is too vast to be cited here.

[33] The present authors are currently engaged in research into the correlates of occupational choice amongst fifteen year olds in Grammar, Secondary Modern and Comprehensive Schools, and intend to re-test the theory on this sample.

Chapter Six

TOWARDS A SOCIOLOGICAL THEORY OF OCCUPATIONAL CHOICE — A CRITIQUE

Margaret A. Coulson, E. Teresa Keil, C. Riddell, John S. Struthers

T he purpose of Dr. Musgrave's chapter,[1] to formulate a theory which would cover first and subsequent choice of occupation, and to see this as a process operating on the individual from birth onwards, is a laudable one. But progress 'towards a sociological theory of occupational choice' has not been greatly advanced by the article. In fact it is felt that there is a lack of a sociological perspective, indicating an excessively individualistic view of society, in which concepts of rôle and socialisation can be used without reference to social structure while references to empirical work contain inaccuraces and misinterpretations which confuse rather than clarify the issue under discussion.

The main theoretical weakness lies in the attempt to explain social behaviour in terms of an oversimplified functionalist theory which rests on a consensus model of society.

This implicit assumption—that the barely mentioned social structure within which individuals play out their rôles is unified and cohesive—creates many problems in regard to occupational choice. Thus, in the economic sphere there may be 'delinquency' or 'deviance', but the possibilities for variation are ignored. 'Deviant occupations . . . recruit . . . individuals who are unable to play normal economic rôles', and 'those who have come to have personalities such that they are willing or able to play occupational rôles of a certain type, namely those that are either looked down upon or that cater for individuals who are slightly unusual.' (p. 100). As Dahrendorf points out in his critique of this type of functionalism, such deviance thus 'occurs for sociologically—and that means structurally—unknown and unknowable reasons.'[2] Further, it is misleading to suggest that there is general consensus as to unusual or deviant (and hence usual and conforming?) occupations, for as Musgrave himself mentions later (p. 104) there is evidence to suggest that stereotypes of occupations vary by social class. Can the choice of occupations such as prison warder, long distance lorry driver, night watchman (the examples given) be understood as patterns of deviant individual behaviour, or would a more useful approach be to consider the evaluations of such occupations in different social groups, and relate these to occupational choice?

Perhaps it is this tendency to think in terms of an overall culture which leads Musgrave to describe the need to get or earn a living as a 'dominant value' when he simply appears to mean that certain social rôles derive from the need to get a living. By ignoring the significance of variation and conflict he is able to define the 'significant others' of the new employee as 'managers and work-mates', without considering that their demands may be very different, and to allow that between home and work there may be different codes of morality without consideration of the conflict which may arise. Nor in his discussion of job changes can he entirely avoid this same (value) orientation towards a static social order, in which only un-usual people change their jobs, or work alone. It is implied that the most desirable situation would be one in which new entrants to the labour force could be perfectly matched to an appropriate occupation in which they could remain throughout their working life—'Frequent job changes do not lead to an efficient economy or the growth of a stable personality' (p. 106). This value is not self-evident, and as Musgrave has to acknowledge, technical changes will require people to change jobs more frequently in the future. Of course, in many professional occupations—such as sociology teaching —frequent job change is not so negatively evaluated. It is a serious failure in Musgrave's chapter that he is unable to establish a theor-etical framework which can account for the extent and direction of occupational changes; to do so would require the consideration of social structure which he so consistently avoids.

This lack of reference to social structure leaves function as an isolated concept so that Musgrave uses it inconsistently, as the following examples indicate: it is stated that the child learns obedience and co-operation in the family, and this may enable him to behave functionally at work. Function is apparently used here to mean the maintenance of the present order of relationships. But the assumption is that the work situation is organised on the basis of obedient workers co-operating unquestioningly with their employers; the obedience and co-operation already learnt at home is functional in that it enables them to do this. But is such a consensus model relevant here? 'The dichotomous 'us-them' view of society characteristic of industrial workers' is discussed by Keil, Riddell, and Green as part of the analysis in Chapter Three, related to the way in which attitudes to teacher and school may themselves be related to the existence of such attitudes at work.[3]

The 'let-out' category of dysfunction is equally misleading. It is suggested that the child's reference groups may be either functional or dysfunctional for choice of occupation. To refer to his family *rather* than to his school may discourage the working class boy from seeking high status and therefore be dysfunctional. Here, 'functional' has been used in a rather different way, as referring to the development of an individual's abilities, but the schools themselves may be dysfunctional in this (if we are to acknowledge the evidence on, for example, streaming), and Kahn, to whom Musgrave refers (footnote 24) points out that 'the schools are more a means than an initiator of (social) ascent'.[4] Later the peer group is suggested by Musgrave as a dysfunctional reference group in that it may represent 'an escape from the values of family and school' (p. 103). The concept of function again seems to assume some notion of a unified value system. As it is, the questions which Musgrave formulates at the end of his chapter cannot be understood within the limited and misleading functionalism which is offered as a basis.

Musgrave's lack of conceptual clarity is demonstrated in particular by his failure to define even the terms which he makes central to his theoretical formulation; socialisation and rôle.

Socialisation is a ragbag term, descriptive of an area of study, and includes a wide range of processes. There are two interpretations which can be distinguished. The functionalist usage which Musgrave follows and which has been criticised above emphasises the 'fitting' of individuals into 'society' and considers the processes involved in terms of the needs of a 'social system'.[5] In another usage, socialisation is regarded simply as the process of social learning. This derives from the proposition that the individual's behaviour in any social situation is a result of the total of his experiences in other social situations up to that time. The processes involved and the mode of summation are of course exceedingly complicated and have been studied in relation to personality structure, levels of cognitive development, informational level, motivational factors, etc., and all these interact in complex ways. If we view socialisation in the first sense, as the means whereby social control becomes internalised, there is a tendency to assume that the various processes involved in the modification are unidirectional in relation to the 'needs of society' and that there is more coherence than is shown by the empirical evidence. But even in this interpretation, for 'deviant' individuals the end result of the process is *not* in this direction and it is reasonable to suppose that, although many others may not be labelled deviant, the socialisation process—a complex summation (or multiplication?)—includes many conflicting experiences.

Musgrave's use of the concept of anticipatory socialisation illustrates the difficulties. It is first defined in terms of prior knowledge of positions and prior rôle rehearsal. 'The individual in anticipation practices taking the values and behaviour prescribed for an occupational role in which he sees himself.' (p. 101). But when the idea is widened to include 'reference groups which may be functional or dysfunctional for the ultimate choice of occupation' (p. 102), we find that anticipatory socialisation is not 'prior rôle rehearsal' necessarily, but may include rehearsal of rôles which are anticipated wrongly. It is difficult to see how one can decide clearly whether any particular experience is anticipatory socialisation or not. The example Musgrave gives of medical students coming to see themselves as doctors whilst still in training illustrates the difficulty (p. 103). It does not seem useful to use the same term both for the process of learning the rôle requirements of an occupation to which the individual is fully committed, *and* for rehearsal of rôles, some of which may (by hindsight) turn out to be in anticipation of later occupational rôles, while others may not be.

The same assumption of unidirectionality is made in the discussion of the relations of values of family, school and peer group criticised above. Musgrave assumes that influences in family and school are operating in the direction of the 'needs of the system', so that peer group values must be regarded as a source of deviance. It appears again in Musgrave's discussion of play, which he considers as 'rôle rehearsal' (p. 103).

This tendency to interpret most social experience as 'positive' in terms of later rôle performance can lead to some strange contradictions. Thus Musgrave writes, 'Inasmuch as the private sphere of life is totally separated from the work sphere a worker may have to operate two codes of morality, the public one which must be learnt at work and which may contradict the private one learnt at home.

Since there is low visibility between these two spheres, socialisation into the separate codes should be easy and their co-existence supported.' (p. 105). But he has previously (p. 102) said, 'Each system has its own particular rôle system, but the father and often the mother, will hold positions in both systems, so that the child has a chance of learning about his parents' "economic rôles".' Not much of a chance however unless one wants to have it both ways at once!

Neiman and Hughes wrote in a review of the literature in 1951,[6] 'The concept of rôle is at present still rather vague, nebulous, and nondefinitive. Frequently in the literature, the concept is used without any attempt on the part of the writer to define or delimit the concept, the assumption being that both writer and reader will achieve an immediate compatible consensus . . . .' One distinction, between position and rôle, made by several writers,[7] seems essential in a theory of occupational choice. There is not complete agreement, but the core is that a rôle is a pattern of normatively approved ways of behaving attached to a position, whereas a position is a location in the social structure: (Linton[8] uses 'status', but this is confusing because of the use of the term status in stratification theory). Neither Banton nor Nadel, whom Musgrave quotes[9], make this distinction, though Nadel's distinction between class and rôle is similar. Nadel distinguishes class as being merely the sharing of an attribute whereas rôle is concerned with behaviour and 'a series of interconnected characteristics'.[10] One might propose that Musgrave's distinction between 'consumer' and 'producer' rôles (p. 99), which in any case does not seem very relevant to his theory of occupational choice, should be considered as a 'class' distinction in Nadel's sense rather than one concerned with rôles in any sociological sense. The distinction between *position* and rôle allows us to separate behaviour from identifiable units of structure, so that, for example, we can compare the rôles of teachers in grammar schools and in primary schools without assuming that because we have a named position (teacher) there is *a* rôle attached to it. When Musgrave mentions consumer and producer rôles and 'the British working man' and 'the British ironworker' (p. 105) he assumes there are identifiable rôles attached to these positions.

This distinction also leads to the crucial area of rôle conflict which Musgrave does not mention. The decision as to the content of a rôle is an empirical one dependent on some agreement on the prescribed ways of behaving in a given position. Musgrave, following

Banton, assumes a high level of rôle consensus and does not take into account the conflicting expectations of others by the occupant of a position.[11] 'Others' are lumped together as if only 'generalised others' existed, ignoring the existence of networks of conflicting demands on the occupant of a position. 'As he becomes socialised into his occupational rôle the self image that he constructs must meet the demands of new significant others, more particularly of managers and work mates. . . . . The definition of the situation that is learnt will allow for some tolerance in the behaviour prescribed; some compromise between self and others will be possible.' (p. 105). ·

An aspect of rôle conflict which Musgrave does mention is the possibility of lack of congruence between the various rôles of the individual, e.g. at home and at work (p. 105). As shown above, however, this distinction is not clearly maintained. Musgrave, following Nadel, assumes a high degree of congruence. 'Our conception of rôles, as interconnected ways of acting laid down by the rules of society carries the implication that the series is always a compatible one.'[12] Thus for Musgrave most rôle learning can be related to the successful performance of latent rôles. He uses the concept of 'latent rôle' exclusively in this way, though in Gouldner's usage,[13] to which he refers, it is possible for latent rôles to have either a facilitating or inhibiting effect on current rôle performance. One might also refer to Benedict's well-known argument that some rôles allowed to children in America are a hindrance in the performance of adult rôles.[14]

Musgrave makes no distinction between rôle requirements defined in terms of expectations of others and rôle requirements in terms of the 'need of a social system'. His lack of distinction finds its most extreme expression in his failure to distinguish between personality factors and rôles. In considering the 'stages' of the socialisation process, he criticises (p. 98) Parsons' and Brim's psychologistic criteria for distinguishing primary and secondary socialisation, but these have the advantage that they do retain some distinction between personality factors in rôle performance and the rôle itself. Musgrave's criterion that 'primary socialisation refers to rôles played in all settings' (p. 99) destroys the distinction, and with it the usefulness of the concept of rôle—if a rôle is played in all settings, how can it be meaningfully defined as a rôle? We have here an example of what Dennis Wrong has termed 'The Oversocialized Conception of Man'.[15]

Musgrave's failure to provide a theoretical basis for a sociology of occupational choice is compounded by his inadequate analysis of existing empirical material. Indeed, although Chapter Three by Keil *et al.* is ostensibly the occasion for his overview and analysis, Musgrave does not seem to have realized that it does represent a summary of much of our available knowledge—the 'ordering of the literature' which he proposes to attempt (his note 38) was undertaken in that paper, for the period up to 1964, although directed, perfectly legitimately in our view, towards the problem of job adjustment. Thus, the sorts of questions Musgrave asks about occupational choice 'How and when the individual learns the stereotypes of the various occupations in the labour force, how he comes to see which occupations are available to him and how he learns the behaviour, values and attitudes needed in the various work situations of his culture or sub culture' (p. 99) ignore that a considerable amount of information is already available to indicate that many young people enter the world of work without any clearly formed ideas about the problems.[16] Ginsberg's notions of a progression from 'fantasy' to 'realism' are accepted as if they were established fact (p. 99), whereas they have been criticised as deriving largely from his theoretical orientation and biased sample.[17] Musgrave's discussion of schools' works visits and the Youth Employment services offers an idealised image of what *ought* to go on, and ignores the evidence as to what actually happens in many cases.[18] Musgrave argues that a reference to home rather than school is dysfunctional for the economy in that it will not encourage aims for high status occupations (p. 101). Apart from the inapplicability of the theoretical concept of dysfunction here, there is some evidence that secondary modern school and working‑class home often reinforce each other in preventing high aspirations on the part of children.[19] Form and Miller are referred to as proposing three developmental phases (p. 101) and their views are rejected as they ignore early developments. However, in their expanded discussion of the problem in *Industrial Sociology* (1951), which Musgrave does not appear to have consulted, they distinguish five periods, laying emphasis on the 'preparatory' work period in which they consider precisely what Musgrave chooses to call 'latent parts of primary socialisation'.[20]

On the other hand, Musgrave feels able to make definite statements as to the importance of some types of children's activities in occupational choice, although no evidence at all exists as to the extent and nature of the influence. For instance, it is not known what effects, if any, play activities have on vocational choice (p. 103). It is not known, but *prima facie* very unlikely, that a child is really 'building up his rôle map' by playing postman (p. 103)—as has been indicated above there is evidence that many children have no such 'rôle maps'—if the metaphor itself has any value. Nor is any information available about Musgrave's assertion that play teaches a child the complexity and interrelationships of the rôles in the occupational structure (p. 103). It is surely more likely that it has the reverse effect by oversimplifying and distorting such relationships. Musgrave argues that any new recruit to industry must have 'the situation defined to him' (p. 105). This phrase is impossibly vague; but it can be stated that this is neither a logical imperative—there is no *a priori* reason why it must be defined—nor, in many cases, is it an empirical actuality.[21] Similar examples of inadequate reference to existing material, or assertion without evidence could be multiplied.

Conclusion

Any adequate theoretical approach to a particular social problem must, in our view, satisfy the following requirements. Firstly, it must take into consideration, and satisfactorily account for, all previous research into the topic; secondly, it must adequately relate this work to general theoretical models currently available in the discipline; thirdly, where special terminology is introduced it must be clearly defined and improve in expression on more usual language. By satisfying these requirements such an approach can provide students with a framework of reference for further investigation. It has been shown that Musgrave's chapter, by reason of its inadequate theoretical assumptions (naive functionalism), imprecise use of the concepts of socialisation and rôle, and inadequate empirical reference, does not fulfil these criteria, and therefore cannot be granted the status claimed for it—that of an approach towards a sociological theory of occupational choice. Nor indeed could any approach which virtually ignores the concept of structure be considered as such.

[1] Chapter Four.

[2] R. Dahrendorf: 'Out of Utopia,' in *Sociological Theory*, ed. Coser, MacMillan, 1964, p. 216.

3 See pp. 76–96.

4 J. A. Kahl: ' "Common Man" Boys,' in *Education, Economy and Society*, Ed. Halsey *et. al.* Free Press, 1962, p. 365.

5 O. G. Brim and S. Wheeler: *Socialization After Childhood*, New York, 1966. 'He (the student of socialization) asks how the work of society gets done and how the necessary man power is trained, motivated, kept alive and functioning throughout the life cycle so that the specified rôles are performed.' (p. 5) 'The prescriptions for rôles in any social system are directed to the successful discharge of the function of that system for society.' (p. 4)

6 L. J. Neiman and J. W. Hughes: 'The Problem of the Concept of Rôle —a Re-survey of the Literature,' *Soc. Forces*, 1951, 30, pp. 141-149.

7 E.g. T. Newcomb: *Social Psychology*, Holt, Rinehart and Winston, Inc., 1950; T. Parsons: *The Social System*, Free Press, 1951; N. Gross, W. Mason and A. McEachern: *Explorations in Rôle Analysis: Studies of the School Superintendents' Rôle*, Wiley, 1958.

8 R. Linton: *The Cultural Background of Personality*, Routledge and Kegan Paul, 1947.

9 M. Banton: *Rôles*, Tavistock, 1965; S. F. Nadel: *The Theory of Social Structure*, Cohen and West, 1957.

10 *Idem.*, p. 24.

11 'For the time being it is necessary to assume in the examination of particular rôles that there is agreement among all the parties affected as to the definition of the rôle in question.' Banton: *op. cit.* p. 36.

12 Nadel: *op. cit.*, p. 65.

13 A. W. Gouldner: 'Cosmopolitans and Locals: Toward an Analysis of Latent Social Rôles, I,' *Admin. Sci. Quarterly*, Dec., 1957.

14 R. Benedict: 'Continuities and Discontinuities in Cultural Conditioning.' In P. Mullahy (ed.): *A Study of Interpersonal Relationships*, Hermitage Press, 1949, p. 297.

15 D. Wrong: 'The Oversocialized Conception of Man in Modern Sociology,' in *Coser, op. cit.*, pp. 112-122.

16 See pp. 79, 83–88.

17 See Chown's attempt to replicate this study. S. M. Chown: 'Formation of Occupational Choice Among Grammar School Pupils,' *Occupational Psychology*, 32, 1958, pp. 171-182, also Keil *et. al.*: *op. cit.*, p. 120.

18 See pp. 86–87. A sociological analysis of the Youth Employment Service would stress the incompatible demands deriving from its requirements to serve its clients' interests, while being dependent on employers' wishes for placement possibilities, i.e. it would locate the Y.E.S. in the social structure.

19 See p. 85.

20 D. C. Miller and W. H. Form: *Industrial Sociology*, Harper, 1951.

21 See pp. 88–89.

Chapter Seven

CONTINUITIES IN THE SOCIOLOGICAL THEORY OF OCCUPATIONAL CHOICE: A NOTE

P. W. Musgrave

M y original paper, reprinted here as Chapter Four, had been followed by the critical analysis of Coulson *et al.* (reprinted as Ch. 6) and also by Ford and Box (reprinted as Ch. 5). My aim in this chapter is to answer the main arguments put forward by Coulson *et al.* in their 'Critique' and at the same time to effect a synthesis of Ford's and Box's work with my original paper. The comments on The Critique will fall under two headings. There is, firstly, what is a definite clarification of my paper and, secondly, there are two major misunderstandings.

1. *Clarification*

The concept of anticipatory socialisation plays an important part in the framework suggested in the original paper. The authors of The Critique note that this concept is used to cover two distinct processes, namely:

(a) prior rôle rehearsal that anticipates a future rôle that is ultimately played,

and (b) prior rôle rehearsal that anticipates a future rôle that is in fact not taken up.

This seems a most worthwhile distinction in this particular context[1] and I would suggest that the latter alternative be termed 'misplaced anticipatory socialization'.

2. *Misunderstandings*

(i) *The Concept of Structure.* One of the main criticisms of Chapter Four is that inadequate attention is given to the concept of social structure. Yet the life cycle of the child is seen 'as a large number of alternative pathways consisting of a series of rôles that are available' to

© P. W. Musgrave 1968 (This article was first published in *The Sociological Review*, Vol. 16, No. 1, March 1968.)

the child (p. 98). The behaviour attached to the positions filled by individuals as they pass through these pathways is categorised as being played in one or more settings. This would seem to be a legitimate way of conceptualising the social structure. However, since at no point in The Critique is this term defined, the criticism can only be attributed to a misunderstanding.

A further structural emphasis is that differentiation is made between rôles located in the production system and those in the consumption system (p. 99). This is an important point since the aim of the paper is to locate occupational choice in sociological theory. One result of this should be that it becomes possible to show which parts of the social structure are relevant to a consideration of the process. Thus the origin of the four stages used in the framework (p. 101) is clear since they are firmly rooted in the pathways through the social structure followed by those undergoing the process of economic socialisation. On the other hand the origins of the influences used by Keil *et al.* in Chapter Three (p. 80) are not at all clear. The same emphasis on structure is seen in the treatment of alternative pathways through the educational system (p. 103). Here the focus is on the way experience of particular types of school influences expectations of the future and, more especially, of future occupation.

The authors of The Critique feel that 'function' is used inconsistently, but, if they had appreciated the point already made that the producer rôles were specifically mentioned to locate the socialisation process in that part of the social system concerned with economic production it would have been clear that the answer to the question 'functional to what?' is here always 'functional to production'. Thus, as correctly surmised, in their first case (p. 125) co-operation learnt at home enables functional behaviour at work, but in their second case (p. 126) the possible dysfunction due to a working class child taking the school as a negative reference group is not simply with regard to the child's abilities, but to this in the context of the maximum use of the 'pool of capability' by the economy.

(ii) *The Concept of Consensus*. The main burden of criticism seems to lie here. Conflict, it is claimed, is ignored and 'consensus' is assumed. Horowitz has identified seven senses in which this term has been used in the recent literature, but once again it is not clear in which of these ways the concept is used in The Critique. Indeed, there appears to be some confusion since in general the authors would seem to mean 'a sharing of perspectives', though doubt is raised as 'rôle consensus' is also mentioned, that is 'accord between rôle behaviour and rôle expectations'.[2]

If one uses consensus in the first sense, then it is undoubtedly true that the framework proposed for viewing occupational choice is in the sociological tradition that works from a starting point of consensus, whereas The Critique wishes to use another sociological tradition that begins from the standpoint of conflict. Assuming the initial reasoning in each case to be sound, the most useful mode of analysis will only be apparent from work accomplished in testing hypotheses based on the two approaches. However, 'a consensus model' need not be as rigid as The Critique implies. Thus rôle expectations 'allow for some tolerance in the behaviour prescribed' (p. 105). Just how much consensus exists on the values governing behaviour in any situation is a matter for empirical enquiry and even partial consensus can be handled satisfactorily using such techniques as Rodman's 'value stretch' hypothesis. Indeed, Caro has recently extended this concept of value stretch 'to actions which are instrumental for the realisation of occupational objectives'.[3] Other empirical studies do seem to have found a considerable measure of consensus on a number of relevant issues, e.g. within (and between) a number of nations on the occupational aspirations of children, and on the hierarchical ordering by children of the occupations in the labour force.[4] Furthermore, and in this same context, a 'rôle map' is not, as The Critique suggests (p. 131), a 'metaphor', but a concept based on empirical work, admittedly with adults, cited in the original paper.[5] In the third chapter Keil *et al.* used the term job 'horizon' in a somewhat similar sense—presumably the quotation marks indicate that the term is used in a metaphorical sense.[6]

As consensus, though not in the rigid sense implied by The Critique, is the starting point for the analysis, the problem of deviance must be raised. The authors of The Critique cite Dahrendorf's view (p. 124) that some deviance is due to 'structurally . . . unknown and unknowable reasons'. This rather pessimistic view is not the only one. As Erikson has said, 'the study of deviance is as much a study of social organizations as . . . of disorganization and anomie'. Here deviance is seen both as 'an important condition for preserving stability' and as a mediator of social change.[7] The point for enquiry is the very structural problem of where the relevant boundaries of normality are drawn, who patrols the boundaries of economic normality and whence they came. The whole field of deviant occupations is wide open to research, since, as The Critique hints, there is no agreement as to what this term means. Yet as long as the concept of economic socialisation is allowed, there is the possibility of economic deviance.

3. *Conclusion*

So far the two main criticisms made by The Critique have been discussed.[8] The position taken is that the framework suggested in Chapter Four is firmly based in the social structure and that a consensus approach, particularly of the flexible type outlined here, can generate hypotheses for testing that are as useful as those likely to come from a conflict approach.

At this point consideration must be given to the way in which the work of Ford and Box relates to Chapter Four. Their approach to the problem of the choice of occupation is through exchange theory, concentrating on the actual choice situation. They specifically state that 'The individual is seen as attempting to realise his occupational values . . . in his choice of employment location' (p. 112). For a general theory of occupational *choice* in their view it is sufficient to take 'occupational values' as given. In one sense this is true, but for many reasons an explanation may be wanted of how these values were learnt. For example, a sociologist of education or a school teacher may be concerned with the links between the family or educational institutions and the economy. The standpoint taken here is, therefore, that, in the present state of knowledge, *pace* The Critique, the most worthwhile method of seeking a sociological explanation of occupational choice is to follow a two stage process. Firstly, the way in which persons learn economic rôles and occupational preferences as they pass through the social structure must be analysed in a framework akin to that outlined in my original paper. Secondly, the manner in which preference becomes choice may best be examined through exchange theory in a way similar to that used by Ford and Box in their Chapter.

University of Aberdeen.

---

[1] A very similar idea has been suggested by H. S. Becker: 'Notes on the concept of commitment', *American J. of Sociology*, November, 1960, pp. 282–3.

[2] I. L. Horowitz: 'Consensus Conflict and Co-operation: A Sociological Inventory', *Social Forces*, March 1963, pp. 177–8.

[3] H. Rodman: 'The Lower Class Value Stretch', *Social Forces*, December 1963; F. G. Caro: 'Social Class and Attitudes of Youth Relevant for the Realization of Adult Goals', *Social Forces*, June 1966, p. 497.

Continuities in Sociological Theory of Occupational Choice: A Note

[4] W. E. Lambert and O. Klineberg: 'Cultural Comparisons of Boys' Occupational Aspirations', *J. of Social Psychology*, February 1964; W. Liversidge: 'Life Chances', *Sociological Review*, March 1962, pp. 27-29.

[5] M. Reeb: 'How People See Jobs: A Multidimensional Analysis', *Occupational Psychology*, January 1965.

[6] See p. 83.

[7] K. T. Erikson: 'Notes on the Sociology of Deviance', *Social Problems* Spring 1962, espec. pp. 308 and 310.

[8] One other point remains:
'Inaccuracies and misinterpretations' (p. 124). At no point is the accusation of actual inaccuracy substantiated, and misinterpretation can only be assumed to mean use of evidence to back a consensus viewpoint rather than the preferred conflict model. Thus The Critique from my standpoint misinterprets Goldthorpe and Lockwood ('Affluence and the British Class Structure', *Sociological Review*, July 1963) in its reference to us-them attitudes in schools, since the authors only consider children as 'traditional proletarians' and do not envisage the possibility that there may be many children who can be termed 'deferentials'. This latter category will in some sense co-operate with the school; this poses a problem for any analysis based on a conflict model.

Chapter Eight

THE ENTRY INTO EMPLOYMENT: AN APPROACH TOWARDS A GENERAL THEORY[1]

K. Roberts

The entry into employment as a sociological problem

Representatives of various disciplines including psychology, economics and education have all examined the entry into employment. They have all defined their own particular problems that the subject matter poses and have attempted to answer them. Before the sociologist enters the field it appears sensible that he should first define his particular interests in the subject. If confusion is to be avoided the questions that the sociologist hopes to answer as a result of his examinations of the entry into employment need to be clearly declared in advance. I would like to suggest that the entry into employment embodies two major social processes. Firstly school-leavers must be differentiated and placed in their various rôles within the occupational system, and secondly they must be induced to accept their new rôles as workers in the specific occupations to which they have been allocated. These processes must take place during the entry into employment in any society with a complex division of labour and in which childhood rôles are not precisely articulated with the specific adult destinations of the young. The sociologist's interest in the entry into employment should be focused upon these two processes of occupational rôle allocation and socialisation. We want to obtain an accurate description of how these processes take place, and to explain why they take place in the manner that they do.

No single social institution or organisation has the performance of these processes as its function. As a result of this state of affairs studies of the entry into employment have tended to be fragmentary, different investigators concentrating upon particular aspects of the topic. Some investigations have dealt with the nature and determinants of the vocational aspirations of school-leavers; other studies have attempted to identify the factors related to entry into different types of occupations; other efforts have been made to describe the structure of the vocational opportunities open to school-leavers; whilst yet other investigations have dealt with the reactions of young people towards work and their attitudes towards their jobs. Further studies have concentrated upon the rôles played by particular organisations such as the schools, colleges and the Youth Employment Service in the entry into employment.

The information that has been produced provides us with a great deal of useful knowledge about various aspects of the entry into employment, but in its fragmented condition it fails to provide answers to the major sociological issues that the entry into employment poses. Data on the ambitions of school-leavers, the factors that influence their occupational attainments, their behaviour in the labour market, the types of jobs they do, and their attitudes towards their work is essential, but the possession of fragmented information on each of these topics does not add up to an account and an explanation of the way in which young people are allocated to different positions in the occupational system, and induced to accept the occupational rôles in which they are placed. What is needed is an overall model or theory, that will relate the various aspects of the entry into employment to one another, and which in doing so will enable us to identify how the processes of occupational rôle allocation and vocational socialisation take place. This lack of a general framework has been lamented before, and the factors that a satisfactory framework would need to encompass have been thoroughly categorised.[2] So far, however, the only genuine attempts to blend the subject matter into a unitary framework have stemmed from the work of developmental psychologists.

Developmental psychology attempts to interpret human behaviour and attitudes in terms of the maturation of the individual's innate capacities. Intellectual abilities and sexual behaviour are frequently treated in developmental terms, and some students of the subject have considered that the entry into employment would be clarified if occupational choice was treated in a similar way. Upon the basis of a research project conducted amongst American high school and college students Ginzberg concluded that occupational choice was essentially a developmental phenomenon.[3] Although we use the same term 'occupational choice' to describe the ambitions of individuals of different ages, Ginzberg found that the occupational choices of individuals at different stages of development were really quite different phenomena. The occupational aims of young adolescents were entertained only as fantasies. It was found that only as the individual progressed through adolescence, and in doing so obtained a growing appreciation of his own interests and capacities, did choices become sensible attempts, made in a tentative manner to relate his abilities and inclinations to an occupational field. During their time at college, students were found to gain some realistic knowledge about what various occupations involved, and only at this stage did their ambitions crystallize upon a firm and realistic occupational choice. A later follow-up study of post-graduate students that Ginzberg conducted suggested that in entering employment and pursuing their careers young people realize ambitions that have gradually developed over a number of years, usually crystallizing before their education was completed, and in realizing their ambitions, Ginzberg argued, people achieve a feeling of self-actualisation.[4]

Ginzberg's studies were based upon samples drawn exclusively from the educationally privileged sections of American society and Ginzberg realized that his theory of occupational choice would probably need modification before it could be applied to other groups. The merit of Ginzberg's work is that it does provide a plausible framework within which information about various aspects of the entry into employment can be co-ordinated. It suggests relationships between ambitions and their determinants, jobs entered, and people's feelings about their work, and from these relationships it is possible to derive answers to the issues of how the products of childhood are allocated to different occupational rôles and how they are induced to accept them.

Super,[5] also working from the premises of developmental psychology, constructed a slightly different theory of occupational choice. Super accepted the idea of occupational choice being a developmental process. He did not consider, however, that ambitions were invariably firmly crystallized at the time of initially entering employment, or that the development of a career always consisted simply of implementing a previously conceived ambition. People do change their ambitions after starting work and careers do change their direction. Studies of labour mobility, however, had shown that careers tended to stabilise as people grew older. Super proposed the hypothesis that during their early years in employment young people's ambitions were both directing and being modified by their own work experience until eventually the two came into harmony with one another, the individuals then settling down in an occupation and experiencing a feeling of achievement and self-fulfillment. Before commencing employment Super envisaged occupational choices developing through similar stages to those suggested by Ginzberg, but whereas Ginzberg attached prime importance to the individual's growing awareness of his own interests and capacities, Super placed greater stress upon the rôle of the individual's social environment in structuring the individual's conception of his interests, abilities and capacities. The self-concept that emerged from the interaction between the individual's capacities and his social environment continued to develop in a similar manner during the early stages of a young person's career until an occupational rôle fully consistent with the individual's self-concept was discovered.

The work of Ginzberg and Super is important because it presents an attempt to co-ordinate our information on the entry into employment. Both Ginzberg and Super stress that we need to consider the entry into employment as a process. No part of the process can be properly understood in isolation. Data on careers, job attitudes, and ambitions only become explicable when placed in a comprehensive framework.

In his discussion Musgrave[6] has proposed that these theories of vocational development can profitably be re-stated in sociological terms, and has suggested that the notion of development can be employed in conjunction with the concepts of socialisation and rôle theory, the individual being conceived as moving between an articulated sequence of rôles in the home, the school system, and the occupational system. Each instance of rôle playing can be considered as a process of socialisation in so far as it structures the range of future rôles available and helps to form the individual's self-image and ambitions. Musgrave's chapter usefully attempts to re-formulate the only theoretical frameworks covering the entry into employment that we possess in a manner amenable to sociological treatment.

In this chapter I shall try to develop further these theories of the entry into employment. I shall do so firstly by reporting the results of an investigation designed to test hypotheses derived from the work of Ginzberg and Super. Secondly, in the light of the results an attempt will be made to extend our theoretical perspectives on the entry into employment.

An empirical test of developmental theories of occupational choice

A study of the occupational behaviour and attitudes of young people conducted in 1965 was designed to test the theories of vocational development proposed by Ginzberg and Super. This study was based upon a survey covering a sample of 196 young men aged between 14 and 23, selected by a random canvas of households in a part of the Greater London Borough that was chosen for investigation. The young men were interviewed about their careers, their attitudes towards their jobs and their ambitions. To a large extent the information collected supplements existing data. In addition to doing this the design of the survey, including young people at various stages in their careers, made it possible to test propositions concerning the processes of vocational development.[7]

Three hypotheses were deduced from Ginzberg's and Super's theories of vocational development.

1. *Young workers' ambitions will gradually become more consistent with their jobs as their careers develop*

Ginzberg's view of vocational development after the initial entry into employment as a process during which the individual brings his occupational choice into reality, and Super's view that ambitions and work experience gradually modify one another until they eventually fall into harmony, both entail this hypothesis.

2. *Job satisfaction will gradually increase as careers develop*

Ginzberg's notion of a career as a self-actualizing experience, and Super's conceptualization of a career as the implementation of a self-concept, both suggest that as their careers develop young workers should become increasingly satisfied with their jobs.

3. *Occupational mobility will decline in frequency as careers progress*

This hypothesis is deduced from Super's theory, which postulates that ambitions and work experience interact until they harmonize with one another, after which the individual achieves occupational stability.

Each of these hypotheses could be tested against the data collected in the survey. In order to test the hypotheses concerning the development of the sample's ambitions and job satisfaction the respondents were divided into four groups. Respondents were categorized according to whether they were employed in manual or in white collar occupations, and according to whether since leaving full-time education they had spent more or less than three years in employment.

1. The ambitions of the respondents were measured firstly by

asking which jobs they were aiming to do eventually, and secondly by asking what sort of job they expected to end up in. Most of the young men possessed aims and expectations that were consistent with the occupations that they were currently engaged in. Within this group a distinction was made between those who whilst wanting to remain in their present occupations were aiming to reach a higher level of employment than they would expect to achieve in the normal course of their careers, and those who were more or less content to remain doing their present jobs, accepting whatever promotion accrued to them. The former group was called 'ambitious' and the latter group 'content'. The remainder of the respondents had aims that were in some way inconsistent with their present occupations. Some intended and expected to move to a different type of work, others wanted but did not expect to be able to enter some other sort of employment, whilst others had no ambitions at all. The total proportion whose aims were different from their present jobs was fairly small, however, and therefore in the analysis all those respondents with 'inconsistent' ambitions have been grouped together.

How the distribution of the respondents' job aims developed as their careers progressed can be seen from the results presented in Table I.

TABLE I

| | | | Occupation | | | |
| | | | white collar | | manual | |
Type of future aim			*under 3 yrs.* %	*over 3 yrs.* %	*under 3 yrs.* %	*over 3 yrs.* %
Content	...	...	39	44	42	47
Ambitious	...	...	39	35	24	20
Inconsistent		...	22	21	34	33
		n =	28	23	38	49

Upon the basis of these results neither a clear cut acceptance nor rejection of the hypothesis is possible. The proportion of young workers with 'inconsistent' ambitions showed no statistically significant tendency to decline as their careers progressed. There was no evidence of a tendency for young people to gravitate into occupations consistent with their aspirations, or to adjust their ambitions to the occupations that were available. On the other hand, those respondents who had been working for over three years were more likely to be content to remain at their current level of employment, and were less likely to be 'ambitious' than were more recent entrants into the labour force. These differences are statistically significant at the 0.5 level, but the diminution of ambitiousness that took place really only appeared to have affected a minority of young employees. Therefore whilst the data suggest that the ambitions of some young people develop in the manner predicted upon the basis of Ginzberg's and Super's theories, this pattern of development certainly could not be called typical of the sample as a whole.

TABLE II

| | Occupation | | | |
| | white collar | | manual | |
	under 3 yrs. %	over 3 yrs. %	under 3 yrs. %	over 3 yrs. %
(a) *How interesting is your job?*				
Very interesting ...	67	50	44	39
Interesting	25	39	38	42
Not really interesting, boring, very boring ...	8	10	18	19
(b) *What are your employers like?*				
Very good	37	41	35	21
Good, fair	59	58	53	71
Not good, poor ...	4	—	12	8
(c) *How do you find the people you work with?*				
Get along very well ...	67	76	59	44
Quite friendly, alright	29	24	29	49
Difficult	4	—	12	6
(d) *How satisfied are you with your job?*				
Very	46	28	44	21
Quite satisfied, satisfied	45	72	56	67
Dissatisfied	9	—	—	12
n =	28	23	38	49

2. The second hypothesis to be tested postulated that as their careers progressed young workers would become increasingly satisfied with their jobs. To assess their job satisfaction the respondents were asked to appraise a number of particular aspects of their work: how interesting they found their jobs, how they rated their employers, and

how well they got along with the people they worked with. They were also asked directly how satisfied they were with their present jobs. With each question the respondents were asked to select one out of five possible answers graded in degrees of favourableness. The results obtained to these questions are presented in Table II.

It is difficult to draw any general conclusions from these results since not all the changes that took place during the young workers' early years in employment were in the same direction. Few respondents in any type of work, or at any period in their careers, appraised any aspect of their jobs unfavourably. The proportion expressing dissatisfaction with some aspect of their work did decline on three out of four questions amongst those respondents who were in white collar jobs. But amongst manual employees on two aspects of their work the older respondents were more likely to reply unfavourably, whilst on the other two aspects it was the younger workers who were the most likely to give unfavourable responses.

Differences did occur between the more and less experienced employees over the degree of favourableness with which the respondents rated their jobs. However, with the exception of the white collar workers' ratings of their employers and their workmates, the changes in job attitudes that took place over time were in the opposite direction to what would have been predicted on the basis of Ginzberg's and Super's theories. Manual workers in particular became less likely to appraise their jobs extremely favourably as their careers progressed. We must conclude, therefore, that the trends in the respondents' attitudes towards their jobs that accompanied the development of their careers fail to support the hypothesis.

Investigators who have asked their subjects to recollect changes that had occurred in their feelings about their jobs over time have found that people report increasing job satisfaction as their careers mature.[8] Cross-sectional studies, such as the one now being dealt with, have never revealed such clear trends, and it is probably dangerous to attach too much validity to individuals' recollections of their past attitudes.

3. The third hypothesis, derived from Super's theory, predicted that the sample's rates of occupational mobility[9] would decline as their careers progressed. In analysing the data on occupational mobility the respondents were not classified according to their types of work. The sample was treated as a whole and the number of occupational changes made per year of employment was calculated.[10] The

results are given in Table III.

TABLE III

Year of employment		O.M.R.		Occupational Mobility Rate
1st	...	0.44	...	(n = 116)
2nd	...	0.26	...	(n = 97)
3rd	...	0.30	...	(n = 73)
4th	...	0.28	...	(n = 49)
5th	...	0.45	...	(n = 31)
6th	...	0.33	...	(n = 18)

Once again it is impossible to affirm or reject conclusively the hypothesis upon the basis of the data on occupational mobility. The propensity of the sample to change their occupations displayed no consistent tendency to either fall, to rise, or to remain stable as their careers progressed. The failure of any consistent pattern to emerge suggests that different modes of career development are to be found in various sub-populations, but because of the small numbers involved in the sample this line of analysis could not be pursued. The rate of occupational mobility in the respondent's first year in the labour force was exceptionally high, and this does suggest a subsequent settling down process after unsteady beginnings along the lines that Super's theory would indicate. After the first year in employment, however, that sample's rate of occupational mobility exhibited no consistent decline. There was no evidence of careers gradually being stabilised, and the failure of such a tendency to be found provides a ground for rejecting the hypothesis.

None of the three hypotheses derived from the theories of Ginzberg and Super have been adequately confirmed and this suggests that although the careers, job attitudes, and ambitions of some young people probably develop in ways one would predict from the theories under consideration, these theories cannot be accepted as satisfactory accounts of the processes that are involved in the entry into employment. Indeed, the results of the investigation, taken in conjunction with other studies of British school-leavers, suggest that amongst young people in Britain at any rate, occupational choice does not play the key rôle in the entry into employment that Super and Ginzberg ascribed to it. Popular commonsense conceives individuals as making up their minds about the sort of work that they wish to do, and then selecting appropriate jobs. Occupational rôles are thought of as being chosen by their players. Popular commonsense however, is not always consistent with social reality, and the idea that individuals choose jobs and then enter them is a proposition that requires supporting empirical evidence before it can be accepted. When the evidence on the interaction between the ambitions and the occupational behaviour of young people in Britain is carefully examined, the typical pattern of interaction seems not to be for jobs to be entered upon the basis of ambitions, but for ambitions to be adapted to the occupations that young people find themselves able to enter. The approach of Ginzberg and Super accepts as its central yet unproven assumption that occupational choice-making is the critical determinant at work in the transition into an adult working rôle.

Three types of evidence support the conclusion that amongst British school-leavers at least, occupational choice is frequently not the determinant of career behaviour. Firstly, there is the fact that most of the occupational mobility that takes place amongst the adolescent labour force is not anticipated in their ambitions. In the survey described above, only 12 percent of those respondents who had been working for less than three years desired and expected to change their occupations at any foreseeable time in the future. But amongst those respondents who had been employed for five years or more, 43 per cent had changed their occupations during their fourth or fifth years in the labour market and there was no reason to believe that those respondents who were less experienced vocationally at the time of the investigation would behave any differently during their fourth and fifth years in employment. Occupational changes are not foreseen in the development of young people's ambitions. All the investigations that have been conducted amongst young workers in Britain have found the overwhelming majority of the respondents to be in possession of ambitions consistent with their current jobs. Eighty per cent of a sample of Sheffield school-boys[11] had no intention of leaving their existing occupations after one year in the labour market, yet it is known that the proportion of young workers who achieve permanent career stability at this early stage is much smaller than this. When questioned, few young employees ever claim to want to move to a different type of work, yet in practice many do so. What seems to happen is that ambitions adjust to occupational changes, rather than changes being planned in order to realize previously developed ambitions.

The second type of evidence supporting the view that it is careers that determine ambitions is that despite the fact that many school-leavers fail to enter their chosen jobs, few are dissatisfied with the employment that they do obtain. Studies that have followed up samples of school-leavers over the transition from school to work have found that many young people fail to achieve their job aims at the time of leaving school. Different investigators have found only about 50 per cent school-leavers realizing their ambitions. Once these 'thwarted' school-leavers are in employment, however, few want to leave their jobs. They claim to be satisfied with their work and adjust their ambitions to the occupations that they have entered.[12]

A third type of evidence suggesting that the ambitions of young people are products of their careers concerns the extent to which school-leavers' 'ambitions' do represent their true vocational aspirations. It is a well-established fact that British school leavers' ambitions are realistically modest.[13] Young people rarely entertain ambitions for jobs falling beyond their educational attainments. School leavers who fail to enter their chosen jobs find it necessary to displace their ambitions horizontally, but in general young people are not over-ambitious. The fact that young people should display such modest ambitions leads one to question whether the ambitions they reveal when questioned by research workers, teachers, or Youth Employment Officers really represent the jobs that they would ideally like to enter, and there is some evidence to suggest that they do not. In my investigation, after they had been questioned about their 'aims' and 'expectations' the respondents were then asked which job they would want 'if (they) could choose from all the jobs in the world'. Fifty per cent of the young people mentioned an 'ideal job' that differed from the aim they had named earlier and many who failed to mention an ideal job did so because they were spoilt for choice. This suggests that the ambitions of many young people represent something other than their own true aspirations. In her investigation Wilson[14] also made a distinction between 'aims' and 'fantasy aspirations'. She asked her school leavers to recall their early ambitions, and found that their current fantasy aspirations bore a close resemblance to their earlier aims. The school leavers seemed to make an effort to adopt realistic ambitions and previous aims that could not be realized were relegated to the realm of fantasy.

To a large extent young people's ambitions appear to be based upon the occupations that they expect to enter rather than upon the vocations that they would ideally choose to follow. Ambitions are anticipations of the direction that careers are going to take. They are products of occupations that individuals are in the process of entering rather than determinants of the patterns that careers take.

This view of the relationship between careers and ambitions is contrary to the relationship embodied in the theories of Ginzberg and Super, and it is also contrary to popular conceptions of the way in which individuals choose to enter jobs. Nevertheless the available evidence, based on studies of young people in Britain, suggests that ambitions are in fact products of careers. Ambitions are chosen on the basis of occupations entered, rather than the reverse.

3. An alternative theory : *the opportunity-structure model*

To account for the fact that school-leavers do enter different types of jobs and pursue careers falling into different patterns there is really no need to postulate any differences between the ambitions of the individuals concerned. Despite the widespread prevalence of the ideology of free occupational choice, different groups of school-leavers do possess differential ease of access to the various types of employment. The occupational opportunities open to any school leaver are structured by a number of factors, the most important of which is that the individual's educational attainments and his freedom of occupational choice are really strictly limited. The type of secondary school an individual attended and his achievements within the school govern the range of occupations he is able to enter. It is true that there are few occupations in Britain where entrance qualifications are rigidly defined and enforced, but at all levels in the occupational hierarchy, and especially at the higher levels, educational attainments are amongst the main criteria used in selection procedures. So whilst it would not be true to say that a school leaver's job opportunities are rigidly determined by his educational attainments, it is the case that the ease with which a school leaver can enter different types of jobs is strongly influenced by his scholastic achievements. Different groups of school leavers are presented with totally different opportunity structures upon entering the labour market. Upon making their exits from the educational system school leavers stand in varying degrees of social proximity to different types of occupations. These varying degrees of social proximity have nothing to do with the ambitions of the individuals concerned. They are inherent in the structure of the educational institutions that the young people are leaving, and the occupational institutions that they are entering, and the close relationship between the educational status of school leavers and the status of their first jobs implies no differences in the vocational attitudes, ideals or values of different groups of school leavers. Different attainments can be accounted for in terms of differential opportunity structures.

Another factor that can influence a young person's job.opportunity structure is the type of home from which he comes. Recruitment to occupations still takes place to a large extent via informal channels. In the investigation reported in this study 35 per cent first jobs and 52 per cent subsequent jobs were obtained as a result of either personal contacts or off-chance enquiries, and other surveys have produced similar findings. A skilled craftsman is still able to obtain an apprenticeship for his son, and a professional man is able to open up opportunities for articled employment on behalf of his relatives. By virtue of the different backgrounds from which they are drawn school leavers stand in varying degrees of social proximity to different types of employment.

Once young people have entered their first jobs the different opportunity structures opened up by the nature of their early occupations can largely account for the subsequent development of their careers. School leavers who enter jobs involving training in either professional or craft skills are rarely occupationally mobile during the early stages of their careers. In the survey upon which this study is based, when the occupational histories of the respondents were compared after their working lives were two years old those in routine white collar or non-skilled manual occupations were found to be by far the most likely to have made an occupational change during their working lives (See Table IV).

TABLE IV

Occupation after two years		Proportion having made no changes %
1. Non-manual with training	...	85 (n = 13)
2. Non-manual, without training	...	66 (n = 15)
3. Manual, with training	... ...	80 (n = 35)
4. Manual, without training	... ...	26 (n = 34)

School leavers who enter jobs involving training find that the opportunities available to them in their initial occupations are superior to any prospects that are available elsewhere. Their training is an investment in skill and status the returns upon which can only be realized by remaining occupationally immobile. Those young people whose initial jobs involve no systematic training are more likely to find job opportunities with comparable prospects to their own in different occupations at all stages during the early years of their careers. Jobs involving training are to a large extent reserved for school leavers and so the young person who initially enters unskilled employment is likely to spend his early years at work moving between a series of different occupations in order to obtain the maximum returns (both economic and psychological) from his labour. His opportunity structure will be less precisely focused than that of the school leaver who initially enters employment involving a course of training.

By far the most highly mobile are young people in non-skilled manual employment. They change their occupations much more frequently even than their counterparts in non-skilled white collar work. The explanation for this is probably that the bureaucratic organisation of white collar jobs provides rewards for seniority that are not available in manual work. Because inertia is positively rewarded in white collar jobs the young person in non-skilled white collar employment has a definite incentive to remain occupationally inert.

Rates of occupational mobility are often taken to indicate a state of vocational maladjustment. The young worker who flits between numerous short-lived unskilled jobs is thought to be in need of vocational advice and guidance, if not psychologically disturbed in general. But really the young worker who enters and leaves a succession of routine jobs in a constant attempt to obtain the highest possible earnings and to ward off boredom is not displaying symptoms of maladjustment. In fact he is making a realistic adjustment to the job opportunity structure that his particular career situation opens up.

In showing how the occupations that school leavers enter, and the sequences of career movements that they subsequently make, are explicable in terms of the different opportunity structures that are opened up to various groups of young people I am proposing an alternative theory of the entry into employment to those offered by Ginzberg and Super. These two theorists interpret careers in terms of the working out of young people's ambitions. Factors such as education and home background are held to influence occupational placement only in so far as they affect the development of vocational aspirations. To Ginzberg a career is a process of self-actualisation during which an individual brings an occupational aim into reality. Super conceives careers in a similar way although he allows for some feedback from the experience of work into the occupational choice-making process itself. The alternative theory that I am proposing asserts that the momentum and direction of school leavers' careers are derived from the way in which their job opportunities become cumulatively structured and young people are placed in varying degrees of social proximity, with different ease of access to different types of employment. The ambitions of school leavers adapt to the direction that their careers take, and are not major determinants of the occupations that young people enter. Evidence has been marshalled from my own and other investigations which supports this alternative theory, and invalidates the hypotheses deduced from the theories of Ginzberg and Super.

In proposing an alternative theory I am not suggesting that the opportunity structure model should be adopted as a theory of universal validity, and that other frameworks should be subsequently dismissed. Simply to oppose the different theories against one another would be quite mistaken. There is no reason to assume that the entry into employment takes place in a similar manner amongst all groups of young people in all societies, and in showing that the theoretical frameworks developed by Ginzberg and Super cannot be applied to school leavers in modern Britain it is not being argued that their theories should be totally rejected.

The models of the entry into employment that we have been considering and testing are situated at the preliminary stage in the process of theory building. They represent initial attempts to blend the many factors that are involved in the entry into employment into integrated frameworks. Before we can determine how the major sociological processes that are involved in the entry into employment are in fact taking place, it is essential that the relevant material should be organized in such a systematic manner.

The next stage in theory construction should not be to decide which of the proposed models possesses universal validity. Theory construction will proceed more profitably by attempting to determine in which particular social contexts the different models of the entry into employment are applicable.

I have shown that amongst young people in Britain the models established by Ginzberg and Super are inapplicable, and have proposed an alternative framework. The intention is that this alternative framework should be treated as an additional method in which the entry into employment can, and in many cases does, take place. Studies of American youth suggest that the theories proposed by Ginzberg and Super probably possess greater validity in the context of American society. In America the ambitions of young people do appear to play the rôle of determinants of the direction that careers take, and aspirations do not appear to adjust so readily to the job opportunities that are available. The next stage in the development of theory concerning the entry into employment will involve systematically comparing groups of school leavers making the entry into employment in different social contexts and identifying the factors that determine the manner in which occupational rôle allocation and socialisation take place.

I conclude by attempting to identify certain attributes of the social situation of young people in Britain that could explain why the opportunity structure model should typify their occupational behaviour during the entry into employment. One condition for the operation of such a model is that job opportunities should be structured in a manner corresponding to the way in which the output of the educational system is graded. That British secondary education is highly stratified is well known. It is also the case that ease of access into different types of occupations is related to the status a young person has achieved at the time of leaving the educational system. The imposition of this type of structure upon the process of the entry into employment (which does not exist to the same extent in all societies) is a pre-requisite for the processes of occupational rôle allocation and socialisation to be determined by the opportunity structure.

A further pre-requisite for the occurrence of this particular type of transition into employment is that the work orientations of school leavers should be sufficiently elastic to adapt to those occupations to which the opportunity structure places them in the closest proximity. Evidence presented earlier suggests that the ambitions of young people in Britain do adapt to the types of work that they happen to find available. This adaptability is not self-explanatory but depends upon the existence of a malleable orientation towards occupational rôles in general. There are three sets of factors operating in the British adolescent's social situation that could explain this type of work orientation.

Firstly there is the ideology of free occupational choice. This ideology does not correspond to social reality, but it does possess widespread currency as a social belief, and, as has often been pointed out, when people believe a particular idea to be true they will react as if it was in fact valid. Young people believe that they are personally responsible for the jobs they have entered. They believe that their employment is personally chosen, and this affects the way in which they react to their occupations. It makes them ready to reconcile their ambitions to the occupations into which they have been allocated. To be dissatisfied with one's occupation would be to engage in self-criticism. The desirability of an individual's occupation, and its worth as a goal for ambitions are things that the young person must defend unless the prospect of an alternative job has already presented itself.

A second set of factors promoting adjustment to whatever type of work the opportunity structure presents, which applies especially to young men, is the male adolescent's need for a personal identity that can be established only by playing an occupational rôle. It is widely believed that the modern adolescent is leisure-oriented and that he attaches only an instrumental significance to his employment, and it is true that most young people do rate their leisure as being more important to them than their work, and that many, especially those in manual occupations, seek little from work other than a secure income. The modest demands that young people make upon their employment could go a long way to explaining why they so rarely feel dissatisfied and frustrated with their work. But it would be wrong to assume that the overt attitudes of young people exhaust the psychological relevance of employment. If there is one conclusion that can be drawn from the inter-war studies of the effects of unemployment it is that the loss of his job means more to the individual than the mere loss of instrumental rewards. Studies of out-of-work young people found that unemployment led to a rapid deterioration of their personalities, self respect was lost, and the individuals concerned became socially withdrawn. A young man needs a job to obtain an adult status in the eyes of the community, and a respect upon which he can establish an identity for himself. Occupational rôles have a central significance in the lives of men in industrial societies. Without a job a man completely loses his social identity. When school leavers are asked to write essays about their future lives, work is nearly always a major theme in boys' essays. For girls work does not possess such a central socio-psychological significance, and unemployment consequently does not bring such deleterious effects. But the male school leaver has a need for 'an' occupation which overrides any preference he may possess for a 'particular' occupation. This helps to explain why the ambitions of school-leavers should so readily adapt to the openings that the opportunity structure makes available.

The third set of factors contributing to the elasticity of school-leavers' work orientations concerns the limited nature of their knowledge about occupations. It is usual to examine differences in job preferences in terms of differential evaluations of the occupational structure, but it is important to remember that the cognitive field of the individual places strict parameters upon the range within which the evaluative preferences can operate. The job information to which a young person has access is strictly limited. The division of labour has produced a multiplicity of occupations, and in industrial societies work is performed in special organisations normally out of the gaze of the general public. Under these circumstances it is difficult for a young person to acquire any sort of comprehensive job knowledge. Parents and teachers are usually ill-equipped to offer comprehensive advice, and the official vocational guidance agencies do not operate on a scale that would enable them to make a substantial impact. Consequently school-leavers know little about the occupations that are open to them, or even about the occupations that they say they wish to enter. Obviously young people have an outline type of knowledge about the range of jobs that are in existence, and they are able to place different occupations in a status hierarchy producing results similar to those achieved with adults. Developing a crystallized vocational aim, however, requires more than a rough, cursory knowledge of what doing a particular job involves. Before he can develop a commitment to a specific occupation a young person must be equipped with a knowledge of the sort of work that is involved, how the occupation is entered, and the type of qualifications and training that are required. Before he possesses this cognitive equipment a young person cannot develop any firm ambitions. If the job information possessed by school-leavers is minimal, and the evidence does suggest that this is so, this will help to explain why young people's ambitions should adapt so readily to the occupations that they happen to enter. It will also help to explain why young workers' ambitions remain closely geared to the occupations they are actually in, because the occupations he has practised will be the only occupations about which the individual possesses sufficient knowledge upon which to erect any concrete aims.

Conclusions

These aspects of the adolescent's social situation that could help to explain why the opportunity structure model should typify the entry into employment amongst British school-leavers are only tentative suggestions offered to indicate the lines along which theory construction could profitably develop. This chapter has taken one step in the development of our theoretical perspectives on the entry into employment. The importance of developing comprehensive models if the sociological processes that are involved in the entry into employment are to be understood has been stressed. Existing models based upon the premises of developmental psychology have been tested against data on the occupational behaviour and attitudes of young people in Britain; they have been found inadequate and an alternative model has been proposed. In the future still further models will probably be developed to describe the entry into employment in various social situations. From there progress will be possible towards determining the specific factors in a social situation that make each particular model operational. It is vital that all future studies in the sociology of the entry into employment should integrate their findings within a general theoretical framework, for it is only by achieving such integration that our understanding of the major social processes involved in the entry into employment can be properly advanced.

University of Liverpool.

[1] This article is based upon the author's M.Sc. (Econ.) thesis, London, 1966.

[2] P. M. Blau, J. W. Gustad, R. Jessor, H. S. Parnes, R. C. Wilcock: 'Occupational choice; a conceptual framework'. *Ind. and Lab. Rev.*, 1956, pp. 531-543, and E. T. Keil, D. S. Riddell, B. S. R. Green: 'Youth and Work: Problems and Perspectives', *Soc. Rev.*, July 1966, p. 117.

[3] E. Ginzberg *et al.*: *Occupational Choice: an approach to a general theory*, New York, 1951.

[4] E. Ginzberg *et. al.*: *Talent and Performance*, Columbia University Press, 1964.

[5] D. E. Super *et. al.*: *Vocational Development: a framework for research*, Teachers College, 1957.

[6] See Chapter Four.

[7] For additional information on the research design and method see K. Roberts: 'The Entry into Employment', M.Sc. (Econ.) thesis, London, 1966.

[8] E. Ginzberg *et. al.*: *Talent and Performance, passim.*

[9] Movements between occupations rather than between jobs were analysed since it is an occupational change that is most likely to signify a change in the direction of an individual's career and ambitions.

[10] To have broken the sample down on this question according to their types of employment would not have affected the direction of the results and would have made the number of cases at the more advanced career stages unnecessarily small.

[11] M. P. Carter: *Home, School and Work*, Oxford, 1962.

[12] For evidence on this point see M. P. Carter: *op cit.*, G. Jahoda: 'Job attitudes and job choice among secondary modern school-leavers', *Occ. Psych.* Vol. 26, pp. 125-140, and 206-224, and M. D. Wilson: 'The vocational preferences of secondary modern school-children', *Brit. J. Ed. Psych.*, Vol. 23, pp. 97-113 and 163-179.

[13] T. Veness: *School-leavers*, London, 1962.

[14] M. D. Wilson: *op. cit.*

Chapter Nine

SOME THEORETICAL PROBLEMS IN THE STUDY OF YOUTH*

S. Allen

Introduction

Young people in industrialised societies share in a common experience of being considered non-adult and are excluded from full participation in adult society. They are admitted into adult status by formal and informal processes, which can be abrupt or gradual and which in Britain take place at different ages in different areas of social activity. This situation is frequently contrasted with non-industrialised societies in which the transition from childhood to adult status is institutionalised and clearly marked by formal ceremonies. This contrast is explained by a variety of factors, such as the reduced significance of kinship based organisations in allocating adult status, the increasing differentiation accompanying the division of labour and the degree and rate of social change. It is also seen as giving rise in industrialised societies to conflict and discontinuity, which are usually characterised in terms of the emergence of youth cultures, youth movements and the problems of youth which are not present in other types of society. The sociological explanations advanced to account for youth problems and cultures contain biological and psychological assumptions as well as assumptions about the nature of the processes and relationships which characterise industrial and non-industrial societies. There is a dominant approach based on integrative models of social analysis in which common value patterns play a major part in articulating social relationships. The problems of youth then become organised into an explanatory scheme in which adjustment to the major value orientations and symbols of a particular society is stressed. The process of such adjustment is assumed to give rise to the problems and stresses of adolescence in modern societies and the coalescence of youth into cultural groups to emphasise 'their problematic, uncertain standing from the point of view of cultural values and symbols'.[1] This kind of social analysis

---

* Paper presented to the Yugoslav National Conference of Sociology, Split, Yugoslavia, 15th February, 1968.

© S. Allen 1968 (This article was first published in *The Sociological Review*, Vol. 16, No. 3, November 1968.)

is derived from the normative functionalist models most highly developed in the work of Talcott Parsons. Criticisms of this approach are increasingly made on the grounds of its theoretical inadequacy; that it stresses stability and continuity, that it is unable to account for structural change and conflict and so on.[2] But so far there is little criticism of the use of concepts and emphases drawn from this approach and applied to the analysis of problems, particularly social problems.

Theoretical Considerations

In investigating the position of coloured, immigrant youth in Great Britain this model of an integrative social system articulated through common values is inadequate and moreover misleading. It leads to conceptualising the problems in terms of value differences and sees the resolution of these problems in terms of adequate socialisation for integration into British society. Each of the characteristics, colour, immigrant and youth can be the basis of social differentiation. But even where such differentiations exist they cannot explain the behaviour of these categories. Indeed in order to understand the operation of these characteristics it is necessary to use a radically different approach.

The social position of youth cannot be separated from the overall social structure in which it is located nor can the approach to youth, as a sociological problem, be understood apart from the general theoretical scheme which is used, implicitly or explicitly, to define and analyse the problem. Perhaps the most thorough-going attempt to deal with the social position of youth in recent years is the work of S.N. Eisenstadt, *From Generation to Generation*.[3] Eisenstadt's analysis of the position of age groups, youth movements and so on seeks on a comparative and historical basis to specify the conditions under which such phenomena will exist. His aim is both theoretical and practical and he claims relevance for his work to the understanding of present day youth cultures and problems. It is my contention that, whatever the merits of Eisenstadt's attempt at a comprehensive analysis of the problem on a theoretical level, and however suggestive his data, his work has little relevance either to the explanation, in a sociological sense, or to the understanding in a practical social way of the position of youth and the structural conditions of which it is a consequence. It is not my aim to give a textual criticism, which is impossible in a short study, but to examine the basic assumptions used in this work and in a much more fragmentary way in other work on youth and to discuss an alternative approach which I consider to be more satisfactory theoretically and more relevant in practical approaches to the problem. Eisenstadt states that 'The crucial importance of age relations in all societies and of age groups in all universalistic societies is clearly seen in the fact that the smooth transmission of social heritage, various attempts at change and various manifestations of discontinuity are largely, even if not wholly, effected through them.'[4] Whilst the relations between those of different ages are of significance in all societies, to elevate these relations to a position in which stability, change, continuity and discontinuity are seen to be articulated through them is questionable for simple, relatively static structures; for complex, rapidly changing structures it is extreme sociological naïveté. Social relationships have to be understood as part of a dynamic process, in which social situations are the consequence of structural contradictions operating at different levels and with different intensity. Differentiations such as colour, immigrant and youth involve a consideration of the dialectical inter-relation of economic, power and ideological structures.

Generational Analysis within a Structural Context

The social world of men is passed on to succeeding generations as an objective social reality which each new generation does not create. Each new generation must individually and collectively live in the world of social relations and through action re-affirm or challenge it. Part of this world is the structure of legitimation passed on for acting in one way rather than another, which is learned within a system of rewards and penalties. But this is not the totality. The externality and objectivity of the world of social relations is not a matter of definition and redefinition by all social groups irrespective of the position in which they find themselves. Age relations (including youth) are part of economic relations and the political and ideological structures in which they take place. It is not the relations between ages which explain change or stability in societies, but change in societies which explains relations between different ages. Karl Mannheim in his generational analysis maintained that generational separation in terms of number of calendar years was an inadequate foundation for an analysis of social process and change. He distinguished between (1) a generational location in which people were located merely by accident of birth and biological rhythm; (2) the generation as actuality, those who shared a common destiny within a generational location and (3) generational unit which participated in this common destiny but responded differently to it.⁵ Such distinctions point to the necessity of analysing sub-groupings within any one generation and the relations between such sub-groups and other age groups in order to explain differential responses.⁶ In complex (what Eisenstadt calls universalistic) societies, the experiences of sub-groups with different economic positions, differential amounts of power and differential access to education, housing, occupations, status and so on, cannot be assumed to be similar experiences, either subjectively or objectively, for the members of these groups be they 9, 19 or 90 years of age. In Britain the experience of a 19 year old working class youth is strikingly different from that of a middle or upper class person of the same age. This is not simply a difference of economic or social level but a difference which permeates every aspect of life. Comparison of these groups has shown, for instance, a relationship between the forms of language learning and thinking that are acquired through different social environments.⁷ Nor does the existence of inter-generational social mobility between classes diminish the differences which exist in the class system. In societies with class systems the position of youth cannot be understood without reference to this system.

I would go further than this and maintain that in no society can we understand the position of youth unless we first ask what structures the everyday lives of members of the society, what groups develop in relation to these structures and what articulates the relational aspects of these groups. That is, we have to have an overall model which will enable us to select and give priority to those parts of the system which are consequential for other parts.⁸ In societies without private ownership, and therefore without classes based on the ownership and non-ownership of productive property, it cannot be assumed that all factors have an equal weight in determining life chances and social experience. In such societies generational experience may play a more determining rôle in social relations, but this is problematical, a matter for investigation within a framework which hypothesises the relative autonomy of this factor and others such as sex, region, ethnic and strata or family origins in relation to economic and political power. An empirical enquiry based on a multiplicity of factors, without a systematic consideration of the relations within which these factors are operating, can at best give a partial description of processes; it cannot be the basis of an analysis of social relations. In societies with economic, political, religious, regional and ethnic differentiation the social position of youth is not a unitary phenomenon.

Empirical Studies

In their survey of much of the existing European and American literature Keil *et al.* indicate that most research on young people fails to take any account of the realities of the social structure in which the 'problem' being investigated is situated.[9] '. . . general studies of adolescence are overwhelmingly concerned with biological and sexual development, and the major social changes are either ignored or discussed briefly and speculatively.'[10] Out of eighteen general textbooks on adolescence, for instance, not one emphasized the adjustments necessary in starting work, though in most societies the vast majority of people enter their working lives at this time. Many studies concerned with the transition from school to work rely heavily on the stated aspirations of schoolchildren, rather than investigating the actual experiences of starting work. Others assume adjustment to work involves a 'culture shock' deriving from the clash of values between pre-work expectations and the realities of the work situation and discuss this 'shock' on the assumption that all school situations and all work situations are the same. In Britain this latter assumption is quite unrealistic; schools are highly stratified and pre-work experience varies not only with type of school, but also with class, neighbourhood and family differences, whilst work situations can be differentiated along the lines of occupational and skill level, size, age and social composition of work group and so on. Unless these differences are recognised a blanket assumption about 'culture shock' can only obscure rather than explain the complex processes involved in different transitions from school to work.

Nor is there any agreement in empirical work on what constitutes youth. In Britain this has included the years from twelve to twenty-five or a block of years in between; or the basis has been from puberty to marriage. The right to marry, to vote, to own property, or enter legal agreements, to join the army, or drive a car, or drink alcohol in public and countless other formal rights are products of discrete historical processes and are conferred at a variety of ages with little or no reference to capability or lack of it. Those who attempt to use psychological bases as a guide confer an apparent order on this non-child, non-adult status but increasingly these attempts have been queried.

Although many psychological theories conceive of getting older as a developmental process, often divided into stages whereby human beings pass from immaturity to maturity, much empirical evidence has not supported these simple assumptions. C. M. Fleming comments 'the development of the young human being is both more continuous, more complex and more highly differentiated than the psychologists of the past and popular writers of today would lead us to suppose.'[11] Peck and Havighurst, who divide development into five stages with ideal-type character-types, found only a quarter of their sample approximated to the level of maturity and these were no more likely to be found among adults than among sixteen year olds. They also reported that a 'sizeable minority', 'perhaps over 50 per cent' of the adult American population was still in the first two stages of development.[12] Whatever status is given to such findings and to many others,[13] it seems clear that to accept personality development as a linear, inevitable process through which all normally endowed human beings pass to a stage of 'adult maturity' is not a useful basis on which to begin to analyse youth. In terms of physical development adolescence may well be the peak period for such development, whilst social development or maturity is assumed to belong to adult status. The 'ideal-typical adult' is part of a deeply embedded and pervasive ideological structure. Social adolescence, that is behaviour not appropriate for adults, can be created and for the past two hundred years societies in Western Europe have been creating adolescents.

The existing work on youth tends to present us with an ever-growing list of factors which seem to be influential but little or no attempt is made to specify their interrelation. In the transition from school to work, for instance, the list grows longer, but we are no nearer explaining the relative significance of school, home, labour market, peer group or work experience in structuring attitudes, behaviour and problems in the work situation of adolescents. This ignorance is frequently thought to stem from the difficulties of measuring these influences and the answer to lie in better question-naire design or interview technique. So that instead of asking 'Do you like your job?' and correlating the 'Yes', 'No' and 'Don't Know' with five, fifty or more other variables, we now ask informants to rank money, friends, chances of social mobility and so on, and correlate the answers with job 'satisfaction'. Whilst it goes without saying that questionnaires and interviews can be technically efficient or inefficient and that a mastery of techniques is a necessity for those who propose to use them, the situation has developed, evident in a wide range of empirical research, where the technique dictates the structure of the research. So much so that for some years in Britain and America the 'if it can't be measured, it doesn't exist' kind of sociology was dominant. Such research lends itself to ever more sophisticated statistical handling, but for those who are interested in understanding and explaining social processes it has so far been a peculiarly arid form of endeavour.[14] The dispelling of ignorance will not be achieved through more attention to techniques but through reassessment of the basic theoretical assumptions underlying studies of youth. If empirical research is to be relevant, then structural inter-relationships must be recognised and some overall model developed which specifies these in terms of their hypothesised significance. Empirical work would then no longer be an accumulation of *ad hoc* correlations without social meaning and relevance, but a cumulative process in which we progressively identified the conditions under which different forms of social behaviour developed. I have been able to mention only a few of the theoretical and methodological deficiencies encountered in most of the studies of youth with which I am familiar. The two outstanding problems which sociologists who are interested in explaining the behaviour of young people face if they wish to make use of existing material is, on the one hand, the crude empiricism of much of the work and, on the other, the dominance of a naive functionalist approach based on integrative models of society.

Youth Viewed as Problematic

When youth is viewed as problematic this has consequences for investigation and for policy recommendations. Such a view is widely held by social workers, educationalists, and youth leaders, who face the task of getting youth to act in certain specifically approved ways, to stay on at school or college, to take and hold certain kinds of jobs, to reject delinquent peers, to become politically involved or whatever the specific problem may be.[15] Such ideological and legal contexts do not bind the sociologist in his analysis. Indeed it is necessary to reject problem-solving perspectives in order to carry out an analysis of the causes and consequences of inter-relations between social groups.[16] In a recent text on social problems, 'The selections on youth attempt again to portray *the scope and variety of this problem . . . It is only* under relatively specific conditions, connected with growing social differentiation, and with the diminution of the rôle of the family, that stage *has crystallised as an area of unmanageable social problems.*'[17] From a social science point of view several questions come to mind. What are the unmanageable social problems of youth? Why is it that youth in some types of societies come to be considered as problematical? Problematical for whom? First it would seem that youth is problematical for adults within given social contexts. On closer inspection these social contexts exist within industrialised societies, with developed patterns of the division of labour which produces groups stratified in accordance with certain economic and technical demands. Second, the problems which arise from this division of labour stem from the contradictions inherent in the structure and are unmanageable within that structure. The unmanageable social problem of unemployed youth in the United States, particularly Negro youth, with its far-reaching consequences seen in their most violent form each summer in many urban centres, can neither be understood nor solved in terms of a youth problem.[18] It is an unmanageable structural problem arising out of economic and social relations, and explanations in terms of the characteristics of youth are less useful for its solution than analyses of the structure of employment and the factors making for differential access to jobs.[19] It is not 'deviant' not to be employed, or to take up 'delinquent' occupations if jobs do not exist or the achievement of reward is higher in delinquent than non-delinquent occupations. Nor is it 'unrealistic' to leave school before completing the course, if continuing your education makes only a marginal difference to your occupational chances as seems to be the case for working class youths in Britain and the U.S. It is a popular belief that longer education brings material and social rewards. This may be so only if the education is well beyond that of others within the group or prior social status, in terms of parental origin, is relatively high. Miller suggests '. . . I believe we would find that graduation does not make a great difference for the working-class boy: it is the linkage of graduation with prior middle-class status that makes the difference in the overall results of high school diplomas to occupations. And I suspect that many working-class boys have some awareness of the facts about them.'[20]

The low aspirations of some working class school children have been noted by investigators in Britain, whilst most others aim for a skilled trade, for which apprenticeship rather than longer formal education is the method of recruitment. This latter tendency has also been recorded by investigators in Poland and Germany. In France, on the other hand, handicrafts and small farming are given preference. Mobility aspirations are most frequently reported in work from the United States.[21] In my own research on coloured immigrant youth the stated aspirations tend to be higher than for white boys of the same age and education. This may reflect a combination of a lack of knowledge of the processes by which such jobs are obtained and the structural obstacles to such achievement and a high motivation to get out of the narrow job range occupied by most of their parents, some of whom are well qualified for higher status jobs, or it may be due simply to parental pressure. With a structural framework the explanation of the behaviour of unemployed youth or those who leave school early would not be presented in terms of a 'lack of achievement motivation' or inadequate socialisation to 'common values' (or heritage), but would first assess the behaviour in terms of the realities of the socio-economic situation. The realism or lack of it could then be related systematically to the total social situation in which young people enter work.

A different example of the tendency to reify youth may be found in the political sphere. A variety of characteristics are attributed to present-day youth; in politics the most frequent are apathy and idealism. The process towards political maturity is assumed by many political sociologists in Great Britain and the United States to involve compromise. Or put another way, conservatism increases with age. Further assumptions are made that young people are less bound by habit and old political ties than their elders and, therefore, more responsive to political pressures of the moment. Consequently it is argued it is to the young that we must look for one of the principal sources of political change.[22] Various explanations have been put forward to account for the political behaviour of youth. Apathy is linked with an 'end of ideology' argument; loss of idealism with coming to terms with realities; generational experience, particularly the post-war affluence is used to 'explain' both activity and apathy, conservatism and change. The inconsistency of the assumptions, the contradictory nature of much of the data and the non-discriminatory types of explantation raise questions about the usefulness of the category of youth in relation to political behaviour. In so far as young people are treated in a similar way, for instance in highly industrialised societies the young are excluded from positions of power, then they can be considered as a meaningful category as a first approximation. Their responses to this exclusion cannot be assumed to be 'standard' regardless of their experience. In Britain it may be generally true that young people are 'not very interested' in politics and could therefore be described as apathetic. Such 'apathy' is not confined to the young. Among those who are active two broad groups which are not necessarily exclusive must be distinguished; those formally linked with the system of parties and those involved in 'political' activities. In recent years the second category has included, among others, the Campaign for Nuclear Disarmament, the New Left and groups against the Vietnam War which have generally become known as the 'politics of protest' and have largely arisen since the Suez Crisis of 1956. Discussing the political activity of young people, Abrams and Little came to some interesting tentative conclusions.[23] Four out of five activists came from families with records of political activity; seven out of ten support the same party and activism is related not so much to present experience as the experience of two or three generations ago. Support for different parties is related to overall perceptions of British society, particularly the nature of its class system. In overall terms '. . . there is little reason to treat the young in contemporary Britain as a new political generation. The perceptions and orientations of the age group as a whole are organised in an old frame of reference. Young activists, whatever their first hopes, are constrained to work old institutions and accept old possibilities. The pace of change is set by the political parties . . . British youth has no collective political self-consciousness.'[24]

Put into a more general context, the lack of equality of status, either in controlling the means of power or decision making within a given political structure, is seen clearly between parties and their youth sections in Great Britain. The majority seem to accept this definition of power between youth and adults.[25] Those who try to change the position are likely to find themselves disaffiliated and their section disbanded.[26] The problem of youth is that of being expected to be involved but being powerless. This is not a specific youth problem.

In situations of rapid change where new questions arise which cannot be dealt with by existing institutional arrangements, problems and discontinuities may be seen as, or expressed through, conflicts between generations, but sociologically would be more satisfactorily analysed in terms of the dialectical relation between existing institutions and changes in structural bases of the society, which affect all ages within the society. For instance, institutional arrangements suitable for revolutionary and immediate post-revolutionary situations are not likely to work as the situation changes and new problems arise. The transformation of society is a continuing process within which constant re-analysis has to be made.[27] To conceptualise it as simply a conflict of views or policies between the 'old guard' and the younger generation is to reduce the complexities of social structure to two opposed groups differentiated by age. This is not to say that generational experiences will not differ, and at times may differ markedly, but we add little to our understanding by ascribing such differences to age. When one generation grows up in a world structurally differentiated from the world in which the previous generation was raised, then the questions to be tackled by sociologists concern the identification of the structural differences, the differential impact of these on various sub-groups, and the consequences arising from the lack of congruence between the new problems and the existing institutional arrangements for tackling them. Political apathy or rejection may be a positive symptom of this lack of congruence of political institutions and political problems, and may be as much a characteristic of adults as of youth.

In putting forward a perspective in which the 'problems' associated with youth can be seen as more general problems, many areas frequently associated with youth have been neglected. The aim of the discussion is, however, not to cover 'youth problems' comprehensively but to argue that a new approach to the subject, which puts it firmly into a framework of dialectical structural change, will prove more fruitful both for the analysis of past work and for future research.

University of Bradford.

[1] 'Archetypal Patterns of Youth' in S. N. Eisenstadt (Editor): *Comparative Social Problems*, New York, 1964, p. 140.

[2] See for instance, Hempel: 'The Logic of Functional Analysis' in L. Gross (Editor): *Symposium on Sociological Theory*, New York, 1959, pp. 271 ff. and D. Lockwood: 'Some Remarks on the Social System,' *British Journal of Sociology*, Vol. VII, No. 2, 1956.

[3] S. N. Eisenstadt: *From Generation to Generation*, Glencoe, 1956.

[4] S. N. Eisenstadt: *op. cit.* p. 323.

[5] Karl Mannheim: 'The Problem of Generations', in *Essays on the Sociology of Knowledge*, Paul Kecskmeti (Ed.), London, 1952, pp. 276-320.

[6] Mannheim's explanation is in vague psychological terms, whereas a sociological explanation appears to be more adequate.

[7] B. Bernstein: 'Social Class and Linguistic Development: a Theory of Social Learning', in A. H. Halsey *et al* (Eds.): *Education, Economy and Society*, Glencoe, 1961, pp. 288-314.

[8] For a discussion of this problem of the relation of parts of the system see David Lockwood: 'Social Integration and System Integration', in G. K. Zollschan and W. Hirsch (Eds.): *Explorations in Social Change*, London 1964, p. 244-56; A. W. Gouldner: 'Reciprocity and Autonomy in Functional Theory', in L. Gross (Ed.): *Symposium on Sociological Theory*, New York, 1959; S. Ossowski: *Class Structure in the Social Consciousness*, London, 1963; and in contrast see T. Parsons: *The Social System*, Glencoe, 1951.

[9] See Chapter Three.

I should like to thank the authors for allowing me to see two other papers prepared by them and to record my appreciation for the many discussions I have had, particularly with Mrs. Keil and Mr. Riddell on aspects of some of the problems discussed in this section, both during and after their work on 'The Young Worker: Adjustment to Work Situations and Adult Rôles', a research project carried out at the University of Leicester of which I was an investigator from 1962-64.

[10] *Ibid*, p. 91

[11] C. M. Fleming: *Adolescence*, London, 1948, Revised ed. 1963.

[12] R. F. Peck and R. J. Havighurst: *The Psychology of Character Development*, New York, 1960.

[13] See, for instance, Percival M. Symonds: *From Adolescence to Adult*, 1961.

[14] The remarks by S. M. Miller in relation to aspirations could well be applied to much of the data on occupational choice and satisfaction/dissatisfaction with work. 'I think that in social research we have been too prone to accept at face value solicited answers to deceptively simple questions; we have been willing to accept reliable scaleable items and have paid much less attention to the problems of validity. I do not believe that we understand enough about working class people at least to use indiscriminately the questionnaire techniques that are so widespread . . . I just do not understand the results and suspect them to be largely artifacts of sociological research production today.' S. M. Miller: 'The Outlook of Working Class Youth', a paper presented at the Annual Meeting of the American Sociological Association, Washington, August 31st, 1962.

[15] S. M. Miller's paper, 'The Outlook of Working Class Youth', *op. cit.* discusses this question with reference to educational drop-outs and the campaign to get young people to stay at school longer.

[16] Social problem oriented sociology would seem to have as one of its primary tasks not the solving of the problem, which in any case is likely to be well beyond the power of the sociologist, but a clarification of the ideological content in the definitions of social problems and the mystification functions of such ideologies.

[17] S. N. Eisenstadt (Ed.): *Comparative Social Problems*, New York, 1964, p. 134 (italics are mine).

[18] Nor as a coloured youth problem where race and age differences are adduced as explanations.

[19] The autobiography of Malcolm X contains very vivid descriptions of the socio-economic dimensions of this problem. *The Autobiography of Malcolm X*, New York, 1964.

[20] S. M. Miller: *op. cit.*

[21] See p. 79.

[22] See, for instance, E. E. Maccoby, R. E. Mathews and A. S. Norton: 'Youth and Political Change', *Public Opinion Quarterly*, Spring 1954, p. 23.

[23] P. Abrams and A. Little: 'The Young Activist in Politics', *British Journal of Sociology*, Vol. XVI, No. 4, December 1965.

[24] *Ibid*, p. 331.

[25] F. Musgrove in his work *Youth and the Social Order*, London, 1964, argues that adults impose a special irresponsible status upon the young and then justify their position by denouncing the young for behaving irresponsibly.

[26] The Labour Party has a long history of conflict with its youth section and deep differences on policy questions have led to closing it down on several occasions. With little effort at political education and virtually no attention to policy decisions passed by youth conferences, the conflict continues. The young are expected to work within given policy and without power to change anything.

[27] See W. Hinton: *Fanshen: A documentary of revolution in a Chinese Village*, New York, 1966, for an analysis of the relation between local institutional arrangements and structural change promoted by the Chinese Communist Party in the years before 1949.

Chapter Ten

SOCIAL STRUCTURE, AWARENESS CONTEXTS AND PROCESSES OF CHOICE*

Jennifer Haystead

The purpose in contributing a further conceptual approach to the multiplicity already existing in the area of first job choice is to suggest an alternative to 'variable analysis'[1] and thus one which is more firmly rooted in current sociological theory. Whereas Keil,[2] and Musgrave[3] utilized a rôle theory approach to occupational choice and thus emphasised the importance of examining the way in which status attributes influence the channels through the social structure which particular groups follow, they gave little attention to the way in which these factors influence the actual process of choice. It is therefore proposed in the present chapter that the concept of 'awareness contexts'[4] provides not only a practically useful but also a theoretically fruitful means of representing the definitions of situations carried out by acting individuals, because they can be related to different processes of choice.

It is generally accepted[5] that the choice process occurs over a considerable period of time and that it is largely irreversible because previous involvement in social organisation differentially channels individuals through the social structure so that they arrive at various 'jumping off' points into the occupational hierarchy. However, confusion and disagreement arises because, although many authors define the term 'occupational choice', they fail to clarify the nature of the phenomena they consider suitable for inclusion. Thus the concept of 'choice' is applied to situations in which:

(a) subjects objectively have a choice between alternative courses of action and are aware that these different alternatives exist and that they can choose between them;

(b) subjects objectively have a choice between alternative courses of action but are not aware that these different alternatives exist;

* This study is related to a research project financed by the Scottish Council for Research in Education. I wish to express my gratitude to A. G. Davis and M. P. Carter for many helpful comments.

(c) subjects objectively do not have a choice between alternative courses of action but think that they do; and

(d) subjects objectively do not have a choice between alternative courses of action and are aware that they do not.

Whether a choice is involved in job entry, and if so when, must be treated as empirically problematic if any meaningful explanation of why particular individuals find themselves in jobs X, Y or Z is to be made. To take the 'if' first. We must ask at different stages: 'to what extent is the individual aware that the situation is or will become problematic and that he must choose between alternative courses of action?' Thus, instead of accounting for occupational entry solely in terms of choice within certain broad limits, we can study the process in terms of a 'career', continually taking account of both the choices made by the individual which commit him in certain directions, and the decisions and actions of others (such as parents, teachers, or Youth Employment Officers) which affect him.

The following example illustrates the advantages accruing from this type of approach. The influence of social class on measured intelligence and thus on the type of schooling, academic achievement and level of job entered, has been given considerable attention in research. However, as Hordley and Lee point out,

> ' . . . scholars have been remarkably willing to assume that the proliferation of certificates and diplomas is automatically accompanied by a strengthening of the link between an individual's general educational attainment and his subsequent level of employment'.[6]

Even if it is the case, such factors can only be considered guide-lines to an individual's choice, because to say that choice was influenced by the academic achievement of an individual, tells us only that the individual did not gain entry to a certain range of occupations. It does not tell us when the individual knew that he could not get in. This is an important consideration, because if the individual was both aware of the formal qualifications required for entry and also attempted to assess his ability to gain these qualifications when he first considered which job he might enter (say during his last term at school), his pattern of choices may be considerably different from another situation where the individual is only aware that he does not possess the required qualifications when he applies for the job. In the former case the individual may have ample opportunity to form a new pattern of preferences, and the experience may lead him to search for information about entry requirements which he previously had not considered; whereas in the latter case, where the situation may be perceived as in need of more urgent resolution, the individual may enter the first job offered to him.

In this connection it is evident that, from the point of view of looking at a decision making process, the choice of the same occupation at two different places is equally important in analysis as the choice between two occupations. For this reason the present discussion is in terms of 'jobs' rather than 'occupations' (which here incorporate the dimensions of locus, occupational category and level in the status hierarchy).

With regard to the 'when' of choice, according to Rosenberg,

> 'One of the most perplexing problems in the study of the occupational choice process is that of figuring out when a decision is actually a final decision. When has an ultimate crystallisation taken place?'[7]

Apart from attention to obvious structural influences (for example, a child leaving school at the age of fifteen to enter employment will have to 'decide' earlier than another who has been offered a place at university at the age of seventeen or eighteen) this problem has been largely ignored. Researchers have been content to break in at different points in the choice process and either ignore the amount of consideration given by the subjects to their future job and/or to assume that a choice has or has not been made. The problem as posed by Rosenberg is misleading in itself because the concept of a 'crystallized choice' raises more problems than it clarifies. A few examples should show what I mean:

Example (1) Individual A chooses job X at time T_1, and at times T_2 and T_E. (T_E being the time of entry into the first job.)

Example (2) Individual B chooses job X at time T_1, job Y at time T_2 and job X at time T_E.

Example (3) Individual C chooses job X at time T_1, job X at time T_2 and job Y at time T_E.

In the first example we could say that the choice was 'crystallized' at time T_1; but what would we do in the case of B in example two? Presumably we would say that his choice was not crystallized until time T_E, but it is quite possible that individual A considered other alternatives and went through the same processes as individual B with one minor difference—that is, that the previous choice remained the choice at time T_2. In the case of the third example, if we suppose that individual C did not enter job X (which we previously may have considered to be his crystallized choice) because he could not get this job but nevertheless intended to try again later—would we say his crystallized choice was job Y at time T_E? These difficulties are avoided if we talk only in terms of job preferences at different points in time and the job entered. We can still see when the job entered was first considered without *post hoc* imputation of a particular degree of certainty in the mind of the subject.

Theoretical disagreement arises concerning the stage in the choice process at which the individual is conscious of the fact that he is acting in such a way as to be influencing his future job. To clarify the differences of opinion, the illustration of the economist's tree of decisions (in which the nodes represent choice points and the branches channels through the social structure) is useful. If the choice of a job can be viewed as 'purposive'[8] behaviour, the tip of a branch would represent the desired objective or level of job and the choice at each node would be made with the effects in mind that this decision will have on the attainment of the desired job or range of jobs. If the behaviour was not purposive, then either the individual would progress along one branch without being aware that he could have followed other branches, or the choice at each node would be made without the objective of a job or range of jobs in view. The individual would thus progress along the branches, continually making decisions or having them made by others, thus opening up the possibilities of following new branches and closing off old ones, with no overall objective that these could be considered steps towards; until finally he arrived at the last node before the tip of the branch, which would constitute his job choice—provided that subjectively there was more than one course of action he could take. Katz and Martin[9], although objecting to the term 'adventitious' which carries overtones of 'accidental' theories, maintain that the latter is the most fruitful way to conceptualise job choice. Thus Katz says 'the nub of the *adventitious* formulation is that immediate situational adaptations can constitute the pathway of entry into a particular occupation.'[10] As a result, stated reasons for the choice may appear 'trivial'[11] unless the subject is aware of and can verbalise the way in which his previous actions and involvement in social organisation have limited his present choice. Further, as is evident from Becker's discussion of the concept of commitment,[12] one may not know at the time to what one has committed oneself, but only after the action begin to realise the side bets (in terms of courses taken or not taken at school, or the energy and time expended on a particular interest and so on) that have committed one to follow a particular course of action.

The discussion so far has made the following points. Any explanation of how a particular individual comes to enter job X must first of all consider whether the individual sees himself as being faced by competing alternatives requiring a 'choice' between them; and if so at which points in the process are these alternatives faced. This leads to the second consideration, which is the nature of the alternatives, because the latter will obviously differ between stages of the choice process. Thus, for example, if the choice is between alternative school courses, we must examine the extent to which the child perceives this choice to be related to the future choice of job or a particular style of life associated with a range of jobs. Finally, consideration must be given to the social structural limitations on the range of alternative possibilities perceived by different categories, including those decisions and actions taken by others which effect these perceived possibilities.

When we arrive at this position we can give further consideration to the 'choice process'. So far it has been suggested that the process of choice must be analysed from the perspective of the individual's constructions of reality. The important components of the definition of the situation with regard to this problem seem to be the following: first, the amount and content of the occupational information which the individual possesses. This will differ because of variations in exposure to occupational information through formal channels—such as career talks, interviews with Youth Employment Officers and teachers—and informal channels—such as conversations with parents or friends—and also because of variations in the extent to which the individual engages in a search for information. For example, it may be that boys engage in a significantly greater amount of activity directed towards finding out such things as the financial rewards of jobs than do girls because of the traditional emphasis on the male as a 'breadwinner'. Secondly, the definition of the situation involves the individual's self-conception. Following Kinch[13] I define the self-conception as 'that organisation of qualities that the individual attributes to himself', and I understand the self-conception as emerging in interaction, so that social rôles both constitute the organising framework in which the self-conception develops and are themselves an integral part of it. Thus the distinguishing content of any individual's self-conception is established during the interplay between the succession of self-images and his goals and values.[14] In turn an individual's self-conception is hypothesised to guide his action and to influence his interpretation of events and other actions.

The conceptualisation of 'awareness contexts' by Glaser and Strauss[15] suggests a possible way in which the important aspects of an individual's definition of the situation with regard to the problem under consideration could be analysed. They give a general definition of an 'awareness context' as 'the total combination of what specific people, groups, organisations, communities or nations know about a specific issue';[16] and they outline four possible types of awareness context which they found to be empirically relevant to the problem of the patient's and other interactants' awareness of the patient's dying. An 'open' awareness context is said to prevail when each interactant is aware of his own identity and his identity in the eyes of the other. A 'pretense' awareness context prevails when both interactants are aware of the identity of the other but pretend not to be. A 'closed' awareness context prevails when one interactant does not know either the other's identity or his own identity as viewed by the other. Finally, a 'suspicion' context prevails when one interactant suspects the identity of the other and/or the other's view of his identity.

The issue in our case is which job 'should' this individual try to enter. Whereas in the example given by Glaser and Strauss an interactant was either aware, suspicious, or unware; in our case many more degrees of awareness are possible because of the various dimensions of knowledge. These include knowledge of the typical job requirements in terms of entrance qualifications, other personal characteristics required or preferred by employees, and competition for entry into this job. Also knowledge of job characteristics in terms of rewards and costs (such as the amount of pay, type of work, hours, training required, chances of promotion and so on). And finally knowledge of the characteristics of the individual in terms of his ability to gain the typically required formal qualifications, his other personal characteristics which may influence his chances of getting a particular job (such as possessing a particular skill, accent or appearance), and his value hierarchy in terms of the rewards and costs that are important to him. The important interactants as regards the choices which ultimately result in an individual's entering a particular job would probably be parents and other relatives, peers, teachers, Youth Employment Officers and/or employers.

Rather than trying to outline all the logical possibilities of knowledge and no knowledge in these areas, I suggest that the following are likely combinations and will exert significant differences on the process of choice.

	'Open' awareness context	'Closed' awareness context	'Partial' awareness context		
(1) Awareness of choice ...	+	—	+	+	—
(2) Knowledge of job requirements ...	+	—	—	—	+
(3) Knowledge of job characteristics ...	+	—	—	—	+
(4) Knowledge of characteristics of individual ...	+	—	—	+	+

+ represents knowledge
— represents no knowledge

An open awareness context, at one extreme, would be the case where the individual himself and all the people offering suggestions, guidance and information were aware that the individual faced a choice between alternatives and possessed complete information about all the possible jobs and attempted to assess his ability to attain and perform them. Obviously this is rarely if ever the case, particularly as there are often no definite requirements for a particular job but rather typically perceived requirements or typical constructions of reality. However, it is more plausible to suggest that for one or a limited number of jobs everyone involved has their own conceptions of these factors. An extreme example of a closed awareness context would be when the individual whom the issue concerns and the people with whom he is interacting are not aware that he can take alternative courses of action and do not possess information about job characteristics and requirements nor about the relevant characteristics of the individual. A partial awareness context would exist if the individual and his interactants possessed knowledge of some of these areas but not others. The examples of partial awareness contexts I have given in the above scheme are: first, where they are aware that a choice is faced but have no knowledge on which to base a decision; secondly (a modification of the first), where they are aware that this is a choice situation and are familiar with the personal characteristics of the individual but have no comparable knowledge of job characteristics and requirements; and thirdly, where, although they possess all the relevant knowledge, they do not realise that this is a choice situation. If account was taken of which kind of interactors possess which knowledge, a very complex description of an awareness context and different types of contexts could be developed. However, for the present purpose of developing a working model from which to derive testable hypotheses about the choice process, the distinctions made above will probably suffice.

To organise a study of the choice process as it is influenced by an individual's changing definitions of the situation, a modification of Glaser and Strauss' paradigm would be useful. The component parts would be a description of:

(1) the given type of awareness context

(2) the structural conditions under which the awareness context exists

(3) the consequent influences upon job choice and the process of choice

(4) the influence of social structural attributes directly on the processes of choice

(5) changes in either self-conceptions or information about jobs that transform the contexts along with the structural conditions for the transformations

(6) the behaviour of various individuals as (or if) they attempt to manage changes of awareness context (e.g. by a search for occupational information) and

(7) the consequences of different awareness contexts and transformations on the process of choice and thus on the final choice or entry into a particular job.

The type of awareness context prevailing would depend on first, the stage at which, if ever, the individual and the important interactants were aware of the fact that the individual had a choice between alternative courses of action, and that his choice would effect the job ultimately entered by the individual. Secondly, the range of knowledge of the job characteristics and typical requirements outlined above of both the individual whom the issue concerns and the people with whom he is interacting. And thirdly, the extent and type of consideration given to an analysis of self by the individual and of the individual's characteristics as outlined above by other inter-actors. Thus the influence of social structural attributes on the aware-ness context means that the factors considered in a choice will differ. Remembering that job choice is an accumulation of prior com-mitments, consciously or unconsciously made, and that for some children the choice has to be made at the age of fifteen or sixteen whereas for others it is a more gradual process of narrowing the field by choices (such as which courses to undertake at the higher education level) with perhaps more opportunity to become socialised into an occupational rôle, it becomes evident that social class, through its influence on the academic achievement of the individual, is an important attribute. Social class may also influence the type of aware-ness context prevailing through the emphasis on the importance of a 'career', or a 'secure job', which may differ more markedly be-tween boys and girls in the working class than between the sexes in the middle classes.

The influence of different awareness contexts upon the choice process brings us to a consideration of the way in which a choice is made between competing alternatives. There is general agreement amongst authors who have paid any attention to this problem[17] that the choice consists of a compromise. As Simon states:

> 'In an important sense, all decision is a matter of compromise . . . . . The environmental situation inevitably limits the alternatives that are available, and hence sets a maximum to the level of attainment of pur-pose that is possible. The final decision will depend both on the relative weight that is given to the different objectives and on the judgment as to the extent to which any given plan will attain each objective.'[18]

Discussion of the manner in which an individual arrives at a decision has been confused by the job, occupation, or level of occupations being considered as the 'end' and the chosen means of attaining this end being treated as more or less 'rational'. Thus, when job choice is treated as purposive behaviour in that actions are considered to be guided by an occupational goal, it is 'rational' in so far as the individ-ual selects alternatives which are conducive to the achievement of the previously selected goals.[19] However, as Katz points out, the 'adventitious' approach to the choice process does not imply irrational behaviour. Rather, the extent of rationality we attribute to the utilization of means is dependent upon what we are considering as the end.

> 'To be sure the adaptations may not be rationally geared to occupational choice but may instead be addressed to other problems that seem to be more pressing at the time. This may be irrational, or nonrational, as far as occupational choice is concerned, but entirely rational as far as coping with immediate circumstances.'[20]

As sociologists we are interested in the ways in which social structural factors affect the process of choice irrespective of whether these processes are judged by any formal criteria to be 'rational' with respect to the attainment of any analytically defined goal. Thus Garfinkel, following Schutz,[21] makes an important contribution when he says:

> 'Instead of the properties of rationality being treated as a methodological principle for interpreting activity, they are to be treated only as empirically problematic material. They would have the status only of data and would have to be accounted for in the same way that the more familiar properties of conduct are accounted for.'[22]

Three of the most applicable of the possible 'rationalities' outlined by Garfinkel[23] have already been introduced into this discussion. They are: first, the degree of awareness of the possibility of exercising a choice and the amount of consideration given to the choice; secondly, the clarity and objectivity of the individual's definition of the situation; and thirdly, the extent to which the individual anticipates the alterations which his actions will produce on both this goal and other goals or courses of action (which was implied in the reference to the realisation of commitment involved in a particular course of action). However, the 'search for means' has not been mentioned. Here Garfinkel refers to the fact that an individual looks for rules of procedure which in his past experience gave the practical effects he now desires, to the frequency of this search and to his ability to employ techniques that worked in other situations in the present situation. The influence of social structural attributes on the way in which a choice is made, is an area which has been of little concern to either sociologists in general or occupational choice theorists. However, relationships which could be profitably examined are the ways in which different socialization patterns and previous experiences (for example as between different social classes and the sexes) influence the way in which they manage a situation in which alternative courses of action are open to them. For example, it may be that practice in decision making in other areas, such as choosing one's own clothes or spending one's pocket money, may enable the individual to balance the rewards and costs accruing from a particular line of action in a more far-sighted way. Similarly it may be that some groups attach more importance to decisions which are seen to be related to one's future job and this may result in differences in the amount of time and energy expended in reaching a solution. Finally, it is possible that some kinds of home background are more likely to present the child with the opportunity to make up his own mind rather than merely to acquiesce to the opinions of parents, which would mean that a different strategy would have to be adopted by the child.

In sum, whereas existing research has based its postulation of a particular process of choice on an assumed type of rationality, it is proposed here that only when we have answered the questions about how different social structural groups make a choice when they perceive themselves to be faced by competing alternatives, can we see in what sense these courses of action could be described as 'rational'.

The first problem is to establish how different categories make a choice when they see themselves as faced by competing alternatives —which may be along a status dimension, a situs dimension or both— or simply between alternative jobs within the same occupational status and situs group. Sherlock and Cohen's[24] research in this area provides a useful illustration of the influence of an open awareness context on the choice process. These authors suggest that in the case of the pre-dental students they studied, a 'minimax' strategy was employed in the choice of dentistry as an occupation. That is, dentistry was chosen because it combined high rewards with a reasonable degree of access.

> 'Medicine, although possessing greater rewards, was rejected because of difficult access; while law, university teaching and accountancy were rejected because of perceived lower rewards.'

The 'minimax' principle was originally a suggestion of a possible normative approach to decision making under uncertainty. In this situation the individual was assumed to know all the possible alternatives and all the consequences which might result from each alternative, but the uncertainty arose in that the probabilities of specific outcomes were unknown, or perhaps not even meaningful. It was suggested that 'economic man', who was assumed to make his choice so as to 'maximise' something, should select that alternative which had as it worst outcome the loss which was smallest. Attempts have been made to modify the characteristics of 'economic man' for use in descriptive theories of decision making, notably by Simon.[25] He points out that 'administrative' or 'social man' makes his choice using a simplified picture of the situation that takes into account just a few of the factors he regards as most important and relevant for his purposes, that he has a limited knowledge of the possible alternatives and consequences, and finally, Simon suggests, social man 'satisfies' rather than 'maximises'. That is, he chooses that alternative which is satisfactory rather than the best possible alternative. These characteristics of social man bring the demands on his computational abilities into a more realistic perspective. Although Sherlock and Cohen do not discuss this point it would seem that the pre-dental students were operating their strategy in these limited terms as it was an action 'performed by living human beings in situations defined by them'[26] and it could perhaps be more clearly termed a 'minisat' than a 'minimax' strategy. Methodological inadequacies, however, prevent their study from providing substantial support for even this.[27]

If the type of process described by these authors was to be an adequate representation of the procedures utilized by a particular group, it would mean, first, that an open awareness context prevailed. They assume that the subjects were aware of the fact that they could choose between alternative courses of action and that these alternatives differed chiefly with respect to the situs dimension; that they had knowledge of other alternatives in terms of the requirements and characteristics such as financial rewards; and that they attempted to implement their own value hierarchy in terms of the rewards and costs that were important to them. Secondly, it would mean that the subjects were capable of balancing the rewards and costs accruing from the various alternatives considered. Given these necessary characteristics, it becomes obvious that this type of strategy could only be a description of the procedure for a limited number of the population.

To illustrate further the way in which awareness contexts could influence the process of choice, we will take an example at the opposite extreme. This would be where choices up to the point of entering the labour market (for example, choice of school courses) were made in a relatively closed awareness context with respect to the future job. This would seem to be most likely for adolescents classified by the school system as 'low achievers' because they will not have faced or have had brought to their attention the choice situation of further education' to the same extent as their 'higher achieving' peers. They are also required to make an earlier job choice for they cannot delay entry into employment by prolonging their period of formal education. They have thus had less time to think about their future careers. As they have probably been socialised into expecting different kinds of rewards from work (for example, monetary rather than 'self-fulfilment') their whole conception of the meaning of work may differ and thus the importance attached to making a decision. Evidence that this is the case for some fifteen year old school leavers is provided by Carter's[28] study of a hundred boys and a hundred girls selected at random from five of Sheffield's secondary modern schools in 1959. He mentions that

'Children were keen to get started no matter what the job was, especially if their friends had already obtained jobs. They, too, wanted to get fixed up as soon as possible. The idea of waiting for the job of their choice did not occur to most of them'.[29]

This, in turn, would preclude any sustained attempt to change the awareness context by a positive search for information. In fact, in our example,

'Children's *knowledge of the employment structure of Sheffield was very limited*, and as a result several found themselves in jobs which they had not thought of at all until the opportunity occurred. Knowledge of vacancies was even more limited'.[30]

Other indications that the awareness context was relatively closed were the fact that some children remembered very little about the Youth Employment Officer's school talk and that few children were interested in the guidance and discussion aspects of their interview with the Youth Employment Officer. Further only

'Two-thirds of the children remembered that their teachers had spoken to them about jobs. Most children were vague about what had been said . . . . . The vagueness was due to the children's lack of interest, but also to the brief and casual way in which employment had been mentioned . . . . '[31]

Similarly, Carter points out that the ability of the majority of parents to advise on the choice of work was very limited and that there was little attempt to discuss the subject of work. Finally,

'Only one-quarter of the boys and two-fifths of the girls had discussed what jobs to aim at with friends who were still at school, or who had left school before them.'[32]

As a result the children's first awareness that a choice situation exists may be when alternatives are presented to them by such people as parents, teachers or Youth Employment Officers. As the alternatives presented in all probability will be those 'suitable' for them in terms of educational qualifications, the factor of 'ease of access' may not be treated as significant or, alternatively, be thought of in terms of the mechanisms of application (for example, if a relative offers to put their name on the list of applicants at the place where he works). It may be unimportant which job is entered if there is little difference in the rewards and costs of the presented alternatives. Given that the rewards are similar, the final choice may be based on a comparison of the costs of entering the different jobs—such as the distance from home. Alternatively it may be only the rewards which are perceived as differing significantly, so that the choice is made by weighing the advantages of, for example, getting more pay as against going to work at the same place as a friend. These 'low ability' adolescents could perhaps also not be expected to perform a complicated balancing of factors to the same extent as the students studied by Sherlock and Cohen.

To summarize the argument in conclusion. The actual process of first job choice has been neglected. It is suggested that rather than constructing rational models of choice for testing, it is more useful to examine the types of rationality exhibited by different groups. This approach then focuses on the problems of, first, whether the subjects are 'aware' of the fact that they are faced by competing alternatives. Secondly, it emphasizes the importance of examining their definition of the possible alternatives. The concept of awareness contexts provides a means of expressing different types of situations which may exist and which can then be related to varying processes of choice. We would expect that variations in alternatives available, knowledge about these alternatives, the degree of previous commitment to a particular alternative or range of alternatives and the subject's awareness of this, will influence the way in which a choice is made. Finally, if we examine the different types of rationality of choice exhibited by groups occupying varying social structural positions, attention must be given to the amount of consideration given to the choice. This may be influenced by such things as the age at which a choice must be made, the amount of time before a definite commitment is required, and whether the individual has previously or regularly made important decisions and has thus implicitly or explicitly worked out some kind of decision making procedure. Only when we have documented the ways in which both previous experiences and particular awareness contexts at different points in time influence the actual processes of choice, can we attempt to present an integrated picture of the way in which choices are made by particular groups and thus account for the final entry into a job.

University of Aberdeen.

[1] H. Blumer: 'Sociological Analysis and the "Variable"', *Amer. Sociol. Rev.*, 21, 1956, pp. 683-690.

[2] See Chapter Three.

[3] See Chapter Four.

[4] B. G. Glaser and A. Strauss: 'Awareness Contexts and Social Interaction', *Amer. Sociol. Rev.*, 29, 1964, pp. 669-679.

[5] This stems from the work of E. Ginzberg, S. W. Ginsberg, S. Axelrad and J. L. Herma: *Occupational Choice: An Approach to a General Theory*, Columbia U.P., New York, 1951.

[6] I. Hordley and D. J. Lee: 'The Alternative Route—Social Change and Opportunity in Technical Education', *Sociology*, 4, January, 1970, p. 41.

[7] M. Rosenberg: *Occupations and Values*, Free Press, New York, 1957, p. 81.

[8] The classification of 'purposive' and 'adventitious' approaches to occupational choice was suggested by B. Sherlock and A. Cohen: 'A Strategy of Occupational Choice: Recruitment to Dentistry', *Soc. Forces*, 44, 1966, pp. 303-313.

[9] T. E. Katz and H. W. Martin: 'Career Choice Processes', *Soc. Forces*, 41, 1962, pp. 149-154.

[10] T. E. Katz: 'A Comment on "The Strategy of Occupational Choice: Recruitment to Dentistry"', *Soc. Forces*, 45, 1966, p. 120.

[11] Remarked upon by T. Caplow: *The Sociology of Work*, McGraw Hill, New York, 1954, p. 218.

[12] H. S. Becker: 'Notes on the Concept of Commitment', *Amer. J. Sociol.*, 66, 1960, pp. 32-40.

[13] J. W. Kinch: 'Research Note. A Formalized Theory of the Self-Concept', *Amer. J. Sociol.*, 68, 1963, pp. 481-486.

[14] R. H. Turner: 'The Self-Conception in Social Interaction', in C. Gordon and K. J. Gergen (Eds.): *The Self in Social Interaction: Classic and Contemporary Perspectives*, Wiley, New York, 1968, pp. 93-106.

[15] Glaser and Strauss: *op. cit.*, 1964; and B. G. Glaser and A. L. Strauss: *Awareness of Dying*, Aldine, Chicago, 1965.

[16] Glaser and Strauss: *op. cit.*, 1965, p. 670.

[17] Notable examples are Ginzberg *et al.*: *op. cit.*; P. M. Blau *et al.*: 'Occupational Choice: A Conceptual Framework', *Ind. & Lab. R.*, 9, 1956, pp. 531-543; D. E. Super: *The Psychology of Careers*, Harper, New York, 1957; Rosenberg: *op. cit.*; B. S. Philips: 'Expected Value Deprivation and Occupational Preference', *Sociometry*, 27, 1964, pp. 151-160; F. G. Caro and C. T. Philblad: 'Aspirations and Expectations: A Re-examination of the Bases for Social Class Differences in the Occupational Orientations of Male High School Students', *Sociol. and Soc. Research*, 49, 1965, pp. 465-475; Sherlock and Cohen: *op. cit.*; and J. Ford and S. Box: See Chapter Five.

[18] H. A. Simon: *Administrative Behavior*, Second Edition, Macmillan, New York, 1957, p. 6.

[19] For example Ford and Box on p. 112, suggest that 'There is now general agreement that this phenomenon is to be viewed as a *rational process* by which certain desired ends are weighed against the perceived probability of their attainment.' Their footnote 16 points out that they believe it will more usually be a *Wertrational* than a *Zweckrational* process, presumably because either an end may not be weighed against others, and/or account may not be taken of the effects of other goals or courses of action which the attainment of an end may produce. (See M. Weber: *The Theory of Social and Economic Organsation* (edited by T. Parsons), Macmillan, New York, 1947, footnote p. 115.) However, because they do not discuss the different levels of choice in terms of the competing alternatives at different stages in the choice process, they imply that both university undergraduates and fifteen year old school leavers exhibit the same type and degree of rationality in the process of arriving at a decision.

[20] Katz: *op. cit.*, pp. 120 and 121.

[21] A. Schutz: 'The Problem of Rationality in the Social World', *Economica*, 10, 1943, pp. 130-149.

[22] H. Garfinkel: 'The Rational Properties of Scientific and Common Sense Activities', in *Studies in Ethnomethodology*, Prentice-Hall, New Jersey, 1967, p. 282.

[23] Garfinkel: *op. cit.*, pp. 262-283.

[24] Sherlock and Cohen: *op. cit.*

[25] H. A. Simon: 'Rational Choice and the Structure of the Environment', *Psychol. Rev.*, 63, 1956, pp. 129-138 and 'A Behavioural Model of Rational Choice', *Quart. J. Econ.*, 69, 1955, pp. 99-118.

[26] A. Schutz: 'Common Sense and Scientific Interpretation of Human Action', in M. Natanson (Ed.): *Philosophy of the Social Sciences*, Random House, 1963, p. 345.

[27] See Katz: *op. cit.*, and also B. Sherlock and A. Cohen: 'Adventitious Versus Purposive Occupational Choice: A Reply to Katz', *Soc. Forces*, 45, 1966, p. 282.

[28] M. P. Carter: *Home, School and Work*, Pergamon, Oxford, 1962.

[29] Carter: *op. cit.*, p. 149.

[30] Carter: *op. cit.*, p. 150.

[31] Carter: *op. cit.* pp. 101-102.

[32] Carter: *op. cit.*, p. 100.

Chapter Eleven

SOME FACTORS AFFECTING THE CAREER CHOICE AND CAREER PERCEPTIONS OF SIXTH FORM SCHOOL LEAVERS

Stuart R. Timperley and Alison M. Gregory

Much discussion at present surrounds the relationship between those sections of society concerned with the supply and demand elements of manpower—the educational system and the world of work. The concern has been with the wider needs of society and the more specific needs of organisations on the one hand, and the freedom of individual choice on the other. The importance of this relationship and its inherent difficulties has been commented on by Crichton in discussing the implications of the changing social context for the personal policies of organisations. She states that 'education of individuals in a democratic society must necessarily be more than a vocational preparation for work. Yet work is so dominant in importance . . . . . that the relationship between education and employment is a vital one.'[1] The need to improve the link between the educational system and the world of work has been referred to by Ginzberg as one of our most intractable manpower problems.[2] It is not only the relationship between the educational and employment systems that it is causing concern, but, as the Robbins Report pointed out, there exists a need for much closer co-operation between the institutions of higher education and the schools.[3]

It has been noted that the educational and occupational systems are very closely related in industrial societies, and that the fit between them is very close.[4] Certainly the systems do relate, but the relationship is not a simple one, as Blau has pointed out.[5] Most theoretical discussions of occupational choice refer to the entry into employment as part of a process, though opinions are divided as to the extent and complexity of this process. Blau refers to occupational choice as 'a process involving a series of decisions';[6] Ginzberg regards it as 'a developmental process'.[7] Super, whilst adopting the developmental approach of Ginzberg, draws attention to the 'compromise process' involved.[8] British writers, too, in arguing for an adequate theoretical framework, have emphasised that occupational choice is a

© Stuart R. Timperley and Alison M. Gregory 1971 (This article was first published in *The Sociological Review*, Vol. 19, No. 1, February 1971.)

part of a process. Roberts argues that the sociologists' interest in the entry into employment should take into account the two processes of occupational rôle allocations and socialisation.[9] Keil, in discussing reactions towards working life, indicates that entering the world of work and developing in it is a process.[10] In discussing the limitations of this approach, Musgrave argues that a theory of occupational choice should cover the whole process of first choice of occupation and take account of influences operating on any individual from birth onwards as well as covering subsequent job choice; this he sees primarily in terms of the process of socialisation,[11] a concept suggested by Keil.[12] The rationality of the process of occupational choice is emphasised by Ford and Box, when certain divided ends are weighed against the perceived probability of their attainment.[13]

Clearly there are different theoretical orientations to the concept of occupational choice, but as Ford and Box indicate, it would appear that 'most sociological discussions of occupational choice have converged'[14] and that it is possible to discern a pattern underlying most of these theories; a pattern which White refers to as the 'process of occupational choice'.[15]

Of course, occupational choice itself is but part of a wider process. Merton has referred to recruitment, occupational choice and allocation to occupations as simply three aspects of the same process, in that they are all concerned with the flow of personnel into the employment system.[16] Ensuring the best possible fit between the educational and employment systems is a manpower planning problem at both organisational and national levels; a problem of matching the supply characteristic of the labour force with the demand feature of employment opportunities.[17]

This chapter is concerned with the effectiveness of the flow of personnel from the school sixth form into the higher education and employment systems, and represents an attempt to examine the aspirations and expectations of sixth form leavers, the information which influences their career perceptions and their image of industry. Most entry into employment takes place at one of three points: at the minimum school leaving age, after a sixth form course, or on the completion of a course of higher education. The research reported here is part of a larger project to investigate not only the entry into employment of young 'high talent manpower' or 'strategic human capital',[18] but the utilization or socialisation of such manpower by the employment system, as this will obviously affect subsequent job mobility.

The research was carried out at thirteen secondary schools in the Merseyside area. Five of the schools were boys' grammar schools, four were girls' grammar schools, one was a girls' direct grant school, and there were three mixed comprehensive schools. Questionnaires were sent out to these schools to be answered by students mid-way through their final sixth form year and who were about to take Advanced level subjects in the G.C.E. examinations. 431 replies were received, from 233 girls and 198 boys. The major areas of interest in this enquiry were educational intentions, career aspirations and expectations, the relative importance of information sources in choosing a job and the general image of industry and commerce. In addition, relevant information was obtained on subjects to be taken at 'A' level and parental occupation.

Career Aspirations and Expectations

There have been doubts expressed as to whether or not choice is made in terms of an occupation, a job or a career; and whether or

TABLE I

Career Aspirations of Sixth Form School Leavers

Sector of Economy		Total		No. specifying Job	No. not specifying Job
			Numbers wishing to work in each area		
Agriculture	... ...	14	3.3%	8	6
Industry and Commerce	...	113	26.4%	76	37
Professional Practice	...	20	4.7%	16	4
Medicine	... ...	30	7.0%	22	8
Education	... ...	114	26.4%	57	57
Government Service	...	37	8.6%	27	10
Armed Forces	... ...	3	0.7%	3	0
Church	... ...	0	0%	0	0
Journalism Arts Entertainment	...	44	10.1%	27	17
Research	... ...	44	10.1%	30	14
Other	... ...	9	2.1%	8	1
Non respondents	... ...	3	0.7%	—	—
Total	...	431	100%	273	154

not a choice is actually made, or whether it is more appropriate to talk in terms of 'drift'[19] or in terms of orientation to particular 'settings'.[20] It is contended here that it is most meaningful in this context to ascertain initially the *area or sector* of the economy in which a student desires or expects to work, and then to determine the degree of specificity which they express for a *particular occupation or job* within the chosen sector.

The students were asked, first, to identify which of the listed sectors of the economy they would *most like* to work in, and, if possible, to specify the job they would most like to do within the chosen sector. Results are shown in Table I.

The industrial and commercial sector and the educational sector are each aspired to by over a quarter of the sample and are by far the most desired career areas. Other sectors which appear desirable include journalism, arts and entertainment (10.1 per cent), research (10.1 per cent), government service (8.6 per cent) and medicine (7 per cent). The significance of these aspirations can really only be seen, however, in conjunction with the expectations of the students, and accordingly they were also asked to indicate

TABLE II

Career Expectations of Sixth Form School Leavers

		Numbers expecting to work in each area		
Sector of Economy		Total		No. specifying Job	No. not specifying Job
Agriculture	7	1.6%	4	3
Industry and Commerce ...	132	30.6%	75	57
Professional Practice ...	13	3.1%	9	4
Medicine	28	6.5%	17	11
Education	158	36.6%	59	99
Government Service ...	35	8.1%	13	22
Armed Forces	2	0.5%	1	1
Church	0	0%	0	0
Journalism ⎫ Arts ⎬ ... ... Entertainment ⎭	12	2.8%	6	6
Research	14	3.2%	4	10
Other ... ′... ...	5	1.2%	4	1
Non respondents	25	5.8%	—	—
Total ...	431	100%	192	214

the sectors of the economy they *expected* to work in, and again, if possible, to specify the job they would most like to do within the chosen sector. Results are shown in Table II.

The relationship between aspirations (or preferences) and expectations has been noted by Blau, who sees the eventual course of action on which an individual decides as reflecting a compromise between preferences and expectations.[21] Super also refers to the inter-relationship between aspirations and expectations, in that the eventual choice is seen as a compromise which is constantly being modified by experience in searching for a career.[22] In this instance it is interesting to note the stability between the aspirations and expectations of those students wishing to enter both medicine and government service. Both show a very small drop from aspiration to expectation, but it is apparent that the experience of students wishing to enter these categories has, if anything, hardened their commitment to these sectors.

Perhaps the most interesting points to emerge are the decline of the more glamorous areas—journalism, arts and entertainment —as from aspirations to expectations (10.1 per cent to 2.8 per cent); and the increase in the numbers of students expecting to enter industry and commerce (26.4 per cent to 30.6 per cent) and education (26.4 per cent to 36.6 per cent). In addition, there is an interesting but forseeable increase in the numbers of non-respondents to the questions on expectations.

It would appear that there is an element of fantasy in the desire of over a fifth of the sample to enter the arts, journalism and entertainment, and research sectors, as only a small number expect to work in these areas eventually. These are the two sectors where there is a significant drop when expectations are considered, and this must be examined in conjunction with the increase in numbers expecting to enter industry and commerce, and education. In fact, these two major areas, together with the non-respondents, are the only sectors which actually increase when expectations are considered, and it is assumed that they account for those individuals who were unconvinced as to their abilities to obtain jobs in the areas of their choice. Given these circumstances, it is possible to agree tentatively with the conclusions of Liversidge that the aspirations of school leavers in this country are of a realistic nature.[23] There are, however, certain qualifications to be made at this point, mainly concerning the confusion that surrounds the two concepts of aspirations and expectations. It has been said, for example, that 'investigators have noted, and sometimes been dismayed by the realism of the aspirations of some young people in this country.'[24] Yet Roberts in saying that 'it is a well established fact that British school leavers' ambitions are realistically modest', indicates that these ambitions appear to be based on occupations they expect to enter rather than on their aspirations.[25] Liversidge, too, in talking of a 'startlingly accurate appraisal of life chances by school leavers',[26] appears to interpret life chances in terms of expectations rather than aspirations. The difficulty lies in the interpretation given to the concept of aspiration. In this context it appears that for more than three-quarters of the sample their aspirations and expectations coincided—a fact which does illustrate the inter-relationship between the two factors and that aspirations are realistically based. Yet there is still the fact that over one-fifth of the sample do not feel that their aspirations are likely to be met, and accordingly expect to enter other sectors—in fact industry, commerce and education. To this extent, therefore, their expectations are realistic or modest.

The fact that this minority appear to have accepted that they actually will go into industry and commerce or education, highlights a not altogether satisfactory situation; namely that these areas are likely to become 'dumping grounds' for those students who do not think they will succeed in working in the sector of the economy in which they would ideally choose to work (analysis shows that as many as 15 per cent of the total sample may fall into this category). This is further emphasised by an examination of the specificity of job choice within each of the areas. Taking the two major sectors of industry and commerce, and education, it is clear that the number of students able to specify a job within these sectors is very similar in terms of both aspirations and expectations. The real difference comes with those students unable to specify a job in the sector within which they expect to work; an increase from 37 to 57 students in the case of industry and commerce, and from 59 to 99 students in the case of education.

The concept of job specificity can also be utilized to illustrate the fact that some students have a fairly strong commitment to an occupational area, and that whilst aspirations can be seen in terms of levels of particular jobs or professions (as in the classical level of aspiration theory[27]) it can also be examined in terms of aspiration to work in a particular economic sector. For example, the numbers of students wishing to enter medicine and government service were 30 and 37 respectively, of whom a relatively high proportion could be specific about the job they wished to do (22 and 27). The number of students expecting to work in these sectors remained constant (28 and 35), but the number of people able to specify jobs in these sectors dropped considerably. It would appear that, for certain reasons, students were determined to work in their desired sectors, even if they were unable to obtain their desired job.

Sex, Family Background and 'A' Level Subjects

Given that the two sectors of industry and commerce, and education account for the aspirations of over half the sample, it might be useful at this stage to examine the characteristics of those sudents who wish to enter these two sectors (particularly as it appears they also expect to enter these sectors), as well as examining the characteristics of the sample as a whole.

The sample was composed of 46 per cent boys and 54 per cent girls (see Table III).

TABLE III

Sex Distribution of Sample of Sixth Form Pupils

Sex			Total		Those wishing to enter Industry and Commerce		Those wishing to enter Education	
Male	...	...	198	46%	78	68.5%	22	19.3%
Female	...	...	233	54%	35	31.5%	92	80.7%
Total	...	...	431	100%	113	100%	114	100%

A significant point emerges from an analysis of the sex of the students wishing to enter industry and commerce and of those wishing to enter education. Of the students wishing for an industrial or commercial career, there are twice as many males as females (78:35). Amongst the students wishing to enter education the balance changes completely and it can be seen that there are four times as many females as males in this category (22:92). The situation exists, therefore, where nearly half of all female leavers desire to work in the education sector, whilst only 22 per cent of the male leavers wish to do so.

In terms of social class distribution (see Table IV) there appears to be a normal distribution, with most of the students coming from the intermediate and skilled classes. However, those students wishing to enter industry and commerce were more likely to come from the third social class category (skilled), and a higher proportion of those wishing to enter education come from the first social class category (professional) than was the case for the group wishing to enter industry and commerce.

TABLE IV

Social Class Distribution of Sixth Form Pupils

Social Class		Total	Those wishing to enter Industry and Commerce	Those wishing to enter Education
Professional	...	43	9	15
Intermediate	...	154	41	41
Skilled	...	174	48	39
Partly Skilled	...	17	4	5
Unskilled	...	7	3	2
Non respondents	...	36	8	12
Total	...	431	113	114

An examination of the subjects being taken at 'A' level (see Table V) raises a number of issues; perhaps the most important of which is that over 70 per cent of all those wishing to enter the educational sector were taking either languages or general arts subjects at 'A' level, and that only 12.3 per cent were taking science subjects. If this is taken a stage further, it can be seen that of the 168 people taking science 'A' levels, only 73 wanted to go into either industry and commerce or education. Even allowing for the fact that some of the remainder will modify their aspirations and expect to enter these sectors, this does not alleviate the manpower problem of schools, industry and commerce in recruiting scientists.

A further breakdown by sex, 'A' level subjects and orientation to industry and commerce or education, illustrates the same interesting sex differentials. For example, taking those students wishing to enter industry and commerce, then of those taking science subjects (60), four-fifths were likely to be male; of those taking general arts subjects (36), three-quarters were male; and of those taking languages (16), four-fifths were female. Even greater differentials occur amongst those students wishing to enter education. Given that nearly three-

TABLE V

Advanced Level Subjects to be Taken by Sixth Form Pupils

Subjects	Total		Those Wishing to enter Industry and Commerce	Those wishing to enter Education
Science	168	38.8%	60	13
General and Practical	23	5.8%	1	18
Languages	84	19.4%	16	35
General Arts ...	156	36.0%	36	47
Total	431	100%	113	113

quarters of these students were taking general arts or language subjects, it appears that over seven times as many female as male students
fall into this category; and that even in the other subject areas—
science and general and practical—there are more females than males.
The problem of the lack of science teachers would therefore appear
to be even more specific to male science teachers, and the excessive
proportion of potential women arts and language teachers must give
some cause for concern.

One other breakdown was attempted in order to see if there was
a relationship between the students' mothers' employment situation
and the students' aspirations. Just over half of the mothers were
either in full- or part-time employment and, again taking aspirations
to work in the two major sectors, it would appear that those students
with an educational orientation are more likely to come from homes
where the mother is in full- or part-time employment than are those
with an industrial orientation (see Table VI).

TABLE VI

Mothers' Employment Situation of Sixth Form Pupils

Mothers' Employment	Total		Those wishing to enter Industry and Commerce		Those wishing to enter Education	
Full-time ...	97	22.4%	22	19.5%	26	23.0%
Part-time ...	126	29.0%	29	25.6%	38	33.6%
Non working ...	205	47.3%	62	54.9%	48	41.7%
Non respondents	3	1.3%	0	0.0%	2	1.7%
Total	431	100%	113	100%	114	100%

Educational Intentions

It is to be expected that the great majority of sixth form leavers wish to enter full-time higher education, and this was apparent in this study, for of the total sample, some 87 per cent hoped to enter higher education after leaving school. Of course, this high figure is made up of students who possessed different probabilities of entering higher education, and an attempt was made in the questionnaire to differentiate between these perceived probabilities, and to relate this to the aspiration to enter certain sectors of the economy (see Table VII). Students were asked if they would be continuing their full-time education after leaving school, and were required to reply according to their degree of certainty.

TABLE VII
Further Education Intentions of Sixth Form Pupils

Educational Intentions	Total		Those wishing to enter Industry and Commerce		Those wishing to enter Education	
Definitely intending to continue ...	234	54.2%	44	38.9%	91	80.2%
Hoping to continue and thinking it likely ...	135	31.5%	48	42.5%	20	17.4%
Hoping to continue and thinking it unlikely	12	2.8%	1	0.8%	0	0.0%
Definitely not intending to continue ...	31	7%	14	12.4%	1	0.8%
Don't know ...	19	4.5%	6	5.4%	2	1.6%
Total	431	100%	113	100%	114	100%

From this further breakdown it can be seen that the 87 per cent of the total wishing to continue to higher education is made up largely of groups with slightly different probabilities of actual entry, i.e. those who definitely intended to continue (54.2 per cent), those who hoped to continue and thought it likely (31.5 per cent), and those who hoped to continue and thought it unlikely (2.8 per cent). There could be a number of reasons for the individuals choosing any of these categories; for example, those with the greater feeling of certainty could represent the more able students who thus felt more confident about their chances of entry, or it could be that they had already been accepted for higher education, or perhaps it could be explained in some cases by entry into certain areas being conditional upon the student undertaking higher education. It certainly seems reasonable to assume that, to some extent, the group who felt more certain of entry represented students who conformed to the above descriptions. If one therefore assumes this, it is interesting to compare those students aspiring to industry and commerce with those wishing to enter education, in terms of the firmness of their educational intentions.

The degree of certainty of entry into higher education appears to be very much more positive among those with an eventual desire to enter the educational sector of the economy. Of course, entry into education is very much dependent on the student first having been through some part of the higher education system, and this obviously is reflected in the high degree of certainty illustrated. Of those students wishing to enter industry and commerce, over 80 per cent were hoping to enter higher education, but half of these were slightly less certain about their chances of doing so. It would appear, therefore, that the expectations of entering higher education are less certain amongst those aspiring to an industrial or commercial career than amongst those aspiring to an educational career. It could be a fruitful area for further research to investigate the reasons for this disparity, as there are likely to be implications for the personnel policies of industrial and commercial organisations. For example, if it could be shown that the lower expectations of entry into higher education of students wishing an industrial or commercial career were borne out in practice, then industry and commerce could be recruiting people for whom an immediate industrial or commercial career was essentially a second choice. In addition, the question could be asked whether or not industrial and commercial organisations regard it as inevitable and/or satisfactory that their potential recruits have a lower expectation of entering higher education.

One tangible point that can be made at this stage relating to recruitment policies in general, is that the students available for employment immediately after leaving the sixth form will consist of two main groups; first, those who actually wish to leave at this stage (and it should be noted that the process leading to this decision may well be extremely complex), and secondly, those who have not been accepted into the higher education system (in other words their aspirations and very probably their expectations have not been met). A recent sixth form survey in one hundred northern schools, for example, showed that some ten per cent of all sixth formers intending to enter higher education would in fact have to enter employment,[28] and there is no reason to think that this present sample will differ very significantly in this respect. Following on from this, it is probably incorrect to talk in terms of sixth form leavers as students who have decided that they really want to enter employment at this stage. It is likely that of those actually leaving to enter employment, half will regard immediate employment as a second best choice, and that of the other half the reasons for wishing to enter employment may have little to do with a well thought out decision about the benefits of early entry. Keil, for example, points out that 'choice' is probably too strong a word to use, in that it indicates some rational assessment of abilities and opportunities which does not really characterise sixth form leavers.[29]

Sources of Information on Career Choice

Given the complexity of the process of movement from the sixth form to the world of work, it follows that one of the most important influences on an individual's career choice, or perception, is the amount and quality of information he or she receives about sectors of the economy, occupational areas and specific jobs. A number of writers have emphasised the importance of adequate information in the process of career choice, and at the same time have drawn attention to a situation in which there is a lack of such information. Blau, for example, draws attention to the way in which occupational choice is restricted by lack of knowledge about existing opportunities,[30] and Carter has argued that much subsequent job changing arises out of inadequate help and guidance during the process of job choice.[31] Roberts, in discussing the limited nature of the knowledge of school leavers about occupations, draws attention to the fact that not only is the job information possessed by school leavers minimal, but that it is also difficult for a young person to acquire any sort of comprehensive job knowledge.[32]

The information which a student gets about possible future careers can come from a number of sources. Musgrave sees the family, the school and the peer group as important influences in the context of pre-work socialisation, and formal outside influences, such as the Youth Employment Service, as related to the stage of socialisation concerned with entry into the labour force.[33] Regardless of the specific theoretical framework, these information sources appear to be generally acceptable. For the purpose of this research it was assumed that information on careers within different economic sectors could be classified as coming from three major sources: school, home and external sources. Students were presented with a list of twenty-one possible sources of information, classified within the three major areas, and asked to identify those sources which provided them with a large amount of information, with some information, and with no information. The results are shown in Table VIII.

TABLE VIII

Sources of Information on Careers used by Sixth Form Pupils

Sources	Total		Those wishing to enter Industry and Commerce		Those wishing to enter Education	
Group I—School						
1. Private talk with careers teacher	61	14.4%	16	14.2%	17	14.9%
2. Careers lesson or group talk by careers teacher ...	25	5.8%	5	4.4%	13	11.4%
3. Literature provided by careers teacher ...	89	20.6%	90	79.5%	33	29.0%
4. Film show by careers teacher	18	4.2%	6	5.3%	6	5.3%
5. Visits to local industry arranged by the school	18	4.2%	8	7.1%	3	2.6%
6. Careers conventions arranged by the school ...	118	27.4%	25	22.0%	44	38.5%
7. Teachers other than careers teachers ...	92	21.4%	23	20.4%	30	26.1%
8. Lessons other than careers lessons	26	6.0%	5	4.4%	10	8.8%
Group II—External						
9. Careers conventions organised by the Youth Employment Officer ...	41	9.5%	16	14.2%	6	5.3%
10. Group talks arranged by the Youth Employment Officer	9	2.1%	2	1.8%	5	4.4%
11. Private talk with Youth Employment Officer ...	32	7.4%	11	9.7%	1	0.8%

TABLE VIII—Continued

Sources		Total	Those wishing to enter Industry and Commerce		Those wishing to enter Education	
12. Talks by representatives of prospective employers ...	37	8.6%	8	7.1%	10	8.8%
13. Literature from prospective employers ...	44	10.2%	13	11.5%	10	8.8%
14. Prospectuses of universities and colleges ...	316	73.5%	78	69.0%	99	87.0%
15. Press advertisements for jobs ...	20	4.7%	7	6.2%	4	4.0%
16. Radio and television programmes	32	7.4%	5	4.4%	7	6.2%
17. Periods working in organisations, e.g. holiday jobs	57	13.2%	5	4.4%	12	10.5%
Group III—Home						
18. Parents or relations ...	92	21.4%	21	18.5%	32	28.0%
19. Parents' friends ...	44	10.2%	5	4.4%	15	13.2%
20. Friends at university or college ...	98	22.8%	15	13.2%	41	36.0%
21. Friends already working ...	37	8.6%	11	9.7%	7	6.2%

These results indicate those sources of information which provided the students with a large amount of information about future careers. The fact that nearly three-quarters of the sample thought they obtained a lot of information from the prospectuses of universities and colleges is to be expected, given the fact that 87 per cent of all the students hoped to enter university or college. This does, in fact, relate to another point, which is that these results refer only to quantity of information and not to quality, so that although 73 per cent obtained a large amount of information from prospectuses, it does not follow that the prospectuses provided the right information in the best possible way.[34] The same applies to all other sources listed as providing a large amount of information.

The following comments, therefore, relate to the sources actually used. The major point appears to be that, apart from the high utilization of prospectuses, there is a distinct levelling out amongst the three major sources (school, home and external), tending to bear out the point made by Keil that 'family, neighbourhood, peer groups, education received, influences from mass media, the extent of formal vocational guidance all need to be considered' as influences on occupational choice.[35] However, within these three areas there are variations between individual sources, and one interesting aspect of this is the slight impact of the Youth Employment Service. There has been much discussion and criticism of the rôle of the Youth Employment Service,[36] and the results here tend to support these criticisms and indicate the lack of success of the Service in the provision of information. It is, perhaps, only fair to point out that this could be due to a number of factors—for example, shortage of trained staff, an emphasis on other guidance areas such as job changing, or even an over-emphasis on the fifth form leavers.

Within the school itself it would appear that the school careers teachers provide more information in a purely formal capacity (e.g. distributing literature) than in an informal or guidance capacity, where their rôle compares unfavourably with that of other teachers. Hill has in fact pointed out that the careers teacher is a lot less influential on choices of career than might be expected, in that he found a near equality of influence of subject master and careers master in his study of the career choices of grammar school boys.[37] (Although these results do not support his other conclusion that the careers master is less of an influence than the Youth Employment Service.) One further comment in the context of school sources, relates to the fact that nearly four-fifths of those students wishing to enter industry and commerce obtained a lot of information from literature provided by the school's careers teacher. This should leave no doubt as to the importance of this area for industrial and commercial organisations who are interested in recruiting at this level, but it would be of interest to know whether or not the information provided by this source is satisfactory, or whether the importance of the source reflects inadequacies in more personal or informal methods of providing information and advice.

The most influential school source of information appears to be the careers convention organised by the school, and this is certainly one way of bringing home to sixth formers the possibilities of different careers in different occupational areas, but again it would perhaps be fruitful to have some indication of whether this type of convention does provide the right sort of information, or whether they only succeed in over-glamorizing certain sectors and occupations. (The tendency for senior personnel to represent organisations at careers conventions is one manifestation of this.)

An examination of the home sources of information indicates that the two most important home sources are parents and relations, and friends already at university or college. This latter source (which appears to be especially important for those students intending an educational career) reflects the fact that the majority of the respondents wished to enter a university or college. The importance of parents and relations as influences on career choice has been noted before, as has the fact that this can be either a positive or negative influence.[38] The point has also been made that with local and national changes in technology, changes in job skills, and in the demand for labour, it is unfair to expect subject teachers and careers teachers to keep abreast of such changes,[39] in which case it could be said that it is even more unfair to expect (and hence less likely) that parents and relations will be able to cope in this respect. Certainly given the results above, that parents and relatives do provide a lot of information for 21.4 per cent of the respondents, attention should surely be focused on the quality and accuracy of this information and the way in which this situation could be improved.

Finally, there appear to be some interesting differences, in terms of major sources of information untilized, between those students wishing to enter industry and commerce and those wishing to enter education. Those with an industrial orientation appeared to rely very heavily on literature provided by the schools' careers teacher and appeared more likely to obtain information from the Youth Employment Service—in both cases more so than the educationally orientated. Those wishing an educational career utilized schools' career conventions, subject teachers, university and college prospectuses and home sources rather more than those desiring to enter industry and commerce.

The Image of Industry

The final section of this study is concerned with the students' perception of the world of industry, and represents an attempt to examine the relationship between the perceptions of those wishing to enter this sector and the perceptions of those wishing to enter education.

Students were given a semantic differential test intended to illustrate their perceptions of industry. There were, in all, nineteen choices and the positive scores were added to give an indication of degree of favour towards industry. (Results are shown in Table IX.)

TABLE IX

The Image of Industry held by Sixth Form Pupils

Score Area	Total	%	Wishing to enter Industry and Commerce	Wishing to enter Education
0— 3	43	10.2	6	18
4— 6	73	17.0	13	19
7— 9	82	19.3	13	27
10—12	76	17.2	14	25
13—15	47	11.0	21	6
16—18	59	13.7	33	8
Non respondents	51	11.6	13	11
Total	431	100	113	114

The results are of interest when a breakdown is attempted of the perceptions of those with an industrial and commercial orientation and those with an educational orientation. It can be seen that a much more favourable or positive view pertaining to industry is held by those with a desire to enter that area, than is held by those with a desire to enter education. Yet it should be of concern that some 30 per cent of those wishing to enter industry and commerce have a distinctly negative view of their proposed future occupation, and that the great majority of those with an educational orientation view industry with varying degrees of disfavour.

There is nothing new in the fact that the general view of industry held by school leavers is rather poor, as Willings has pointed out, yet it could be suggested that much of this is due to the fact that the information the students get about careers in this sector is inadequate.

Conclusion

This study has been concerned with analysing some of the factors influencing the career perceptions and choice of sixth form school leavers. It has indicated that the aspirations of many sixth formers are realistic in nature, and that aspirations must be examined in the context of expectations. The fact that education and industry are to some extent 'dumping grounds' for those whose aspirations are regarded as unlikely to be met has also been highlighted.

An attempt was also made to examine the major sources of information utilized by the sixth form leavers, and it appeared that many of the sources from which a lot of information was obtained were formal sources, and that generally the sources reflecting personal guidance were less significant. One area which is in need of further examination in this respect is that of the quality and effectiveness of each of the various sources. The final area of interest in this paper was the students' perception of industry, and a generally unfavourable impression was revealed (even to some extent amongst those desiring an industrial or commercial career).

In view of the vast investment in education at all levels, it is a cause of much concern that the flow of young high talent manpower from the educational system into the employment system is not as effective as it might be. Further research is obviously needed urgently to ascertain what further weaknesses exist at key points in the process of occupational choice, or perhaps occupational drift.

School of Business Studies, University of Liverpool.

[1] A. Crichton: *Personnel Management in Context*, Batsford, London, 1968, p. 170.

[2] E. Ginzberg, *et al.*: *A Manpower Strategy for the Metropolis*, Columbia Univ. Press, 1968.

[3] *Higher Education*, Report of the Committee of Higher Education, Cmnd. 2154, H.M.S.O., London, 1963.

[4] 'The Employment Frontier', *Trends in Education*, January, 1967, p. 3.

[5] M. Blaug, M. Preston and A. Ziderman: *The Utilization of Educated Manpower in Industry*, Oliver & Boyd, London, 1969.

[6] P. M. Blau, J. W. Gustad, R. Jesser, H. S. P. Ames and R. C. Wilcock: 'Occupational Choice: A Conceptual Framework', *Industrial & Labour Relations Review*, Vol. 9, No. 4, July, 1956, p. 536.

[7] E. Ginzberg *et al.*: *Occupational Choice*, Columbia Univ. Press, 1951.

[8] D. E. Super: *The Psychology of Careers*, Harper, New York, 1957, pp. 165-289.

[9] See Chapter Eight.

[10] See Chapter Three.

[11] See Chapter Four.

[12] Keil, Riddell and Green: *op. cit.*

[13] See Chapter Five.

[14] Ford and Box: p. 111.

[15] S. White: 'The Process of Occupational Choice', *British Journal of Industrial Relations*, Vol. VI, No. 2, 1968, p. 166.

[16] R. K. Merton: *The Student Physician*, Free Press, Glencoe, 1957.

[17] D. Pym: 'Technical Change and the Misuse of Professional Manpower', *Occupational Psychology*, Vol. 41, No. 1, 1967, p. 1.

[18] F. Harbison and C. A. Myers: 'Education, Manpower and Economic Growth', McGraw-Hill, New York, 1964, p. 16.

[19] L. G. Reynolds: *The Structure of Labour Markets*, Harper and Brothers, New York, 1951.

[20] G. Psathas: 'Towards a Theory of Occupational Choice for Women', *Sociology and Social Research*, Vol. 52, No. 2, 1967, p. 265.

[21] Blau *et al.*: *op. cit.*, p. 535.

[22] Super: *op. cit.*, p. 187.

[23] See Chapter Two.

[24] Keil, Riddell and Green: p. 82.

[25] Roberts: p. 148.

[26] Liversidge: p. 58.

[27] K. Lewin, T. Dembo, L. Festinger and P. S. Sears: 'Level of Aspiration', in J. McV. Hunt (Ed.): *Personality and the Behaviour Disorders*, Vol. 1, Ronald, New York, 1944, pp. 333-378.

[28] 'Sixth Form Survey', *Trends in Education*, No. 7, July 1967, p. 46.

[29] Keil, Riddell and Green: p. 82

[30] Blau *et al.*: *op. cit.*, p. 535.

[31] M. Carter: *Into Work*, Pelican, Harmondsworth, 1956.

[32] Roberts: p. 155.

[33] Musgrave: *op. cit.*

[34] D. Willings: 'Fitting the Man to the Job', *Personnel Management*, August, 1969.

[35] Keil, Riddell and Green: *op. cit.*

[36] See for example, Carter: *op. cit.*

[37] G. B. Hill: 'Choice of Career by Grammar School Boys', *Occupational Psychology*, 35, 1965, pp. 279-287.

[38] Willings: *op. cit.*

[39] C. J. Gill: 'Counselling in Schools', *Trends in Education*, April, 1967, p. 8.

Index

ability 15, 29, 58–9, 72, 79, 117, 172
see also attainment
Abrams, P. 167
achievement 16
adaptation: mechanisms 41; to available work 153, 155
adjustment 76–96, 88–91; and choice 28
adolescence *see* youth
adults 165; status 158
advantages held by individuals 16
age relations 160–2
alienation 16
Allen, S. 51–3
allocation processes 15–16
alternative occupations 42, 179–80, 182; appraisal of 48; awareness of 36
ambition 140–4, 148, 152, 155; and knowledge 155; factors in 51–3
America 153
appraisal of chances 33–5
apprenticeships 76, 88–9
aptitudes 21 *see also* ability
ascription 16
aspirations 41–2, 58–75, 130, 143–4, 162; career 189–93; national differences in 78–82; level of 165–6; unfulfilled 90
attainment, educational 149, 172, 182, 193–4 *see also* ability
attitudes 80–2, 87–8
awareness concepts 171–86; types of 176–82

Banton, M. 128
Becker, H. S. 49
Bernstein, B. 53, 83
Blau, P. M. 31–3, 187, 191, 198
blue collar workers 15
Box, S. 35–6, 45–6, 136, 188
boys 62–75, 193–5
Brim, O. G. 129
Bullock, R. 39–40
Burns, T. 27

Campbell, J. W. 64–5
Caplow, T. 111
career 29, 140, 142–3; aspirations and expectations 189–93; attitudes 87;

information 198–202; perception of 187–206
careers convention 201–2
Caro, F. G. 135
Carter, M. P. 86–7, 183, 198
challenge 47
chemistry students 113–20
Cherret, P. 39–40
choice, occupational 19, 33; motivation of 32; nature of 23; processes of 31–2, 44–8, 171–86; restricted 23; secondary 120; theory of 111–37; use of the term 13–14 *see also* preference
class, social 58, 68–74, 172
clerical work 89
closed awareness 176–82
Cohen, A. 181, 184
Coleman, J. S. 85
colleagues 19
compromise 28, 29, 32, 112
conflict 125, 134–5; between children and parents 84; between children and teachers 39; between generations 158, 168, 170n; internal 48; of attitudes 88; role 128
consensus 134–6
Coulson, M. A. 45
counselling *see* vocational guidance
Crichton, A. 187
Crowther Report *Early Leaving* 89
crystalization 25
culture shock 162
Cunnison, J. 85

Dahrendorf, R. 124, 135
decision making 48; accidental 21; and committment 49–50; process of 24–5, 173–86; rationality in 35–7
deprivation 43; economic 23
deviancy, occupational 124, 135, 165
Dill, W. R. 37
dissatisfaction 25, 148; *see also* satisfaction
division of labour 15
Douglas, J. 83
dysfunction 126, 130, 134

Early Leaving (Crowther Report) 89
economic factors 17